MEDITERRANEAN
SEA of AZOV
BLACK SEA
Bosphorus
Constantinople
Nicaea
Bursa
ANATOLIA
GREECE
Lemnos
Edessa
Corfu
Ambracian Gulf
Chios
Smyrna
Gulf of Patras
AEGEAN SEA
Ephesus
CILICIA
Antioch
SYRIA
MOREA
Budrum
Marmarice
Bay of Antalya
CYCLADES
DODECANESE
Milos
Rhodes
Tripoli
CYPRUS
Beirut
Sidon
Damascus
Khania
Candia
Tyre
CRETE
TERRANEAN SEA
Jerusalem
Damietta
Alexandria
Cairo
RED SEA

The Shield and the Sword

By the same author

THE GREAT SIEGE

DRAKE

THE SULTAN'S ADMIRAL

MEDITERRANEAN: PORTRAIT OF A SEA

CLEOPATRA

ERNLE BRADFORD

The Shield and the Sword

The Knights of St. John,
Jerusalem, Rhodes and Malta

E. P. Dutton & Co., Inc.
New York   *1973*

Foreword

ANYONE WHO UNDERTAKES TO WRITE THE HISTORY OF THE KNIGHTS
Hospitaller of St. John of Jerusalem of Rhodes and of Malta is at once
faced with formidable difficulties: for indeed the history of this illustrious
Order is in the large part the history of the Mediterranean covering some
700 years, not to mention the activities of the Order in other parts of
Europe and the New World: thus from its earliest beginnings in the
eleventh century until the present day—a span of more than 900 years!

Ernle Bradford has already given evidence of this scholarship in his
previous books, *The Great Siege* and *The Mediterranean, Portrait of a Sea*, and
it is not surprising, therefore, that in his latest book *The Shield and the Sword*
he has once again demonstrated his skill as a narrator and his integrity as
an historian.

From the very first pages we sense the thrill and drama of the story of
these medieval Knights who were members of a religious order, with their
heroic courage, their idealism, their profound Christianity and inevitably
their human weaknesses.

The military progress and prowess of the Knights Hospitaller of St.
John, as they were then known, is recorded with historical accuracy while
in every chapter the golden thread of the Order's unwavering fidelity to
its saintly founder's injunction: 'to care for our Lords the sick and our
Lords the poor' is always present. We follow the saga of the great sieges
of Rhodes and of Malta, the defeat of the enemy and then the period of
worldly grandeur in Malta, to end, alas, in the cession of the island to
Napoleon, the darkest hour in the history of the Knights of St. John.

It seemed at that moment that the Order had reached its conclusion,

48699

yet the story continues to relate its survival and then its almost miraculous renewal in the twentieth century.

Ernle Bradford has written a concise and moving history of the Order of St. John and not the least of his achievements is to have included all the essential facts within the narrow space of some 300 pages.

The Sovereign Military and Hospitaller Order of St. John of Jerusalem of Rhodes and of Malta, to give it its full title, is today, as the final chapter indicates, perhaps more active and certainly more widespread than at any time in its 900 years' history.

Its sovereignty dating from the capture of the island of Rhodes in 1310, making it one of the oldest sovereign states in Europe, is now officially recognised by thirty-eight states with which the Order maintains diplomatic relations.

The work of the Knights of St. John remains unchanged since the days of its founder, to care for the sick and the poor regardless of race, language or religion. This work goes on today in the leper settlements of Africa and elsewhere, in the earthquake area of the Andes, in the swamps of Bangladesh, in the riot-torn streets of Londonderry and Belfast, in the fighting zone of Vietnam where volunteers of the German ambulance corps of the Order have already sacrificed their lives, and in the countless hospitals, dispensaries and homes on four continents.

The Order's 8,500 members in thirty-nine grand priories, sub-priories and national associations, aided by an unknown number of helpers and generous supporters, still maintain their ancient tradition of voluntary service.

Ernle Bradford's *The Shield and the Sword* appropriately enough appears in the tenth year of the reign of the 77th Grand Master, Frà Angelo de Mojana di Cologna. The 'Modern Crusade' is already launched and the Hospitaller's banner of the eight-pointed cross flies as a symbol of international charity and peace in more than sixty countries throughout the world.

QUINTIN JERMY GWYN
Grand Chancellor of the Sovereign Military Hospitaller Order of St. John of Jerusalem of Rhodes and of Malta

Contents

Photographs follow page 100

Maps

Acknowledgments

I should like to express my indebtedness, as always, to the London Library—that institution without which few writers like myself could survive (let alone derive great pleasure). I also owe a great debt to the Order of St. John itself, in particular to the Grand Chancellor and to the Order's official historian, Frà Toumanoff. Both have been kind enough to read this book in manuscript and to amend my faults. Such errors as remain are mine. Finally I would like to express my thanks to many friends in Malta, especially Sir Hannibal Scicluna (who first, as it were, introduced me to this subject many years ago). Without the Royal Malta Library and the Library of the University of Malta this book would not have been possible.

E.B.

Kalkara, Malta.
July 22nd, 1972.

I

Crusaders

THE SOVEREIGN MILITARY HOSPITALLER ORDER OF ST. JOHN OF Jerusalem, of Rhodes and of Malta, is the oldest Order of Chivalry in existence. It is also the third oldest religious Order in Christendom. It is the only remaining offshoot of that period of history known as the Crusades.

For nearly two centuries, from 1096 to 1291, successive waves of Europeans swept down upon the Levant, first of all to recover the Holy Land from the Moslems, and then to try to hold it and other surrounding areas as Christian territories. They came in their tens of thousands—pilgrims, individual men-at-arms, small companies following a feudal lord, and whole armies. The Crusades were more than the famous series of campaigns to which the name has become attached. They were a steady and continuous movement of Latin and northern peoples into that region of the Near East which had become sacred to them because the Founder of Christianity had been born and died there. The Crusades, as generally understood, were the seven great gales out of the west and north that thundered over this eastern land. All the time though, like a tide making up against a shore, there was a steady trickle of pilgrims and freebooters, priests and land-hungry nobles, seeping out of Europe into the brilliant and ever-confusing East.

As an instrument of policy the Crusades were something comparatively new. True, the idea of the Jihad, the Holy War, had long been familiar to Moslems. Had not the Prophet himself enjoined them, 'Fight in the way of Allah against those who fight against you . . . Kill them wherever you find them . . . It is incumbent upon you to fight even though you may dislike it.'? Christians, on the other hand, whose religion was a religion of peace were, in theory at any rate, taught to regard war as evil. The Eastern Church of Byzantium definitely regarded war as evil, and the very last resort after all attempts at diplomacy or bribery had failed. The soldier was not honoured in Byzantium. Indeed, if he killed upon the field of battle—even in defence of his own country—he was barred from receiving communion for three years. The western position was very different. The aggressive and semi-barbarous peoples of the north could not possibly be contained within the finesse and sophisticated code understood by the Byzantines. Even St. Augustine had said that such things as a just war existed, a war against evil at the bidding of God. But this was a little too complicated a thought for Norman barons and their like, whose favourite pastime was laying siege to a neighbour's castle and seizing his land.

The Code of Chivalry had evolved in feudal societies through the necessity for some style of conduct, and of rules for combat and war. It had been largely promoted in its early stages by the famous *chansons de geste,* the songs about Charlemagne and Roland and their companions. Warfare and the heroic spirit had long been regarded in the West, whatever the Church might say, as things that distinguished the noble from the serf. What was new about the Crusades was that they were actively sponsored by the Church and by the Pope himself. They were partly attributable to a religious revival that had begun in western Europe in the tenth century, and which had steadily increased throughout the eleventh. The Crusades can also be seen as part of the eternal interaction between the East and the West which has always been a feature of European and Mediterranean history.

As an instrument of papal foreign policy the Crusades were designed to secure the Holy Places and protect the pilgrim routes. They were also extremely useful in diverting the activities of warring and often lawless nobles into a constructive war outside the confines of Europe. At the root of so much of this activity lay the penitential system of the Church, whereby a priest might enjoin a man at the confessional to carry out some physical or moral penance before being admitted to the sacrament of the Eucharist. The penitentiary pilgrimage was the most important of these. The pilgrim not only atoned for his sins by the suffering and discomfort of his hard and often extremely dangerous journey, but he then enjoyed the blessing of having visited the Holy Places and stood on sacred ground. The Crusaders' aim was to secure the pilgrimage routes and protect the pilgrims from their Moslem enemies. This was the seed from which sprang the Knights Templar, the Teutonic Knights and the formidable Order of St. John.

The First or People's Crusade came about largely on account of the declining powers of the Byzantine Empire and the steady encroachment of the Turks, who were rightly seen as the greatest threat to Christendom. They had seized Jerusalem in 1071 and, although not totally intolerant, they had made the passage of pilgrims even more difficult than it had been when the area had all come under Byzantine rule. The schism between the Church of the East and the Catholic Church was something that had long troubled the papacy. With the decline of Byzantium, if western Christians could establish themselves in the East, there seemed a chance that ultimately the whole of Christendom might be united under Rome. After the terrible defeat of the Byzantine armies by the Turks at Manzikert in 1071 the pilgrim routes through Asia Minor became increasingly hazardous since all the large cities were now in Turkish hands. The Byzantine emperor Michael VII appealed to the West to come to the aid of Eastern Christendom against the Turks. At the time Michael's appeal was unavailing. But that of his successor, Alexius Comnenus, was to be answered.

In 1095 at the Council of Piacenza in Italy envoys from Alexius begged the Pope, Urban II, to send troops to help them recover Asia Minor for Christendom. This time the situation was more favourable for western intervention. Urban II was a strong Pope, who had firmly established the papal position at home. He now looked hopefully east, dreaming of a united Christendom and the recovery of Christian lands held by the enemies of the Faith. Later in the same year, at the Council of Clermont, he made the famous speech which led to the First Crusade. He called upon his listeners to go to the aid of their brethren in the East. Christendom was in peril, and if the Turks succeeded in overthrowing the Byzantine Empire their next objective would be the rest of Europe. Jerusalem itself, he pointed out, was in the hands of the enemies of Christ; the pilgrims who tried to make their way to the Holy Places were suffering as never before under any other Moslem rulers. He called upon the leaders of western Europe to cease their murderous un-Christian feuds and wars, and to unite against the common enemy. The war to which he summoned them was a just and holy one, sanctified by God. Those who took part in it, were they to die in battle, would have all their sins remitted. Life here on earth was miserable at its best and always afflicted by evil. Heaven awaited them. He called upon them to die for their faith and to take up the sword against the enemies of Christ

The response was electric. Urban II had triggered off a thunderstorm that was to roll across the Mediterranean for generations. 'God wills it! God wills it!' his listeners cried. It was November when Urban addressed the Council. His intention was that the crusaders should leave in the summer of the following year. They would march to Constantinople, where the Byzantine emperor would have transports ready to take them across to Asia Minor. They would then clear all the Turks out of the area and free the great cities that lay on the pilgrimage route. After that they would win back Jerusalem, the Citadel of the Faith. As a symbol of their determination not to rest until Jerusalem was restored, they 'took the Cross'—a cross of red material sewn on the back of the surcoats that covered their chain-mail armour.

Urban was determined to keep the whole expedition under papal control, and named Adhemar Bishop of Puy its leader. It is worth noting that Urban himself was of French descent, that the whole enterprise was first projected on French soil, and that the first of the nobles to join the Crusade was a Frenchman, Count Raymond of Toulouse. Over the centuries—although crusaders came from every country in Europe—the dominant influence was that of France or, to be more accurate, Norman France. The Normans were allied by blood and instincts to the Vikings. Hardy, enduring, subject to fits of berserker violence, they were also dourly religious—and wanderers at heart. The appeal of the sun, the sea, and the south, had already taken them into southern Italy and Sicily. They were always land-hungry. It was not only religion that was to drive them in successive waves across the Mediterranean into Greece, Asia Minor, and the Levant.

After Pope Urban's speech crusading zeal swept Europe like a bush-fire. It was not only the nobles and potentates who were determined to become pilgrims and to win through to the Holy Land. Inspired by the Pope's words strange visionaries such as Peter the Hermit and Walter Sans-Avoir began spreading the idea of the Crusade. The result was that, while the Crusade that Urban had called for was gradually taking shape, another completely different one was getting under way. Life in most of Europe was extremely hard for the poor; with little food, and subject always to the domination of their feudal lords, and wracked by the warfare that only too often raged between them. The idea of emigrating to some far-off sunny land, and in the process acquiring merit in the eyes of God and a remission of sins, naturally appealed to thousands of the peasantry. As Sir Steven Runciman remarks:

Medieval man was convinced that the Second Coming was at hand. He must repent while yet there was time and must go out and do good . . . prophecies declared that the Holy Land must be recovered for the faith before Christ could come again. Further, to ignorant minds the distinction between Jerusalem and the New Jerusalem was not very clearly defined. Many of Peter's hearers believed that he was promising to lead them out of the present miseries to the land flowing with milk and honey of which the scriptures spoke.

The First Crusade falls into two parts, that of the princes, and that of the people. The first to leave was the People's Crusade. It was an abject and tragic failure. A large part of the pilgrims never even got as far as Constantinople, while those who did proved a heavy burden on the Byzantines. Alexius Comnenus had asked for a disciplined army, and all he received was a rabble. They had swarmed across Europe like locusts, sacking and burning Belgrade en route, and now they proceeded to act in the same way on Byzantine territory. Finally, unable to tolerate their behaviour any longer, the Emperor placed his fleet at their disposal and had them transported to Asia Minor. After pillaging the countryside that was still under Byzantine control they extended their activities into areas where the Turks were waiting for them. After a number of minor clashes, the whole body of the People's Crusade—some 20,000 strong—marched out to give battle. It was a foregone conclusion. The Turkish bowmen and cavalry massacred them. Peter the Hermit, who had gone back to Constantinople to try to get more help from the Emperor, was one of the only leaders to survive. After the battle was over, the Turks overran the crusaders' camp. They put the men, women and children to the sword, only sparing a few attractive boys and girls destined for their homes and harems.

It was the end of the People's Crusade. The only lesson it had served was to remind its successors that faith alone was not enough. The sword in disciplined hands was the only thing that could open the road to Jerusalem. In the meantime, the 'crusade of the princes' was under way. It had taken longer to organise than had been expected, and it was not until the spring of 1097 that the bulk of what must be called the first Crusade proper was gathered under the walls of Constantinople. Here, together with their knights and men-at-arms, were such potentates as Godfrey of Bouillon, Duke of Lower Lorraine, Hugh, Count of Vermandois, Raymond of Toulouse, Bohemund of Taranto, Robert of Normandy, Count Robert of Flanders, and the Bishop Adhemar. Their names read like a roll-call of European nobility.

Early in May 1097 the first of the crusaders were beginning to cross the Bosporus. Estimates of their numbers vary. Godfrey of Bouillon alone brought an army of 30,000 infantry and 10,000 cavalry, while Bohemund of Taranto was attended by 7,000 knights. In all, by the time that late-comers and their men-at-arms had arrived and crossed into Asia Minor, it is probable that something like 150,000 were engaged in the invasion. After a month's siege Nicaea fell to them, then Tarsus, and finally Antioch. It was during their occupation of Antioch—at a time when they themselves were besieged by a large Turkish army and morale was low—that there occurred the discovery of the Holy Lance, said to have been the one that had pierced the side of Jesus. There can be little doubt that the whole episode was carefully organised by some canny cleric bent on raising the crusaders' morale. If so, he succeeded in his intent. The army marched out of the city and gave battle to the waiting Turks. The result was a complete victory for the crusaders. From now on they felt convinced that Christ Himself was with them, and that He would lead them into Jerusalem.

It was an age of relics. Men prized and cherished relics of the saints as well as wonderworking images or, for instance, paintings attributed to St. Mark. In Constantinople where the greatest collection of relics from the Holy Land and Asia Minor had been collected there was the True Cross on which Christ was crucified, the drops of blood he had shed at Gethsemane, the rod of Moses, and the stone on which Jacob had laid his head to sleep. At a later date, the Hand of St. John the Baptist in its jewelled reliquary was to inspire the Knights of the Order named after him to incredible acts of courage. The fact was that superstition, religious belief founded on fear or ignorance, often worked. If one believed in the irrational one could also meet situations that would otherwise have seemed hopeless with irrational bravery. The crusaders, for instance, were even further encouraged in their march down the coast of Judaea by an eclipse of the moon. They took this to mean that the Crescent of their enemies was likewise due for eclipse.

On the morning of June 7th, 1099, the army reached the summit of a hill (Montjoie or Mount Joy as pilgrims had earlier named it), and saw Jerusalem spread out before them. In view of what happened later it is worth quoting William of Tyre's description of their reaction:

When they heard the name Jerusalem called out, they began to weep and fell on their knees, giving thanks to Our Lord with many sighs for the great love which He had shown them in allowing them to reach the goal of their pilgrimage, the Holy City which He had loved so much that He wished there to save the world. It was deeply moving to see the tears and hear the loud sobs of these good people. They ran forward until they had a clear view of all the towers and walls of the city. Then they raised their hands in prayer to Heaven and, taking off their shoes, bowed to the ground and kissed the earth.

Jerusalem was one of the strongest fortified cities in the world. Ever since its capture by the Romans in the reign of the Emperor Hadrian it had been the keypoint to the whole area and the walls had been added to constantly over the centuries, first by its Byzantine and later by its Moslem rulers. The siege of Jerusalem lasted for a little over a month. That it did not take longer was largely due to the fact that the crusaders were inspired by the vision of a priest, in which he assured them he had been told that if only they would all fast and walk barefoot round the walls the city would fall to them. (On a more practical basis the arrival of a number of Christian ships at Jaffa had recently provided them with the sailors and technicians, the wood and materials, with which to construct siege engines.) They had been disheartened and suffered heavily from the heat under the scorching July sun, but now the army's morale once again revived. On July 15th the walls were finally breached and the Christians swept into the citadel and home of their Faith.

The capture of Jerusalem, like that of Antioch before it, was marked by scenes of such blood-lust and cruelty that it is hard to believe these feudal lords and their followers had the slightest conception of that faith in whose name they had undertaken their expedition. The cross of the Prince of Peace was on their surcoats but in their hands was the hammer of Thor. The governor of the city and his personal bodyguard were allowed to leave —but only in return for a vast ransom. The rest of the Moslems, men, women and children, were butchered in their thousands. Mosques were pillaged and the Dome of the Rock was sacked and plundered. Even some Moslems who had paid a large ransom and taken refuge in the mosque of al-Aqsa (above which waved a banner to show that they were to be spared) were slaughtered to a man. The city ran with blood. The Jewish community fared no better than the Moslem. When they too took refuge in their main synagogue the building was set on fire about them. The crusaders had burst into the city at noon. By nightfall, 'sobbing for excess of joy', they fell on their knees in the Church of the Sepulchre, bowing their heads over their blood-stained hands.

The massacre after the fall of Jerusalem appalled even some of the crusaders. Its effect upon the Moslem world was traumatic. Whenever, in the centuries that followed, attempts were made by Latin rulers to come to some accommodation with the Moslems the memory of that day rose up and prevented it. The East had seen the *furor Normannorum*, the rage of the Norsemen (from which the Christian Church itself had once prayed to be spared). The Moslem world would never forget it, and would become equally fanatical in its determination to expel these Christians from the lands that they had seized.

The intolerance of the western Europeans in religious matters was far in excess of anything known in the East. For centuries the Byzantines had traded with their religious enemy, and it was only the onslaught of the Turks upon their empire that had prompted them to call for western help. In Constantinople itself there was even a Moslem quarter and a mosque—something that provoked the contempt and anger of the crusaders. The Moslems, for their part, had usually shown a reasonable degree of religious tolerance in the territories under their control. They had permitted Christians to visit the shrines of their faith and, as has been seen, had allowed a large colony of Jews to settle in Jerusalem. The governor of the city, who had waited throughout the months while the crusaders made their way through Asia Minor and Syria—knowing full well that Jerusalem was their target—had made no move against the pilgrims and other Christians within his city walls. Even when the army had moved down from Montjoie and encamped against Jerusalem he took no violent action against them. The Christians were merely expelled, and allowed to go and join their co-religionists. Among those who probably left Jerusalem before the siege began was a certain Brother Gerard.

2

The Order of St. John

BROTHER GERARD WAS THE HEAD OF A HOSPICE FOR PILGRIMS WHICH had been established in Jerusalem about 1080. It was certainly in existence at the time that the First Crusade reached the city. It was not a hospital in the modern sense, although no doubt it had facilities for treating the sick. A hospice was essentially a place for rest for pilgrims, where they could sleep and get food. The one in Jerusalem seems to have been founded by merchants from Amalfi, that important Italian shipping centre which provided many pilgrims with their means of transport to the Holy Land. Then as now, a traveller had to pay for his passage in advance. (The term 'passage money' was to acquire considerable importance in the later history of the Order of St. John.) The hospice seems to have been dedicated to this saint, although exactly which of the Johns is open to debate. Later it was always assumed that the patron saint of the Order was John the Baptist.

The hospice came under Benedictine rule and was administered by Benedictines from Amalfi. It is very likely that Gerard himself was an Italian from this gracious little city, which had at one time during the ninth century shared with Venice and Gaeta all the Italian trade with the East. The development of the compass is said to have reached Europe through Amalfi. Its naval code, the *Tavolo Amalfitano,* was recognised throughout the Mediterranean until the late sixteenth century. The merchants who set up the hospice in Jerusalem were not being entirely philanthropic. There were practical reasons why shipowners and traders dealing with the East should want to have a rest house in Jerusalem. Not only did they have their own merchants and agents going there, but quite a large part of their business was the transport of pilgrims. Life was rough and tough in those days and travellers could expect little or nothing in the way of comfort whether afloat or ashore. At the same time a 'shipping line' that could, as it were, offer its own insurance in the form of guaranteed lodgings, and even medical treatment, was certain to prove attractive.

Legend has it—and it is possibly no more than legend—that Brother Gerard was not expelled from Jerusalem along with the other pilgrims, but that he stayed there throughout the siege and helped the crusaders by supplying them with bread. As Riley-Smith writes:

. . . the city under siege was the scene of his performance of the miracle required by his hagiographers. It was said that, together with the other inhabitants, he was ordered to help defend Jerusalem. He knew that the crusaders outside the walls were hungry, and so each day he took small loaves up onto the parapet and hurled these at the Franks instead of stones. He was seen by the Arab guards who arrested him and took him before the governor. But when the loaves were produced in evidence of his crime, they had turned into stones and he was released.

Forgetting the matter of the bread into stones, it seems somewhat unlikely that a friar who ran a hospice for Christian pilgrims was allowed to remain in the city during the siege. On the other hand our authorities for this period unanimously declare that this was so, and that Gerard was of the greatest assistance to the besieging army. The only logical explanation would be that—hospitals being rare enough at the time—the city's governor allowed him to remain so that he and his assistants could look after any of the garrison or citizens who were injured during the fighting. One thing is certain; after the capture of Jerusalem by the army of the First Crusade, the fortunes of the small foundation over which Gerard presided were made.

It is quite clear that the foundation administered by Gerard was of the greatest value to the army and the pilgrims who now thronged Jerusalem. The Hospital inevitably expanded, and in those days when dying men made lavish gifts to the Church, and when men who survived also paid their dues, it was inevitable that the Hospital should benefit.

Evidence that it enjoyed great favour is shown by the fact that Godfrey of Bouillon, who became the first ruler of Latin Jerusalem, made the Hospital a gift of some land. His example was to be followed over the

The Syria and Levant coast of the Mediterranean

years by many others who wished to record their thanks for the services of Gerard and his helpers.

Godfrey of Bouillòn had refused to be called King of Jerusalem on the ground that no man should be called a king in the city where Christ had died on the cross. His successor, Baldwin of Boulogne, did not take such a pious view of things and had himself crowned, thus creating the Latin *kingdom* of Jerusalem. He too took the Hospital under his care and protection, and after a victory over an Egyptian army presented the Hospital with a tenth of all the booty. He thus established a precedent which was to make the Hospital one of the richest Orders in the world. His example was soon followed by many rich ecclesiastics in the East, who gave it a tithe of their revenues.

The saintliness of Brother Gerard has often been stressed by historians of the Order that he founded, and there is no doubt that he was indeed a good and noble man. He was also eminently practical—as have been many saints—and an excellent organiser. Before he died in 1120 he had so firmly laid the foundations of the Order that it has endured into the twentieth century. It was recognised as an independent Order by the papacy seven years before his death, by which time it had become the owner of large properties in France, Italy and Spain. With these extensive possessions the Hospital began to establish daughter-houses in Europe along the pilgrimage routes. Out of the small seed of the original hospice in Jerusalem there developed a giant oak with branches extending into all Christian countries (for the daughter-houses in their turn received tithes and donations which enabled them to establish yet further hospitals). All the main ports of embarkation for pilgrims were soon equipped with a Hospital operated by the Order of St. John; Marseilles, Bari, and Messina, to name but a few.

The Order that Gerard founded anticipated by many centuries all subsequent organisations devoted to the care of the poor and the sick throughout the world. In his ideals he echoed the Founder of Christianity. Members of the Order were enjoined to consider the poor as 'our lords, whose servants we acknowledge ourselves to be'. They were also to dress as humbly as did the poor. The nobility of Gerard's aims and life would be hard to equal at any time, but in the twelfth century, when the western world was based on the feudal concept of lord and serf, they were exceptional. His epitaph is hardly an exaggeration: 'Here lies Gerard, the most humble man in the East and the servant of the poor. He was hospitable to all strangers, a gentle man with a courageous heart. One can judge within these walls just how good he was. Provident and active in every kind of way, he stretched out his arms to many lands in order to obtain whatever was needed to feed his people.'

He was succeeded by an almost equally remarkable man, Raymond de Puy. The latter built upon Gerard's foundations, but in doing so changed the direction of the Order so that for centuries to come its hospitaller side —although always strong and important—became overshadowed. While the original members of the Order of St. John had been concerned only with the Hospital, the feeding of the poor and treatment of the sick, a new branch was to be grafted on to it which would be mainly concerned with the protection of pilgrims on the route from the sea to Jerusalem. The military protection of pilgrims might seem little more than a logical extension of the Order's principal rule—to look after the poor—but it was to evolve into a militant Christianity designed to fight Moslems wherever they might be found. The establishment of the military Orders in the East was in itself an inevitable outcome of the sack of Jerusalem, which had inspired a fanatical hatred of Christians throughout the Moslem world. One good deed may sometimes lead to another, but it is certain that an evil one will almost inevitably breed its fellow.

The transition of the Servants of the Poor into the Soldiers of Christ really began in the early twelfth century. In 1136 the Hospitallers were given the important castle of Bethgeblin in the south of Palestine to hold against the Moslems, who had control of the port of Ascalon. This in itself is evidence enough that the military arm of the Order had already come into being—for who would give a fort to a company of Hospitallers? It is clear that Raymond de Puy had already applied to the Pope for the right to develop a military arm of the Order, and that permission had been granted for him to do so. The establishment of the Knights Templar, a purely military Order designed to fight against the enemies of the Faith, had already set a precedent.

The Templars, or 'The Poor Knights of Christ and of the Temple of Solomon', were the brainchild of a French knight who had seen the necessity of a special fighting body to protect the pilgrims in the Holy Land. Much that was later to be adopted by the Order of St. John may have stemmed from the Templars; for instance the institution of a 'Grand

'Master' as head of the Order, whereas among the Hospitallers their head had previously only been known as 'the Administrator'. Thus on to a hospital tending for the poor and the sick was grafted the whole fiery body of medieval chivalry and feudalism.

Politically, these Latin knights and barons now busy establishing themselves as eastern rulers from Antioch to Jerusalem brought no more than the same simple conceptions of justice, law and order, as obtained in their own northern lands. At the same time the military Orders, that of the Templars, of St. John, and a little later of the Teutonic Knights (who started as a Hospitaller Order but soon became only military) developed a style of discipline coupled with their medieval notions of chivalry that was something new. The Templars bore on their surcoats the red cross on a white ground which had originally been adopted for the soldiers of the First Crusade; the Knights of St. John a white cross on a red ground— 'The white Cross of Peace on the blood-red field of War'; and the Teutonic Order a black cross on a white field. All co-religionists, all defenders of the Holy Places and of the pilgrims, they were often at loggerheads with one another. The dissensions between those hot-blooded nobles, only too conscious of their birth, their quarterings, and their battle honours (as well as the different 'clubs' to which they belonged), was not to be conducive to a sensible and united policy towards the affairs of the East.

Outremer (Overseas) as the Latin colonies were called was always destined to be a failure. Dependent on a long line of communications across the Mediterranean from Europe, and established in shifting pockets of territory that were almost constantly harassed by an enemy who had the hinterland to himself, it is surprising that *Outremer* held out as long as it did. This, despite their constant dissensions, must be held to the credit of the crusaders and their fighting qualities. At the same time, man being man the world over, it was also to some extent largely the internal quarrels of the various Moslem states that prevented a concerted drive to get rid of the Christians. Whenever a Moslem leader of any real calibre emerged and united his co-religionists, the Europeans were almost invariably destined for disaster.

At this stage in their history the rules of the Order of St. John seem to have been fairly simple. Their first duty was the care of the poor. This in its turn meant the necessary collection of alms and of their tithes, whether in the Levant or in Europe. The brothers who worked in the Hospital were both priests and laymen. In the early stages there seems to have been little distinction between fighting laymen and those who merely served in the Hospital. All, however, took strict vows of poverty, chastity and obedience to the rules of the Order. It was not until after the middle of the twelfth century that there began to appear a stronger military aspect to the Knights. By this time they already had command of several castles in Syria including the famous Krak des Chevaliers which they were to turn into the most formidable fortress in the East—so much so that a Moslem was to liken it to 'a bone stuck in the throat of the Saracens'.

It is probable that these castles were largely manned by hired mercenaries, for the militant arm had not yet sufficiently developed for them to have been held entirely by the Order. Most of the castles were the gift of Count Raymond of Tripoli, who was anxious to have the powerful Hospitallers as his allies against the constant enemy incursions into his territory. He was also well aware that the Order had ample funds with which to maintain and improve them. By 1168 it is clear that the military side of the Order had developed considerably: we find it sending 500 knights together with a suitable number of mercenary troops as its contribution to a crusading venture into Egypt.

By the time that Raymond de Puy died the future development of the Order had been clearly established. Despite the admonishments of more than one Pope—that the Hospitallers should confine the military side of their activities as much as possible and stick to their original Rule as laid down by Brother Gerard—the Knights Militant had arrived upon the scene.

3

Crusaders in the East

THE EUROPEANS WHO RULED IN THE EASTERN STATES SUCH AS JERUSALEM and Antioch, and smaller principalities like Tripoli, never numbered more than a few thousand. Even with the addition of their men-at-arms, the poorer Latin settlers, the merchants, priests and others, they were little more than a handful, holding on to their lands by castles and the sword— and also by judicious treaties with local Moslem rulers. Being so few it was hardly surprising that it was they who were influenced by their neighbours and their surroundings, rather than the reverse. Many centuries before, although they had come in far greater numbers, the Greeks who had spread over the same area after the campaigns of Alexander the Great had become largely orientalised. If the Greeks with their superior culture had been so transmuted it was natural enough that these comparatively simple and unsophisticated Latin nobles would soon become imbued with the light and the colour, the luxury and the languor of the East.

Used as they were to the cold rains and even colder winters of Europe, to the long twilights, and the brief temperate summers, the brilliance, blue skies and blinding light of these strange lands affected them like a drug. Listening to the biblical stories from their priests in their homelands they had probably never envisaged that Christ Himself had been an oriental, and that the Holy Land was a far remove from the settings in which they had pictured Him. The ultimate failure of the Crusades and the crusading Orders in the Near East was partly attributable to the material aims of Latin nobles, whose private quarrels often took precedence over their real obligations. The records show that they often lived in ostentatious splendour, honouring chastity more in the breach than the observance, and were

constantly at odds with one another. At the same time they brought to
this exotically unfamiliar environment the typical feudal system of Europe.
In Palestine, since most of the Moslems had emigrated after the Norman
conquest, the Latin peasant farmers were largely tied to the land, paying a
percentage of their revenues to the local lord. In other areas agriculture was
run on the basis of the farmers—whether Europeans or native—carrying
on much as before, although subject always to any demands that their
local ruler might make of them. As Sir Steven Runciman puts it, 'The
villagers' dealings with their lord were conducted through their headman,
called sometimes by the Arabic name of *rais* . . . On his side the lord
employed a compatriot as his factor or *drogmannus* (dragoman), an Arabic-
speaking secretary who could keep the record.' It was from estates such as
these—quite apart from those bequeathed to them in Europe—that the
Order of St. John largely drew its revenues.

The Latin conquerors, who had initially despised the Byzantines for
the way in which they traded and had diplomatic treaties with the Moslem
enemy, soon found out that it was only by these means that they could
continue to hold on to their possessions. This pragmatism was reinforced
by their contacts with Byzantines of the Orthodox Church, with Moslems
of different sects, and with the Jews. Removed from the intellectual and
spiritual security of their small European communities they found themselves in contact with many different streams of thought. The overall
result was that they became more tolerant, more broad-minded and,
indeed, easy-going. In the military Orders this process was less easily
observable, but it existed none the less. It was impossible for all except
the most dedicated man to observe that in the kingdoms of the East life
was totally different from that which they had known in Europe.

Between the invaders of these eastern lands and the surrounding inhabitants there began a form of communication, a tolerance even, that
was found extremely distressing by the newly-arrived European, hot for a
chance to save his soul by fighting the infidel. If one may make the com-
parison, the situation was not unlike that of an officer newly arrived from
Britain in the India of the nineteenth century. The old regulars who had
been there long before him, or were even descended from several generations of Anglo-Indians, accustomed to the climate and the ways of the
land, saw things with a very different eye from that of the new
arrival. The newcomers to *Outremer* for their part found the settlers'

acquiescence in the *status quo* incomprehensible, irritating, and un-Christian.

The permanent Latin inhabitants of these eastern states certainly lived a considerably more pleasant form of life than they would have done in their native countries. The draughty discomfort of a Norman castle—with the weather baying outside and the dogs baying in the Great Hall—was replaced by elegance and splendour. The castles had refinements far beyond those of Europe. The Byzantines who had built their houses upon earlier Greek and Roman techniques and traditions had been emulated by the Moslems, who in their turn were copied by the resident crusaders. There were efficient sewerage systems—unknown in medieval Europe—piped water supplies in a number of cities, and in areas where water was scarce great underground cisterns ensured that even through the long hot summers the citizens or the soldiers did not go short of fresh drinking water.

The interiors of the houses with their beautiful carpets, hangings of damask, feather beds, and elegant furniture, amazed the newcomer. He was used to the rough furnishings of a Norman hall, where crude oak coffers, travelling beds stuffed with straw, and long simple tables were all designed so as to be easily transportable if the lord of the house decided to move to one of his other domains. In *Outremer* the furniture which had evolved through Greek and Moorish taste was designed with elegance and comfort in mind. The houses sparkled with beautiful glass (early examples of which, when they reached England, seemed so astonishing that they were thought to be the work of fairies). Feather beds, comfortable cushions, stuffed pillows, tapestries and silks all reached western Europe from the crusaders' contact with the East. Exquisite faience had long been a product of Syria, and Egyptian glassware had been famous for centuries. Even articles from the Far East like porcelain sometimes reached the Levant through the Arabic trade across the Indian Ocean. The rough woollen clothes worn in the north were replaced by silks. The settlers adopted the burnous and the turban when at home, whether in castle or town house. On campaigns they wore a white surcoat made of linen over their chain mail, and an Arabic kerchief or keffiyeh over their helmets.

All this was eminently sensible and practical, but it seemed shocking to the visitor fresh from Europe. Some of the cities still had public baths, a relic from Roman days, but in the private houses of the rich or the nobility baths were almost a commonplace. Like their husbands the Latin ladies adopted the clothing of the East, wearing long silk dresses over which went a brief, heavily embroidered tunic. Jewellery of a quality unknown in Europe for centuries sparkled on wrists, fingers and hair, while the perfumes of Syria and the incenses of Egypt added to their and their homes' attractions.

The castles of the great military Orders like St. John were certainly more austere than those of the married nobility, but even here life was more gracious than in the palaces of their monarchs back in Europe. Part of the success of the Hospital in Jerusalem, and later in Acre, was also undoubtedly due to the fact that the Hospitallers had acquired an awareness of sanitation and hygiene that had disappeared from their homelands with the fall of the Western Roman Empire. The idea of serving the sick off silver dishes undoubtedly originated during these years, for silver and gold were not outstanding luxuries in the Levant. Of inestimable value to the Hospitallers in their treatment of the sick was the fact that—in Syria especially—the traditions of Greek medicine had survived the centuries. The works of Galen were to provide the physicians of St. John with an excellent backbone for their study and practice of medicine.

The induction of a new member into the Order was a moving and deeply serious event. It was the crowning moment in a man's life; a moment which divided him from being an ordinary secular Christian into a servant of God. From now on he was dedicated first of all to the care of the poor and the sick, and secondly to their defence. It has been said that the campaigns in which the Order took part were more often offensive than defensive, and this was often true. On the other hand, while they were attempting to preserve Jerusalem and the Holy Places and keep the pilgrimage routes open, it was not enough merely to wait until they were attacked. If they made a foray into Egypt, for instance, in company with the Templars, it was with the object of checking at source what would undoubtedly have grown into an even greater threat to the Latin kingdoms. Their later activities in Rhodes and in Malta may be read in a different light, but certainly in the centuries in the East it needed little casuistry to justify their militance.

No records exist as to the exact form that the induction of a new candidate took in this period of history. It probably did not vary much from that of later centuries. An aspiring brother came before the Chapter of a convent and, as Riley Smith writes, asked the Master or the brother presiding for membership of the Order. The president asked his Chapter if it was agreeable, because no one could be received without the assent of the majority of the brethren present. He then addressed the candidate: 'Good friend, you desire the company of the House and you are right in this, for many gentlemen earnestly request the reception of their children or their friends and are most joyful when they can place them in this Order. And if you are willing to be in so excellent and so honourable company and in so holy an Order as that of the Hospital, you are right in this. But if it is because you see us well clothed, riding on great chargers and having everything for our comfort, then you are misled, for when you would desire to eat, it will be necessary for you to fast, and when you would wish to fast, you will have to eat. And when you would desire to sleep, it will be necessary for you to keep watch, and when you would like to stand on watch, you will have to sleep. And you will be sent this side of the sea and beyond, into places which will not please you, and you will have to go there. It will be necessary for you therefore to abandon all your desires to fulfil those of another and to endure other hardships in the Order, more than I can describe to you. Are you willing to suffer all these things?'

Once committed there was no turning back. The novice had to promise that he was neither married, nor in debt, nor subject to any other lord—let alone another Order. At a later date when distinctions of noble birth were all important for the knights militant, his family tree and necessary quarterings were investigated before he might even be interviewed. If he was received he swore to live and die in the service of the Order, in chastity and without personal property, and to regard the sick and the poor as his lords and masters. It was a hard oath for a young man to take, but at this date in history it was most definitely meant, and rigorously enforced. Some of the violence and love of battle that marked the militant arm of the Knights of St. John must surely be ascribed to a repression of the natural instincts; a repression that could only find its release in that death of which 'the little death' is no more than a pale mirror.

4

Eternal warfare

THE SECOND CRUSADE IN 1148 WHICH HAD BEEN LARGELY PROMPTED BY the fall of Edessa—that ancient Christian city known as the 'Eye of Mesopotamia'—was a complete failure. It was indicative of what was to come in the years ahead. The Latin kingdoms in the East could never be held if the surrounding Moslem sea were to unite and come against them in one great flood tide. As Sir Ernest Barker commented, '. . . the ignominious failure of a crusade led by two kings brought the whole crusading movement into discredit in western Europe.' The Hospitallers had been prominent in the campaign, and Raymond de Puy himself was one of those present at the council of war when the fatal decision was taken to attack Damascus. It was the inability of the army to take the city that led to the collapse of the Crusade, and there were some who held that the Hospitallers were largely to blame. It is a curious fact that it is not until thirty years later that one finds the first mention in the statutes of the Order of there being a military arm attached to it. By the 1160s, however, one hears of the office of a Marshal, a purely military title. It is quite clear by now that the Hospitallers had followed the Templars into becoming 'soldiers of Christ' as well as being 'servants of the poor'.

By the end of the twelfth century the Order of St. John was rivalled only by the Templars in its wealth and power. It had come a long way from the simple hospice run by Brother Gerard, and was now in possession of such great castles as Krak des Chevaliers, Margat, and Belvoir. Even in Jerusalem there appears to have been a powerful military arm attached to the great hospital. Their original vocation nevertheless was still impressed upon them—that it was the sick and the poor who gave the orders, and it was the duty of the brethren to obey them. Revenues were set aside from various estates to ensure that white bread, for instance, was given to the patients; and clothing, blankets, food and wine were regularly distributed free. Unlike the Templars, who made a distinction in dress between those who were entered as knights and those admitted as sergeants (because they were not of noble blood), the Hospitallers all wore the black mantle. It was not until the second half of the thirteenth century that the caste system hardened. By this time the military side of the Order had become predominant, all the principal offices being held by knights. The Marshal was ranked second only to the Grand Master. At one time or another the Order of St. John had as many as fifty castles in the Levant, some little more than fortified towers, but others immense complexes dominating the whole of the surrounding countryside.

Military architecture developed under the Knights of St. John and the Templars to an unprecedented extent, far eclipsing anything hitherto known in western Europe. The castle which had first been introduced by the Normans into England during the conquest was essentially a circular earth-mound surrounded by a dry ditch. The mound was flattened at the top which was then surrounded by a wooden palisade. This was perfectly adequate against the attacks of men armed with the simple weapons of the time and had enabled the Normans to dominate the country. The logical extension was to convert the palisade into a stone wall, and then to put buildings inside it. In other parts of the countryside, where some natural hill or rock stronghold presented itself, they had little more to do than adapt and improve upon the position.

The crusaders in the East found castles and fortifications already erected by the Byzantines and the Moslems. By a sophisticated graft of western upon eastern styles they evolved some of the grandest and most powerful castles in the world. This indeed they had to be, for the Latins lived surrounded by an actively (or always potentially) hostile population. The main advance in military architecture was the use of flanking towers to protect the line of a wall. Before the age of gunpowder, the battering ram, sapping and mining were the only ways of breaching a wall. It was essential, therefore, that the teams of men engaged with battering rams could be shot at along the curtain of the wall. Mining was largely defeated by building the castle upon a base of solid rock.

Whereas in western Europe the single defence line that had evolved

from the stake palisade was usually considered sufficient, in the East—
where the besiegers might be expected to throw thousands of men for day
after day at the defences—it was soon realised that a second line needed
to be built within the outer. Inside that again, as the last place of resort,
was the keep. This was usually a tower, slightly larger than all the rest, and
sometimes built into the enceinte itself. The castle of course was always
made strongest along its most exposed front. 'Because of the shortage of
manpower,' as Quentin Hughes points out, 'impregnable sites had to be
chosen and exploited. Strong keeps built after the manner of the French
castles became a feature of these fortresses, and concentric rings of defences,
built one inside the other and rising higher and higher, were constructed,
so that those defending the outer walls were covered by fire from positions
behind and above them.' T. E. Lawrence called Krak des Chevaliers
'perhaps the best preserved and most wholly admirable castle in the world'.
To see it rising out of the Syrian foothills with a little fine-blown cirrus
cloud feathering above it is to experience an emotional shock—to under-
stand suddenly what the Crusades really meant. 'I am the kingdom, the
power and the glory' are the words that these walls shout to the sky.

The rivalry of the various factions in the Latin kingdoms of the East
was largely responsible for their ultimate downfall. By 1187 conditions in
the kingdom of Jerusalem were so bad that it was on the brink of civil war.
There could have been no worse moment for the Europeans to engage in
their internecine strife, for the shadow of Saladin was on the horizon. This
brilliant and remarkable man, the first Ayyubite Sultan of Egypt, was by
birth a Kurd from Armenia. Educated at Damascus, that great centre of
Moslem learning, he was a devout Mohammedan (his name means
'Honouring the Faith'), and the possessor of so many virtues that he would
have been rare at any time in history. Honest, brave, chivalrous to a fault,
he was devoted to children, and invariably generous and hospitable—as is
shown by his treatment of captives, as well as by his many gifts to Richard
Cœur de Lion. Saladin was lucky in the fact that his life spanned the
period when the Moslem East had reached a point when there was a
genuine desire for unity among the Faithful. It had become clear to many
men that it was only because of the constant dissensions and religious
divisions between the Moslems that the Franks had managed to retain a
hold upon their lands. Saladin with his intense religious zeal was to unite
them. Islam to him was everything, and he was determined to drive these

Christian interlopers into the sea. 'Let us purge the air of the very air they breathe,' he said.

Despatched by Nur-ed-Din, the ruler of Syria, to assist in the conquest of Egypt he succeeded so well in his task that he was made vizier. It was during this period that four different Christian expeditions were sent to Egypt by King Amalric of Jerusalem, all of which ended in heavy Christian losses, particularly among the Templars and the Hospitallers. On the death of Nur-ed-Din Saladin set about the conquest of Syria. For nearly ten years he was engaged in encircling the Christians, town after town falling to him, so that by 1186 the Latin kingdom was completely surrounded by Saladin's empire.

A four years' truce which had been concluded between Christians and Saracens was almost immediately broken by the Lord of Montreal, Reginald de Châtillon, who ambushed a Moslem caravan and refused to surrender his plunder. Saladin had probably been expecting that something like this would happen. He could control the territories under his command and ensure the obedience of his subjects, but the anarchic Latins with their divided interests and warring factions had no such similar discipline. He intended to impose it with the sword. His orders went out, and soon the whole East began to stir.

In the summer of 1187 Saladin reviewed his troops, about 20,000 men, 12,000 being his formidable cavalry, magnificent horsemen who were to prove so deadly to the knights. On July 1st, he crossed the Jordan and the invasion had begun. One part of his army was sent against the town of Tiberias which swiftly fell to them, only the castle under the command of Eschiva, Countess of Tripoli, managing to hold out. (The wives of these Latin nobles in the East regularly showed as much courage and spirit as their men. There was no safe place, as it were, back behind the lines. When a castle or a city was attacked by the enemy the women were as much in the battle area as anyone else.) In the meantime the Christians had rallied their army, contingents from the Templars and the Hospitallers, and others from Tripoli and Antioch. The Patriarch of Jerusalem had even sent the most holy of all relics to ensure the success of their arms, the relic of the True Cross. This had been discovered in Jerusalem in the fourth century. (Within a comparatively few years Saint Cyril, Bishop of Jerusalem, was to remark that the whole world was full of relics of the Cross.) To expose a relic so precious in those days is an indication of the concern felt about the safety of the kingdom. No doubt someone remembered what inspiration the men of the First Crusade had received from the discovery in Antioch of the lancehead that had pierced Christ's side.

Saladin meanwhile had personally joined in the siege of the castle of Tiberias, leaving the main body of his army in the hills around. He was taking a calculated risk, but he felt confident that the Christians would not leave the castle to its fate. If they fell for the bait he was confident about the outcome. The army assembled against him was about equal in numbers to his own: composed of some 1,200 knights, 4,000 mounted sergeants, probably a similar number of foot-soldiers, together with local mounted bowmen. They were encamped at a place called Sephoria where there were a number of wells. Between them and Saladin lay a burnt-out barren plateau. It was a question of who would cross it first.

There was considerable division of opinion among the Christian commanders. The more hot-headed naturally said that they should set off right away for the relief of Tiberias. The cooler among them, and this included the Hospitallers, were in favour of delaying and making Saladin come to meet them. Even Count Raymond, whose wife was besieged in the castle, said that it would be folly to cross the plateau. Tiberias, he pointed out, was his city and Eschiva was his wife—but that was no reason for the army to hazard itself. Unfortunately, Guy, King of Jerusalem, who was in overall command, allowed himself to be persuaded by the party in favour of relieving Tiberias at once. It was a fatal decision. Saladin had lured his enemy into a death trap.

Early on the morning of July 3rd, 1187, the Christians left their camp at Sephoria and began their march. (It is blazing on that plateau under the eye of the lion-sun of summer, and there are no water-holes or wells.) The plateau shook, danced with mirage, and through the wavering bars of heat the horsemen began to emerge—not to join battle, but to swoop and sting like desert hornets. The whole enterprise was illogical in the extreme, and the only justification that can be found for the army's advance was that Guy, as feudal lord, must necessarily go to the aid of a vassal, whatever the circumstances. The fact that Count Raymond was himself in favour of waiting for the Saracens did not count. Feudal laws and the laws of chivalry dictated Guy's action. In somewhat similar fashion one finds in classical days that generals behaved in what seems now a totally irrational fashion to go to the aid of their 'clients', or even to postpone giving action at a favourable moment because of an eclipse of the moon, or because omens were unfavourable. The Latins of the crusading period, swayed as they were by superstition and by chain-mail codes of behaviour, were every bit as irrational.

Late in the afternoon the rearguard, largely composed of the Templars, was collapsing under the incessant attacks of Saladin's horsemen. The decision was taken to halt the army for the night at the foot of a two-peaked hill known as the Horns of Hattin. The reason for this most probably was that it was known there was a well at this point. But at the height of summer it was dry. Tortured by now with thirst the army encamped to await the dawn-march and, as they hoped, the relief of Tiberias, which would also bring them into possession of drinking water. The Saracens were clearly not going to let them rest. The whole night was taken up by skirmishes, flights of arrows, and the dusty thunder of approaching hooves as other bands gathered around them. At dawn the enemy attacked.

It was a foregone conclusion. Knights, foot-soldiers, sergeants and archers—above all the horses—were exhausted and tormented by thirst. It was not long before the soldiers broke and ran, leaving only the mounted knights and the King of Jerusalem to form a bodyguard around the relic of the Holy Cross. All were overwhelmed. King Guy himself, along with a number of other knights, was captured. Those who were distinguished by the Cross of the Temple or that of St. John were summarily executed. Saladin was normally a merciful man but he knew from past experience that members of the military Orders were dedicated to the extinction of Islam. To allow any of them to be ransomed (always possible with their great wealth) was only to allow another demon to escape and return to battle against his Faith.

5

The armoured men

THE ULTIMATE CONSEQUENCE OF SALADIN'S VICTORY AT THE HORNS OF Hattin was the fall of Jerusalem. This in its turn led to the Third Crusade and to the campaigns of Richard Cœur de Lion (among others) in attempts to restore the Latin Kingdom of the East. But before touching on these later battles, sieges and campaigns—in nearly all of which the Order of St. John was actively engaged—it is important to take a look at the conditions under which these men fought: their arms and armour.

It was still the age of mail. The development of plate armour had begun, but it was not until the fourteenth and even fifteenth centuries that armour, as it is generally understood, became synonymous with the fighting man. Plate armour had been widely used in the Roman world but, after the barbarian invasions of the western empire, it had practically disappeared. The only survivors from ancient days of plate armour were shields, often made of wood, hardened leather, or leather laid over wood, and the helmet. The Normans had evolved a highly efficient type of helmet, which was of conical shape and provided the maximum deflection for any blow aimed at the head. More often than not it had the addition of a bar coming down to cover the nose (the *nasal*) designed to protect eyes, nose and forehead against a swinging sword-cut against the face. The Norman helmet was usually made with a bronze or iron framework, and was lined with plates of bronze or iron. The best and strongest were forged out of a single piece of iron. The inside lining was quilted or padded to afford the wearer a little comfort although, in the midsummer heat of the East, the Norman helmet can never have been pleasant to wear. An alternative to it was the *coif*, a close-fitting hood made out of chain mail.

Chain mail seems to have originated in the East, although the *byrnie*, a mail shirt, is often mentioned in Icelandic sagas. In earlier days only wealthier Europeans were able to afford mail, the lesser ranks being protected by leather or quilted fabric jackets. By the time of the Crusades, the European ironworkers were producing excellent mail—as they had been since the Norman conquest. It was constructed usually with circular rings, designed in five-fold lengths. The *hauberk*, or coat of mail, was sometimes accompanied by leggings of mail. The sleeves might only come down to the elbow, but the tendency was to extend them right down to the wrist, and later, into mittens of mail to protect the backs of the hands. The *hauberk* might reach down to the knees like an overcoat or, in its shorter form, the *haubergon*, be no more than jacket length.

Beneath his coat of mail the knight wore a padded jacket. This was to make it tolerable to the skin as well as to prevent severe bruising or cutting if he were struck. When one reflects that temperatures in the hundreds (F) are common in the East in the summer months, one can only marvel at the physical resilience that enabled men to campaign under these conditions. As Charles Ffoulkes commented: 'It is one of the mysteries in the history of armour how the crusaders can have fought under the scorching sun of the East in thick quilted garments covered with excessively heavy chain mail, for this equipment was so cumbersome to take on and off that it must have been worn frequently night and day . . .'

It had other disadvantages. Because of the weight of the fabric padding, coupled with the even greater weight of the mail, it was hardly possible to take more than a wide swinging cut with the sword arm. Furthermore, as the arm rose so the mail collected in folds at the elbow. At the same time, the action of raising the arm inevitably dragged upward the section of mail between the armpit and the waist. What with its weight, its heat, and its restrictions on fighting movements, chain mail can only be said to have justified its use in a purely defensive capacity. But this was its whole purpose, and when a body of armoured men were defending a tower or castle against far greater numbers of assailants it proved itself by cutting down the number of wounded. It was, as it were, the very inner ring of the human castle within the stone castle walls. Where it failed was under conditions like those that preceded the disaster at the Horns of Hattin. The loosely dressed Saracen horsemen with their mobility and their mounted bowmen had a marked advantage over the steel ring of Christians.

The principal weapon was still the sword although the spear, lance, axe and mace were all used in hand-to-hand combat. The typical Frankish sword as borne by the knights was a descendent of the Viking sword which had conquered England, and large areas of Europe as far south as Southern Italy and Sicily. It had a larger crossguard than its ancestors, but in other respects it differed very little. About three feet long, it was primarily designed for slashing and cutting and, although pointed, was of little use for the thrust. For this reason it was a relatively inefficient weapon for a mounted man and the knights fought best with it when they had dismounted and formed a protective circle, or engaged in a general mêlée. Under its own impetus, coupled with the weight of the man behind it, its cutting power was such that it could cleave clean through helmet and skull right down to the shoulders. Exhumed graves have revealed men who had been sliced open from shoulder to thigh bone, or who had lost whole arms, or even in one case both legs from a scything blow aimed at the knees. Despite its weakness as a horseman's weapon, the long cutting sword continued in use until at a later date the advent of plate armour rendered it ineffective. Once an opponent was almost totally protected by angled, rounded, or fluted metal surfaces the only sword that could be of any real use was one designed for the thrust—to slide up and over a metalled expanse and find the weak point between one metalled area and another. These swords are hardly found until the fifteenth century—long after the drama of the Latin Kingdom of the East had come to an end.

Other weapons used by both knights and foot soldiers during these decades included those usually known as pole-arms or staff weapons. Some of these were descended from agricultural implements such as the billhook or scythe, and others from the spear used since the dawn of history for both warfare and hunting. Among them are to be found long spiked clubs, the pole-axe, the halberd (a long-handled axe with two spikes, one at the top and one at the rear), and the 'bill' with a cutting edge that ended in a hook. The mace, sometimes called the 'morning star' after the German word for it, had a heavy round head studded with spikes and was more of a knight's weapon than a soldier's. Another principal weapon was of course the bow, long used in the East and partly contributory to Saladin's successes against the Latins. The knights themselves employed native and European bowmen, but it was not until the fifteenth century that the English long-bowman would finally proclaim the end of the armoured mounted man.

The Latin kingdom suffered a year of disaster in 1187. After his great victory at Hattin Saladin swept on to capture all the important ports south of Tripoli with the sole exception of Tyre. By October Jerusalem itself was in his hands. The Third Crusade which followed, and in which Richard Cœur de Lion played so prominent a part, failed in its main objective, the recapture of the Holy City. It did, however, serve to prevent the complete expulsion of the Latins, which was always Saladin's objective; and the coast from Jaffa to Tyre was secured. Similarly, the city of Antioch and its surrounding country along with Tripoli remained in their hands, as well as the great Hospitaller fortresses of Margat and Krak des Chevaliers. The death of Saladin in 1193 saved the fortunes of the Latins. Once his commanding personality and dedicated belief in Islam were removed from the scene the Moslems fell into the same disunity that had prevailed among them in previous decades.

What finally emerges from this turbulent period in the history of *Outremer* is the power and prosperity of the two great crusading Orders, the Templars and the Hospitallers. While all the other Franks were impoverished through loss of lands and revenue, being dependent upon their resources in the Levant alone, the military Orders were secure. They had their firm bases in Europe, their lands and houses and income deriving from areas which were secure whatever disasters might befall in the East. It was this strength that was to preserve the Order of St. John through all the centuries that were to follow. The wills of dying men, the revenues of their own properties, the gifts of protected pilgrims and of the sick who had been cured in their hospitals, these were to ensure an economic backbone which spelled survival.

6

An end and a beginning

AFTER THE DISASTROUS FOURTH CRUSADE IN 1204 THE WRITING WAS plain on the wall—*Outremer* could not long survive when Christendom itself was so criminally divided. The Crusade had been inspired by Pope Innocent III, and it had been designed to strike at the heart of Moslem power in Egypt. Deflected by the cunning and cupidity of the Venetians, and in particular Doge Dandolo, the crusaders had first of all sacked the Dalmatian city of Zara, which belonged to the Christian king of Hungary. This in itself was bad enough, but far worse was to follow. Encouraged by the claims of a pretender to the throne of Constantinople (who promised them money and ships to take them to Egypt) and duped by Doge Dandolo, the crusaders found themselves in the position of investing the capital of Eastern Christendom. Weakened by the stupidities and excesses of a recent sequence of bad rulers who had ransacked the Treasury and allowed the imperial navy to fall into decline, Constantinople fell to the army of the Fourth Crusade and was sacked and plundered. It was one of the most miserable events in history. Not only was a great and wonderful city, rich in nine centuries of culture and civilisation, destroyed by these barbarous knights and their followers, but the whole fabric of the Byzantine Empire was shattered. And it was the Byzantine Empire which had been the shield of western Europe. It had provided the springboard from which the most successful Crusade, the First, had been launched, and it had been a buttress behind the Latin kingdom in *Outremer*.

On hearing the news Pope Innocent condemned the crusaders outright. Any hopes that he may have had of effecting a reconciliation between the Western and Eastern Churches were utterly shattered. He saw too as a statesman how detrimental an effect it must have upon Christian interests in the East. In religious terms its principal effect was to continue that division between the two main bodies of the Christian Church which has hardly been eliminated to this day. In secular terms it provided the fatal opportunity for the Latin barons to carve out for themselves small kingdoms and principalities in the prostrate land of Greece. Here they could build their castles, engage in their intrigues and feuds against one another, go hunting, drink the Greek wine—and forget all about the Holy Land.

With this diversion of Latin interest into the lands and islands of the former Byzantine empire *Outremer* received a fatal blow. Who would wish to go campaigning against hardened Moslem warriors, and especially the increasingly powerful forces of Egypt, when they could become rulers over comfortable estates in Greece? In any case, although further Crusades were yet to follow, the old crusading spirit was already on the wane. Even among the Hospitallers and the Templars the old ideals were being increasingly forgotten and a growing secularisation—due almost entirely in the case of the Order of St. John to the dominance of the military caste— was making itself felt. Evidence for this can be found in the fact that, in 1236, the Hospitallers together with the Templars were threatened with excommunication on the ground that they were about to form an alliance with the notorious Moslem sect known as the Assassins.

The latter were a fanatical branch of the secret Moslem sect of the Ismailis, who believed that all actions were morally indifferent. They eliminated their opponents by 'assassination', and were said to induce a blind frenzy among their supporters by the use of hashish, the hemp plant, from which their name derives. It is little wonder that the Pope was indignant at the idea of his 'Soldiers of Christ' coming to any terms with such a despicable branch of Islam. The fact remained that the Hospitallers and the Templars (like the Byzantines before them) had found out that, to survive under the conditions obtaining in the East, it was often necessary to conclude treaties of friendship with the Moslems. In 1238 the Pope issued a bill accusing the Hospitallers of living scandalous lives, including among his charges that they were no longer faithful to their vows of chastity and poverty. They were, he said, greedy and corrupt, in communication with members of the unorthodox Eastern Church, and abusing many of the privileges which their special status gave them. There can be little doubt that many of these charges were true, but the fact was that the Order was so rich and powerful that it could, even while paying lip service to the ruling Pope, more or less afford to disregard the words that were issued in Rome. The seeds of the desire to suppress these wealthy independent Orders was sown as early as the thirteenth century. It was to lead in 1314, to the burning of the last Grand Master of the Templars, Jacques de Molay, to the torture and death of many of them on the ground of heresy, and to the sequestration of their lands and property. The Hospitallers were to be more fortunate. By that time they would have found another role.

The decline of the Christian cause, always abetted by the rivalry and dissension between the Hospitallers and the Templars, was even further accentuated by the added peril of the Tartar invasions from the north and the steadily increasing militancy of Egypt to the south. Jerusalem fell to the Tartars in 1244 and in the same year the entire Christian forces were overwhelmed at Gaza. The Grand Master of the Order together with the Master of the Templars were both captured and taken into captivity in Egypt. This was the worst single disaster since the Horns of Hattin. General ruin threatened the whole Latin cause amid the smoke of burning cities and the surrender of castles and garrisons. The great Hospitaller fortress at Ascalon continued to hold out, until it too fell to the enemy in 1247. Two years later the Hospitallers were among those who took part in the Crusade led by St. Louis of France which was designed to break the Moslem power in Egypt. This ended in disaster, with King Louis himself taken prisoner at Mansourah—only to be released for an immense ransom along with some twenty-five Hospitallers (among others) and the Grand Master of the Order.

The Christians with their constant quarrels had largely encompassed their own ruin during these centuries. Similarly the Moslems. It had already been proved in the days of Saladin that the latter must surely succeed in driving out these foreign interlopers if only they would unite. But like their enemies they were riven by dissensions, both religious, political, and racial. Saladin's successor came in the person of Rukn-ad-Din Baybers, a Turk by birth, who was ultimately to become Sultan of Egypt and of Damascus. Baybers in the course of his violent life, a life marked if ever one was by 'battle, murder and sudden death', not only managed to drive the Latins out of Egypt but set in train the series of

campaigns that were to drive the Latins out of the Levant. As Sir John
Glubb writes,

Although essentially a soldier, Baybers was interested in the administration. In
time of famine, he obliged the rich to feed the poor . . . Whether for religious or
political reasons, he sought the role of the defender of Islam. Stringent orders
were issued against the use of alcohol, against cabaret entertainments and other
forms of immorality . . . Above all, Baybers was a soldier. He frequently rode
down from the citadel of Cairo to the parade ground to watch the troops exercising.
He himself often took a turn and few, if any, of the troopers could handle his
lance or shoot his arrows at full gallop with more skill than the sultan himself.

Neither the Hospitallers nor the Templars come at all well out of this
chaotic period of history. As a contemporary wrote: 'Oh ancient treachery
of the Temple! Oh long-standing sedition of the Hospitallers!' At one
moment in the years following the failure of the Seventh Crusade the
Hospitallers and the Templars even fought on opposite sides. Baybers was
not the man to fail to take advantage of the lunatic dissensions of his
enemies. In 1265, having reinforced all the Moslem castles in Syria, he
led his army into Palestine, giving as his pretext that he was anticipating
a further Tartar invasion. Instead of pressing on to the north, however, he
turned aside and fell upon the fortress of Caesarea. All the defenders were
put to the sword and the city was levelled to the ground. A similar fate
befell Arsoof, and in the following year he laid waste the coastal plain
from Jaffa to Sidon, capturing the important fortress of Safad. The
garrison surrendered on the condition that they might be allowed to depart
unarmed and without any possessions. As soon as they had marched out
they were set upon and massacred. Baybers' aims were the same as his great
predecessor's, but he was no Saladin.

In the spring of 1268 this avenging sword of the Prophet again swept
out of Egypt. The great city of Jaffa was captured and razed to the ground.
Those inhabitants who were neither killed nor enslaved were expelled and
a Turkish colony was planted on the site. Swirling past Tripoli (which he
would have been wiser to besiege) Baybers laid waste all the area around,
killing the inhabitants, destroying the churches, and leaving that rich
and fruitful land looking as though a swarm of locusts had passed through.
Worse was to follow. In May of the same year he suddenly moved his

army northward upon the ancient city of Antioch. The former Roman capital of the East, Antioch had long been the most prosperous of the Latin possessions, being an important centre for oriental trade. Within only four days of his arrival Baybers' men had scaled the formidable walls. Every man in the city was butchered, and the women and children were all sold off as slaves. Baybers handed over Antioch to his troops to loot, and all its riches and incomparable works of art were dispersed among the ignorant Turkish Mameluke soldiery. Determined that Antioch should never again be restored as a Christian enclave in the East the conqueror razed it to the ground. To this day the proud capital where Antony and Cleopatra had once spent the winter together has never recovered from the visitation of Sultan Baybers and his army.

The only reason it seems that Baybers did not take all the remaining Latin castles and fortified places was that he had other preoccupations, among them the Armenian kingdom of Cilicia which, in accordance with his usual policy, he laid waste, killing in the process some 60,000 Christians and enslaving thousands more. A further distraction was the arrival of a small force of crusaders led by Prince Edward of England (which Baybers may have imagined was the spearhead of a large Crusade that St. Louis was said to be preparing). The latter, however, attacked distant Tunis and not Egypt. By that time Baybers had concluded a ten-year truce with Tripoli. In 1271 the great Hospitaller castle of Krak des Chevaliers, sadly undergarrisoned, had fallen to the victorious Sultan. The capture of this superb fortress sounded the death knell of the Order of St. John in the Holy Land and the Levant. When Baybers died at the age of fifty-five in 1277 he had effectively set the seal upon the Moslem reconquest of *Outremer*. It was not only the Christians who had felt the wind of his sword, for he had also successfully thrown back the Tartars and driven them out of the whole area.

The successors of Baybers carried on his policy of total extermination of the Christian settlements. The great Hospitaller fortress of Margat fell in 1285. The knights had been relying upon the fact that a ten-year truce had been agreed upon with the Sultan, but Baybers' successor was no more to be relied upon than Baybers himself had been. The knights and their followers were, however, permitted to leave the fortress for Tripoli, this time without any treachery on the part of their enemy. Four years later Tripoli with its great harbour—one of the chief commercial ports in the

Mediterranean of that time—was besieged by an immense army number-ing, if we are to believe the Latin reports, 100,000 foot soldiers and 40,000 cavalry. After a month's siege the city was carried, and this time no mercy was shown. The city was put to the sword as Antioch had been and afterwards it too, along with its port, was utterly destroyed.

Nothing was now left but Acre. This ancient harbour town in Palestine was the last hope of the Christians in the Holy Land. Situated on the main military highway along the coast, Acre had had the unenviable fate of having been besieged time and time again ever since 1500 B.C. when its name occurs among the conquest lists of the Egyptian Pharaoh Thutmose III. It was destined to fall yet again in A.D. 1291—to yet another army coming out of Egypt. Acre was defended by 800 knights and 14,000 foot soldiers, against whom the Sultan brought an army at least five times the size—some chroniclers maintain ten times.

The city was defended by a double line of walls, the Templars holding the northern sector and the Hospitallers just to their right on the south. To the right of the Hospitallers the walls were defended by the knights of Cyprus and Syria, and next came the Teutonic Order. The southern line of the walls was held by a French detachment, then an English one, and finally Pisans and Venetians holding the area just above the port. On April 11th, 1291, the Sultan Khalil opened the bombardment. He had at his disposal, according to one Moslem historian, the heaviest siege train ever known up to that time. It included over ninety *mangonels* and *tre-buchets*. Both of these had their ancestry in the catapults used centuries before by the Romans. The *trebuchet* was a giant catapult which threw a mass of rock from the end of a long revolving arm, the propelling power being provided by a counter-weight at the shorter end. The *mangonel* resembled a giant spoon and was operated by a windlass. It too could be used for hurling rocks and stones, as well as incendiary materials contained in pottery jars that burst on impact.

On the fourth night of the siege the Templars supported by the English made a spirited sortie from the northern gate of Acre, the Porte St. Lazare, inflicting a number of casualties upon the enemy but failing to destroy the siege engines. A similar sortie a few nights later was made by the Hospitallers but proved no more successful. The disciplined Mame-luke troops were waiting for them and the Hospitallers were forced to withdraw. But the main threat to the defences of Acre came not so much from the siege engines as from the large and efficient body of sappers and miners whom the Sultan had brought with him from Egypt. Day after day the Moslems were undermining the walls, concentrating especially on the strongholds of the protecting towers. The towers of England and of Blois and of St. Nicholas were among the first to begin to crumble. Gradually under the continuing weight of the attack the defenders found themselves being forced back within the second ring of concentric walls.

At dawn on May 18th the Sultan launched a massive assault against the breached and ruined walls of this last Christian city in the Holy Land. As the siege engines continued to fire deep into the city, and as the air was darkened by a blizzard of arrows, the Mamelukes prepared for the general assault. Accompanying them, to inflame their ardour for battle as well as to demoralise the defenders, came no less than 300 camels with drummers continually thundering away on huge sidedrums. The noise was indescribable and the weight of the attacking forces irresistible. By sunrise Moslem banners were fluttering along the walls and the advance columns were already overruning the second line of defences and penetrating into the city. To the north the Templars were holding their own but the main Mameluke attack was thrown against the Hospitallers in the area of the Gate of St. Antony. At this last moment—a moment which had to some extent arisen through the rivalry of the two Orders in the past—the Grand Master of the Templars led a supporting column down to give aid to the Hospitallers. This long area of wall against which was directed the main weight of the attack managed to hold out until well into the afternoon. Then it too was overrun and nearly all the Hospitallers were killed.

Meanwhile, to the south, where the English and French had been holding out against the Mameluke attacks, the evacuation of as many men, women and children as could be accommodated in the ships lying in harbour was already under way. There were not enough vessels, however, to remove anything like the total population of Acre and in the slaughter which later developed thousands were killed and more thousands dragged off to slavery. For the Order of St. John that day marked the end of all their days in *Outremer*. Only a handful of them managed to escape, among them their Grand Master John de Villiers who had himself been seriously wounded in the fighting. The Templars, who had retreated into their great palace at the northern tip of the promontory, managed to hold out for over a week. But in the end the combined weight of the assaults and the continuous tunnelling activities of the besiegers brought down the walls of this, the strongest fortification in the city. The Grand Master of the Temple, Peter de Sevrey, together with some other knights had already been beheaded when they had gone out to try to negotiate a truce in order to save the lives of the women and children who had taken shelter with them. Now, as the battered walls of the palace collapsed, the last of the Templars in Acre along with many of the enemy were buried together in one great smoking ruin.

The whole city of Acre—its fortifications, walls, towers, merchant houses and store sheds, port installations and the warehouses that had harboured so rich a trade for centuries—was set afire and demolished. Within a few days such other few places as had remained within the Latin sphere were abandoned; the people fleeing by sea from such ancient cities as Beirut and Tyre, Haifa and Tortosa. Tyre, which in 332 B.C. had put up the best resistance of all the Phœnician cities to Alexander the Great, was the last to fall to the new conquerors. It was evacuated on July 14th, 1291. But whereas Alexander had brought Greek culture to the East, the Turkish Mamelukes brought nothing but fire and the sword. Baybers and those who followed him, including the now victorious Sultan Khalil, had finally achieved the dream of Saladin—the expulsion of the Franks. But they did not bring with them the Moslem civilisation that Saladin had known. There was little to choose between the desolation that the Mamelukes sowed behind them and that of the Tartar hordes.

Thousands of Christians now flooded the slave markets of the East. These became so glutted that the price of a nubile young woman was no more than a simple silver coin. The Crusades were over. The dream of *Outremer* was over. The Latin kingdom of the East was gone for ever. Henceforth the energies and the violence of the Latins and other western Europeans would largely be directed against one another. A refugee among many other refugees in Cyprus, John de Villiers, the Grand Master of the Order of St. John, wrote that his heart was sick and troubled, and that he was 'overwhelmed with grief'.

Crusaders in exile

THE PLIGHT OF ALL REFUGEES IS INVARIABLY A MISERABLE ONE, BUT THAT of the former Latin settlers in *Outremer* was worse than most. They had lost not only their homes and private property but also their lands. Except for what they brought with them they were penniless. Their presence in the island only served to remind the Cypriots of the disaster that had befallen and, as Sir Steven Runciman comments, 'the Cypriots needed no reminder. For a century to come the great ladies of the island, when they went out of doors, wore cloaks of black that stretched from their heads to their feet. It was a token of mourning for the death of *Outremer*.' The great military Orders on the other hand, although they too had lost castles, property and wide territories, were still immensely rich because of their money and holdings in Europe. In Cyprus itself, the Order of St. John had several estates as well as properties in Limassol and Nicosia. On the southern promontory of the island, where the town and port of Limassol stands, they also had a castle at Colos. It was natural that Limassol should become their headquarters, and within a few years of their arrival they had begun the construction of a new hospital.

The Hospitallers were fortunate in the fact that they still had their original vocation. Even if they, like the other Orders, were demoralised in the immediate years that followed the loss of *Outremer* they were still conscious of their vows that enjoined them to be the servants of the poor and the sick. It was a different matter for the Templars and the Teutonic knights. Deprived of their raison d'être, it seemed as if they must inevitably disintegrate. At first the Templars, acting in conjunction with the Hospitallers, strove to regain their ancient role by mounting commando-type raids on Egypt and the Palestine coastline. In 1300, for instance, a fleet was despatched from Famagusta which landed a small force in the Delta, burnt a village, and then sailed down to Alexandria where they found the defences too strong for them. They next sailed back north and raided what remained of Acre and Tortosa. In a later engagement on the coast they ran into heavy opposition and had to retire, the Hospitallers losing a number of men including one knight. The interesting point about this relatively unimportant excursion is that it is the first time that we find the Hospitallers making use of seapower against the Moslems. It is their first tentative step in the direction of the role of Christian corsair which was later to make them the terror of their enemies and famous throughout the Mediterranean and Europe.

The Templars were less able to adapt and indeed were destined for extinction. Philip of France, who was desperately short of money, had long been casting a greedy eye upon their immense resources and property throughout the land. The opportunity to lay his hands upon the Templars' wealth was presented by the fact that France at this time was under the jurisdiction of the Inquisition. The head inquisitor of France was also Philip's personal confessor so Philip had the tools to his hand. In 1307, at a moment when the Grand Master, Jacques de Molay, as well as nearly all the Templars were in France, the king struck. All were arrested on the grounds of blasphemy and heresy. The charges were centred on the initiation ceremony, when the new knights were admitted into the Order. Now since this ceremony was secret, and since no one but a Templar could state what exactly occured during it, it was possible to levy almost any charge against the Order. If the members denied it the Inquisition could always say that they were lying. On the other hand it was not difficult to extract whatever confession was required by the use of torture. The Inquisition anticipated the trials, the practices, and even the public confessions of Soviet Russia, by many centuries.

The main charges against the Templars were that during the initiation ceremony the candidate was asked to deny Christ thrice, to spit three times upon a crucifix, and to give a triple kiss to the officer admitting him—on the buttocks, on the genitals, and on the mouth. They were also accused of worshipping a mysterious deity, Baphomet, and of indulging in homosexual orgies. The truth or falsehood of the charges against the Templars has long been debated, but the question is one that will never be resolved:

no one can rely upon statements extracted under torture, particularly when the instigator of the charges is known to have had so much to gain by the confiscation of the Templars' lands and money. Nevertheless, it is not impossible that some of the accusations were true. The triple denial of Christ may have been a means, in that simple age, of impressing upon the novice that his dedication to the Order was total, and that it even came before the Founder of the Church which the Order was designed to serve. The anal and genital kiss is a common enough charge against those accused of black magic and witchcraft. The charge of sodomy levelled against the Templars—a sin for which in the Church canon the penalty was death— may possibly be taken seriously. Homosexual relations have always been accepted without much difficulty in the East, and the Templars like all the other Latins in *Outremer* were heavily conditioned by the prevailing atmosphere of the Moslem world that surrounded them. Then again, although like the knights of St. John they had taken the vows of chastity, they were not priests, but arrogant, warlike young males. From the Spartans to the Prussians, homosexuality has always been prominent in warrior castes. In 1312 the Order of the Temple was suppressed and its last Grand Master, Jacques de Molay, was burnt two years later at the stake, while the other chief officers were sentenced to life imprisonment. If Philip's objective had been to secure all their wealth for himself he largely failed, for, except for their property and lands in Castile, Aragon, Portugal and Majorca, all the possessions of the Templars were transferred by papal bull to the Order of St. John. In the end the Hospitallers were the main ones to benefit from the demise of their great rivals.

The Teutonic Order had a quite different fate reserved for it. The last of the military Orders to be formed, the Teutonic Order had begun like the Hospitallers as a nursing service with a hospital in Jerusalem. It had then become dominated by its militant arm. After the expulsion of the Christians from *Outremer* the Order found a new purpose in Europe by becoming the spearhead of the German colonisation of Prussia. The territories that they carved out of pagan Prussia—where they immediately established churches as well as castles—were automatically surrendered to the Pope. He in his turn handed them back to the Order as a fief. Since the Order was engaged in Christianising the heathen, their warfare in Prussia was regarded as a Crusade. Ultimately the Teutonic knights, forgetting almost entirely their original hospitaller function (and even their crusading zeal), were to become a purely politico-military organisation administering vast estates in the newly conquered territory. They represented the first impulse of that German *Drang nach Osten* which was to end so disastrously many centuries later in Hitler's invasion of Russia. The Order itself to all intents and purposes came to an end in 1410 when it was overwhelmed at Tannenberg in East Prussia by King Ladislaus of Poland.

The years from 1291 to 1310 which the Hospitallers spent in Cyprus were characterised at first by a loss of purpose and next by a growing realisation that if the Order was to survive it must change its character. After a number of other minor campaigns similar to their raid into Egypt and Palestine it seems to have dawned upon them that their future lay not so much as a military arm but as a naval one. They were now islanders, and the only possible way whereby they could carry on the war against the Moslems was by sea. As early as 1300 there is a reference to a small fleet belonging to the Order. The title *Admiratus*—Admiral—appears in a deed a year later. It is true that the Knights had owned ships before this, but these seem to have been mainly transport vessels used for bringing troops and stores to Palestine. These they still needed and they used them in Cyprus to bring men and merchandise from Europe to their headquarters at Limassol. But it is in Cyprus that we first hear of the Order owning fighting ships—galleys and galleasses. These were probably intended to be used in a Crusade that never took place—a Crusade for which Pope Clement had been campaigning for some years but which failed through lack of funds as well as through the general decline in the crusading spirit in Europe. It was during this period in Cyprus that an astute Grand Master, William de Villaret, drastically reorganised the Order, tightened up its discipline, secured it further properties and privileges in Europe, and ensured its continued existence.

Nevertheless, although the Knights of St. John had their possessions in Cyprus and had gradually recovered from the moral and material losses resulting from their expulsion from *Outremer*, their position was not satisfactory. The Latin king of Cyprus, Henry, a descendant of the former kings of Jerusalem, was determined that they should not acquire any more holdings in the island. He knew how much power both the Hospitallers and the Templars had exercised in Palestine, contributing to the decline of the kingdom both through their influence and their mutual hostility. He was determined that they were not going to act in a similar fashion in his own country, and made it quite clear to the Orders that they were only present on sufferance. Both the king and his barons viewed the knights with considerable suspicion. Writing of this period in the Order's history Riley-Smith sums up its achievement and character throughout the preceding centuries:

If historians have exaggerated the Order's strength, they have under-emphasised its real historical importance. Not only was it one of the most important institutions in the Latin East, but its officers were great men in many western states. It was one of the first internationally organised exempt Orders of the Church. Its ideal of the care of the sick poor set a standard that was followed by many in the later Middle Ages. It proclaimed, perhaps most characteristically, the crusading ideal: that mixture of charity and pugnacity that had so profound an effect on all western thought in the High Middle Ages. It was an instrument of the popes in the centuries of their pre-eminence, while in its internal history it reflected the changing social and economic structure of Europe: the rise of the knightly class, but also the emergence of a capitalist monetary economy.

The opportunity for securing for themselves a territory which they could truly call their own presented itself in 1306. A Genoese pirate and adventurer, Vignolo dei Vignoli, had obtained a lease of the islands of Cos and Leros in the Dodecanese group in the Aegean. He now came and proposed to Grand Master Fulk de Villaret (who had succeeded his uncle William) that he and the Order should join forces. With their combined ships and men they would capture all the islands in the area—in return for which he would retain a third of the income from them. The fact that the islands were part of the Byzantine empire does not seem to have troubled him. (The Latin kingdom of Constantinople had collapsed in 1261 and a Greek emperor was once again upon the throne.) Grand Master de Villaret listened and approved the scheme, but felt that, in his case at least, he should have papal approval before committing his knights and men against what was, in theory at any rate, the territory of another Christian monarch. That permission was not too difficult to obtain, for the fact was that the Byzantine governor of Rhodes had cast off his allegiance to the emperor in Constantinople and was running his island as a miniature independent state. It was nevertheless a Christian country, the

Rhodian Greeks belonging to the Orthodox Greek Church, and only extreme casuistry could have justified an attack upon it. Fulk de Villaret was lucky. Pope Clement V, who was later to join with Philip of France in destroying the Templars, was a cynical casuist, Philip's creature, and a man of easy conscience.

8

An island home

RHODES IS ONE OF THE MOST BEAUTIFUL ISLANDS IN THE AEGEAN SEA. It is also the most easterly, lying only ten miles south of Cape Alypo in Asia Minor. The channel between Rhodes and the Turkish dominated mainland carried a large part of the merchant shipping passing between the ports and harbours of the north and those of the Levant, Syria, Palestine, and Egypt. The luxuries of the East—spices, silks and sugar—passed their doorstep, as did the grain and timber of the Black Sea. Rhodes was thus admirably suited for the purpose to which the Knights were now to dedicate themselves—the continual harassment of the Moslem world and the disruption of its trade. If they could no longer fight the enemy on land then they would turn to the sea.

The island which was to become the Order's home for two centuries had a long history of military and naval distinction. Rhodian seamen had been famous for their skill and ability in classical times. A Rhodian, Timosthenes, had been one of the foremost scholar-navigators in the days of the Ptolemies, and had been chosen Chief Pilot of the great Egyptian fleet. This tradition of nautical excellence persisted into the days of the Roman Empire and the Rhodians had formed the backbone of the imperial navy in the East. The islanders, native to the sea and its ways from childhood, had subsequently gone on to prove their worth in the navies of the Byzantine Empire, showing themselves master mariners and superb navigators over and over again. If, in the two centuries to come, the Knights of St. John achieved such remarkable successes against the Moslems the credit for them must go not only to their abilities but to the Rhodian seamen who manned the Order's navy.

The island had been called *Rhodes* by the Greeks after the rockroses which abounded there, while its vines in the sheltered valleys on either side of the main mountain range produced one of the most famous wines of the ancient world. Forty-five miles long, with a greatest breadth of about twenty miles, it was rich not only in vines but in olives and carob trees, as well as being blessed with fertile plains growing every kind of cereal. A mountain range, running from north-east to south-west, formed the island's backbone. It reached its highest point almost in the centre, where Mount Anavaro swelled up to a height of nearly 4,000 feet. This provided an admirable look-out point, and from here the coast of Asia Minor could be kept under close surveillance, as well as the archipelago studded with the Dodecanese islands to the north. Far away to the south-west the great bulk of Mount Ida in Crete was visible on a clear day. All over the lesser hills and ranges were dense pine forests, providing excellent wood for shipbuilding—and the Rhodians still built the finest ships in the Mediterranean. The climate was agreeable and healthy, the principal winds being westerly. Most of the summer was enlivened by the northerlies that prevail all over the Aegean; only July and August suffered from hot winds blowing off the mainland of Asia Minor. Numerous streams ran down on either side of the main dividing ridge towards the coast.

There were a number of peasant villages and hamlets in Rhodes, but only one city. This was sited at the eastern end of the island where the classical city had stood, and where that Wonder of the World, the Colossus of Rhodes, a bronze figure of the Sun-God Helios, had once loomed a hundred and five feet high over the city's harbour. It was the harbour that had determined the site of the city. Since classical times Rhodes had been well served by two artificial harbours which the Byzantines had maintained and improved upon, and which the Knights were to make even more efficient and considerably better defended. The northern harbour was the galley port—*Porto del Mandraccio*—with a narrow entrance only about 600 feet wide. The southern harbour was the commercial port—*Porto Mercantile.* Both of these would in due course be protected by impressive fortifications to secure them against enemy attacks. Behind the ports the city of Rhodes rose in an amphitheatre admirably designed for overlooking the harbours and for defending them in time of war. It was here, on the foundation of the classical and Byzantine cities, that the Order of St. John were to erect a complex of fortifications that would be strong enough to

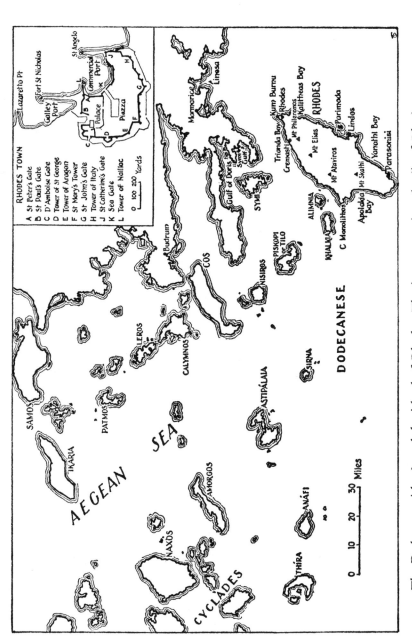

The Dodecanese islands and the island of Rhodes. The inset map gives details of Rhodes town.

RHODES TOWN

A St Peter's Gate
B St Paul's Gate
C D'Amboise Gate
D Tower of St George
E Tower of Aragon
F St Mary's Tower
G St John's Gate
H Tower of Italy
J St Catherine's Gate
K Sea Gate
L Tower of Naillac

0 100 200 Yards

challenge the mightiest armies and fleets sent against it. As early as the first century B.C. the Greek geographer Strabo had described Rhodes in glowing terms: 'The city of the Rhodians lies on the eastern promontory. In its harbours, roads, walls, and other buildings, it far surpasses any other cities. I know of none equal, far less superior to it.'

Grand Master Fulk de Villaret, who will have been well aware of the island's attractions, might well have anticipated Shakespeare's Stefano, 'This will prove a brave kingdom to me.' But first of all he had to secure it, and this was not to prove easy. The Rhodians, as they had shown themselves time and again over the centuries, were as courageous as they were resourceful. As Orthodox Greeks they knew well enough how the Latins had behaved when they had captured Constantinople. They knew also how they had mismanaged the territories that had subsequently come under their control in mainland Greece. For their part they were prosperous through their agriculture, through their current freedom from Byzantine taxation, and from the profits of the piracy which they practised on the Moslem shipping routes. They had absolutely no intention of allowing these Latin invaders to get control of their island, press new taxes upon them and, no doubt, take for themselves the pickings of piracy.

The first landings were made in the summer of 1307 from a flotilla of galleys belonging to the Hospitallers and their Genoese supporters. By the autumn of the year only Pheraclos at the head of a large bay on the east coast had fallen to them. In November, however, they had a stroke of fortune. They managed to capture an important strong point, the fortress on Mount Phileremos, through the treachery of one of the Greeks inside who opened a postern gate to them. (Tradition says at sunset as the sheep were being driven in from the fields the knights—emulating the ruse Ulysses played upon Polyphemus—slipped in under sheepskins.) The possession of Phileremos was important because it put them astraddle the main mountain ridge and less than ten miles south of Rhodes itself. In the meantime, Pope Clement V had optimistically confirmed the Hospitallers in their possession of the island—optimistically because it was to be another two years before the city finally fell.

The long and unexpected resistance of the Rhodians proved a great drain on the Order's resources, so that it even had to go so far as to mortgage its revenues for twenty years to a Venetian moneylender. One thing the Hospitallers learned during this long campaign was that the city they desired was eminently defensible. Indeed, if it could hold out so well with its Byzantine walls and its Greek defenders, what could it not do if garrisoned by the Order of St. John and fortified by all the expertise that they had acquired in the East? In the end the city of Rhodes fell to them not through military operations but through a sheer stroke of luck. The Emperor at Constantinople, hearing of the island's investment, and wanting to restore it to his own control, despatched a ship laden with reinforcements. Carried off course by a sequence of storms, it finally had to run south-east to Cyprus to seek safety. Coming to anchor under the walls of Famagusta the vessel was seized on the orders of a Cypriot knight, who then prevailed upon its Rhodian master to change sides and to talk the Rhodians into surrender. With their reinforcements gone, and with adequate terms presented to them, the citizens of Rhodes had no option but to surrender. On August 15th, 1309, the city opened its gates to the Order of St. John. Fulk de Villaret was now in possession of a fertile and fruitful island with two excellent harbours, as well as a number of usable anchorages along the coasts, and a base from which to operate against the enemy.

What the Rhodian Greeks thought about it all is never mentioned by the commentators—for the commentators are Latins. History is almost invariably written by the victors. One good thing was that in the three years of operations there had been little bloodshed and the Greeks were born adaptors—provided always that their liberty was respected and the practice of the Orthodox religion was tolerated. They may even have consoled themselves with the thought that the Order would bring increased prosperity to their homeland and that it was at any rate better to have these foreign Christians occupying their city than the infidels whose shadow already lay heavy over the waters.

One year later the Order officially moved its headquarters from Cyprus to Rhodes. In the division of the spoils with their Genoese partner, Vignolo, the Knights retained all of Rhodes with the exception of two villages, together with the islands of Lemnos and Cos, from which Vignolo had previously been operating. In return for his assistance Vignolo was to receive one-third of all revenues—which included the proceeds from any profitable piracy. The Order could afford to be seemingly so generous. Vignolo would die one day, whereas the Order of St. John was self-perpetuating. Although heavily in debt for the moment, Fulk de Villaret could afford the luxury of a smile. For the first time since their expulsion from the Holy Land the Order was in possession of a permanent home, and one which gave every indication of being a pleasant and prosperous one. He had an excellent base for the conduct of operations against the enemy and for the first time in nineteen years the Knights had a real raison d'être. More than that, by the Pope's confirmation, the Order was now the legitimate owner of the state of Rhodes. The Order, in fact, was Sovereign. Its only obligations were to the Pope and to its original mission of serving the poor and the sick. Not for them the fate of the Templars. So long as they continued to practise their mission they could feel fairly secure about their lands and legacies in Europe. One of the first things that was immediately set in train was the building of a hospital in the city of Rhodes.

9

Rhodian spring

IT WAS IN RHODES THAT THE KNIGHTS GRADUALLY PERFECTED THE form of their Order; established the greatest fortress town in the Mediterranean; and became the master seamen of the East. With the occupation of Rhodes they also obtained the rulership of the adjacent Dodecanese islands, Cos and Calymnos, Leros, Piskopi, Nisyros, and Symi. Scattered like a necklace across the eastern Aegean—many of the islands were fertile, and nearly all had useful small harbours. These were to prove themselves the outer defences of Rhodes. Just as in Syria and the Holy Land the Knights had built their castles on a series of concentric fortifications, so now they acquired islands that were to serve the same function for their new home. Rhodes was somewhat similar to the inner keep, the last and major strong point of a castle that was now strung out over many square miles of water. At a later date they would also seize and fortify Budrum (St. Peter) on the mainland due north of Kos, as well as Kastellorizo, also on the mainland, about eighty miles due east. Again, like the towers on the outer perimeter of a castle wall the islands provided excellent look-out points. (The name of the island Piskopi means exactly this.) A fortified tower was built here as in several other islands and a garrison was maintained whose duty it was to keep watch on the channel between Nisyros and Piskopi and to light a beacon as a signal to Rhodes if any shipping was seen passing through the strait.

These islands, largely barren today, still had their woods and fertile soil. Of Khalkia a Greek botanist had earlier written: 'There is a place there so exceedingly fruitful that crops mature very early. As soon as one crop has been reaped another can be sown. Two harvests are gathered every year.' All of the islands yielded some profit to the Order, Khalkia also being famous for its shipbuilders, Piskopi producing sage and other herbs from which scented unguents were made, and nearly all of them producing in the small folds of their valleys grain, fruit and vegetables. All round the islands the sea was full of fish—mullet and garfish, octopus and squid, lobster and prawn, and innumerable varieties of rock fish. Grain was one of the only essentials that the Knights later found that they had to import. This they often did by treaties and agreements reached with local rulers on the Turkish mainland—a practice that was actively discouraged by several Popes. But the Knights, who were living 'in the front line', had learned long ago in Syria and the Holy Land that strictures from Rome meant comparatively little, and that it was the judgment of the man on the spot that really counted.

The form that the Order took in Rhodes, based on its earlier organisation, was to prove so efficient that it would last for many centuries. It was the backbone that held the Holy Religion together, and in essence it still survives under the unimaginably different conditions of the twentieth century. At the head was the Grand Master, now, in Rhodes, the Prince of his Sovereign State. The senior officers of each Langue or Tongue were known as Piliers. They, together with the Bishop of the Order, the Prior of the Conventual Church, the Bailiffs of the Convents, and the senior Knights, the Knights Grand Cross—formed the Council, or advisory body to the Grand Master. Not all would be present in Rhodes at the same time, some being away on their estates in Europe and others attending to duties in the hospitals that were strung along the pilgrim routes. All, in any case, if summoned to the defence of the island, were obliged on pain of disgrace to report to Rhodes as soon as possible. The Knights of Justice, the military knights from the great houses of Europe, were required, as has been seen earlier, to give proof of their noble blood. The Novices, the young knights who were just beginning their term of service in the Convent, were required to pass two years of probationary period, during which they must serve one year in the galleys of the Order. This training was essential, for the novices did not necessarily remain in Rhodes but might well return to the priories or the lesser bailywicks and commanderies in the countries of their origin. There they would have to report themselves to their superiors. The latter might second them to other duties either military or diplomatic. But there was never any doubt left that the minute the call came from their small island home in the eastern Mediterranean they must report for duty and make all haste to the defence of the Order. Some, on the other hand, might remain the whole of their lives in Rhodes, this being dependent not only upon their inclination but on the manpower situation in the fortress city.

The Piliers or senior officers of the eight Langues were each assigned a special function, thus the Pilier of Italy was the Admiral, of France the Hospitaller, of Provence the Grand Commander, and of England the Turcopilier or commander of the light cavalry. Inevitably there was some rivalry between the Langues, just as there was equally a fierce competitiveness betwen individuals to rise to the top and acquire one of the principal offices. The method had its advantages as well as its drawbacks for the rivalries, when kept under control by a firm Grand Master and Council, served to promote efficiency in battle. On the other hand the competitive spirit, particularly between hot-blooded young noblemen, could lead to quarrels and dissension and even to open rebellion. This indeed happened during the rule of Fulk de Villaret, and in 1317, the man who had done such great service to the Order was removed from office, and a rival Grand Master voted into his place. But all in all there can be little doubt that the system worked; if it had not it would never have survived the centuries that lay ahead.

The Grand Master, who was naturally a Knight of Justice, was primarily elected by his fellow Knights of Justice. All must have spent three years sea-time in the caravans, three in the Convent, and have thirteen years seniority in their office. The election was not as simple as it sounds, for there was also separate voting in the Langues, the Chaplains and Serving Brothers being entitled to the vote. The final result, after three different stages of voting, produced a grand total of sixteen electors who cast their votes for the next Grand Master. In addition one Knight was elected to give the casting vote should the sixteen reach an equal division in their votes. It is evidence of the intensive lobbying that must have gone on that the seventeenth vote was quite often called into play. What is not surprising, in view of the preponderance of French in the Order, is that during the Rhodian years nearly seventy-five per cent of the Grand Masters were French.

What must never be forgotten is that although later in Rhodes, and later still in Malta, the Order became more relaxed in its ways it was still pre-eminently a religious Order and as strict in its disciplines as any community of monks. In the thirteenth century, as Riley-Smith points out, 'The brethren retired to bed after complines, rising for matins. They slept clothed in woollen or linen garments and must be silent in the dormitory.' In fact, it seems from quite an early date that they did not all sleep in a common dormitory. Certainly by the time that they had erected their elaborate buildings in Rhodes, with separate auberges or hostels belonging to each Langue, it will probably have been only the novices who shared a common dormitory. The Knights kept all the Feasts of the Church, as well as a number of others specifically related to the Order. A conventual Mass of St. John the Baptist was held once a week, and the deaths of all brothers were commemorated on the appropriate anniversary each year. The brothers were bound to abstain and fast at all the ordained times, although those who were engaged on caravans or other campaigns were allowed to eat meat, eggs and cheese—except on Fridays or during Lent. On the other hand on ordinary days it is clear that they ate quite well—and in view of the requirements put upon them it is hard to see how they could have managed otherwise. Meat, fish, eggs, cheese, bread and wine provided the staple diet, although the rules of the Order specifically stated that they should only be provided with bread and water. This meant that there was always an easy punishment available to discipline a member, who for his part could hardly complain since that was all the rule said that he should get to eat in any case. At a later date it becomes clear that the austerity of their life became considerably relaxed; but in these early years in Rhodes, constrained as they also were by financial problems, it is likely that the Knights and the other brethren came nearer to the original rules than they had done for a long time past.

The first necessity on taking up their residence in Rhodes was to improve the fortifications. These, though adequate for the capital of a small island, could hardly be considered strong enough for the home of the Order, for it was almost inevitable that in due course their activities at sea would provoke a Moslem reprisal. As the defences stood they were adequate for the old type of siege where catapults, *trebuchets* and *mangonels* battered the walls, while sappers did their best to undermine them. What was to change the whole balance of power in the fourteenth century was the arrival of gunpowder upon the scene. (A manuscript at Oxford dated 1325 shows an illustration of a gun.) Once the gun was produced in any quantity the old type of fortification had to be completely remodelled. For the moment, however, the Knights were untroubled by that distant thunder on the horizon, and contented themselves with merely improving and strengthening the existing Byzantine fortifications. These were on the old principle of high, fairly thin curtain walls, the gateways guarded by towers, and with sentry-ways running along the tops of the walls between one tower and another. Machicolations, projecting structures through which boiling water, oil, or rocks could be dropped on attackers, completed the pattern of a fortified city in those days when the long bow and the crossbow were the principal hand weapons for besieged and besiegers alike.

Despite the disciplines of their vocation and the duties of their profession the Knights were not entirely engaged with the problems of re-architecting their new city and of preparing their ships for future action against their enemies. They must soon have discovered for themselves the extraordinary beauty of their island home. Not even the most dedicated ascetic could have failed to appreciate that in Rhodes they had acquired a kingdom which was a microcosm of the whole Greek Mediterranean. Behind the city the land rolled away to the south in rich folds of farm lands, sprinkled with white Byzantine chapels and swaying with fruit trees. In the valleys the grape vines rustled. Beyond all this rose up the island's spine, limestone hills purple when the sun set over the long wind-curled acres of the Aegean. At dawn, when the light began to tremble over the Asia of their enemies, the Carian mountains marched out threateningly as if to remind them of the almost limitless power of the Turk. The air was scented with pines and thyme, arbutus, myrtle, and the innumerable other herbs that covered the hillsides. Valleys like Petaloudes echoed with the chuckle of water—the most wonderful of all sounds in hot lands—while the butterflies rose in confetti-like clouds among the rocks.

10

Death to dragons

TWO YEARS AFTER THE KNIGHTS HAD OCCUPIED RHODES A BATTLE TOOK place which was quite unconnected with the Moslem enemy. It has passed, if not into history, at least into legend. A Provençal knight, Dieudonné de Gozon, slew a dragon . . .

In a valley below Mount St. Stephen, a little south of the city of Rhodes, a dragon had established its lair and, in the manner of its kind, was given to preying upon the peasantry—particularly country maidens. A number of Knights at one time or another had gone out to give battle to the dragon but all had lost their lives, with the result that orders had been issued by the Grand Master that the beast should be left severely alone. Dieudonné de Gozon, however, was determined to free Rhodes from the menace, and had a model built conforming to the descriptions of the dragon given by those who had seen it. He then trained dogs to attack it, with the intention of killing it himself while it was engaged by the dogs. When he felt that the training period was over, Dieudonné rode out to the valley. He found the dragon in its lair and slew it. For his disobedience he was dismissed from the Order. So great was the public outcry, however, that the Grand Master was forced to reinstate him. Whatever the truth of the story (and it is possible that some large snake or even a Nile crocodile had established itself near a lake in the valley) the existence of Dieudonné de Gozon cannot be doubted. He is ever afterwards referred to in the Order's archives as 'The Dragon-Slayer'. He went on, undoubtedly assisted by his popular fame, to become Grand Master in 1346.

But the dragon which was to engage the attention of the Knights for centuries to come was the rising power of the Turk swirling out of the East

—ever the home of dragons. Two years after they had established themselves at Rhodes the Order was faced by the first naval challenge from this
great enemy. A Turkish squadron of some twenty ships attacked Amorgos,
the outermost island of the Cyclades. Now Amorgos is over a hundred
miles to the north-west from Rhodes, so at first sight this might have
seemed little challenge to the authority of the Knights over the islands that
came within their control. But it was, on the other hand, only fifty miles
due west of Cos. A Turkish occupation of Amorgos would threaten not
only Cos but Calymnos and Leros, the northernmost bastions of the
Order's small empire. It is probable indeed that the Turks had no
intention of establishing themselves in Amorgos—although there was a
good harbour at the capital Katapola—but were only bent on plunder and
rapine. (The women of Amorgos had been famous for their beauty since
classical times.) Fulk de Villaret nevertheless saw this as a first threat to
his outer defences and sent the Order's fleet north immediately. In the
subsequent encounter the Turks were defeated and lost nearly all their
ships and men. From this moment on the word spread swiftly throughout
the Aegean that there was a new power operating in the sea. In many a
remote island that had once been protected by the Byzantine fleet, the
inhabitants must have felt the first stirrings of hope, that they would not
always be subject to piratical raids. The Cross of St. John was now being
extended over the 'wine-dark sea'.

In the same year as their victory at Amorgos the Knights in company
with the fleet of the King of Cyprus overwhelmed an Ottoman fleet in the
strait between the island of Samos and the famous and ancient city of
Ephesus. All this within two years of first establishing themselves in their
island home is indicative of the fact that the Order took their duties
seriously and that they were remarkably efficient. Yet, perhaps because
the scene of their activities was so remote from Europe, there were not a
few princes, Popes, and prelates, who complained that the Order was too
powerful for the little good it did. Popes cast greedy eyes on its rich
revenues and, after the destruction of the Templars, there were always
those who had in mind the ultimate ruin of the Order. It was in this
political arena, about which we know less than the battles and land
campaigns of the Order, that the power and influence of its members in
Europe were constantly deployed.

That the Order of St. John did not suffer the same fate as the Templars must be largely attributed to two facts; firstly its affairs were well-managed; and secondly its activities were seen by the papacy as the possible herald of further Crusades. What must always be remembered is that Rhodes was only the spearhead of a lance that was supported and directed by the strong shoulder of the Order's holdings in Europe. Without the activities of the priorities, bailywicks, and commanderies in Italy, Spain, France, Germany, and England, Rhodes would have been no more than a distant island in the Aegean Sea which would have been overwhelmed within a matter of years. Money paid for the Order's galleys, money paid for the defences of the city, and money paid for an elaborate spy network throughout Asia Minor and the Near East which kept the Grand Master and his Council well informed of the movement and intentions of their enemies.

Other successes marked these early years, among them the defeat of a Turkish fleet off Smyrna, with the Order fighting alongside the ships of France and Venice. The Venetians were always glad of the Order's assistance in policing the Aegean, for they had large holdings and interests in the islands which formed stepping stones for their trade with the East. In 1345 a major success was achieved with the capture of Smyrna, one of the most important trading posts on the coastline. In little over thirty years the Knights had extended their protecting power and influence over all the southern Aegean, and they were now holding one of the major cities of Asia Minor. It was no small achievement. Smyrna remained an important advance outpost of the Order until 1402, when it fell before the inexorable advance of the Tartars under their ruler Timur the Lame.

In 1365 that dream of so many Popes once again revived and the crusading spirit flashed once more through Europe. Pope Urban V, moved by Peter I, King of Cyprus, and finding a useful tool in a well-known Carmelite preacher, proclaimed a new Crusade. Although few of the greater nobles came from England—with the exception of the Earl of Hereford—and none from Germany, there was a substantial French contingent. Many lesser knights and their men-at-arms came from all over Europe, even from as far afield as Scotland. In the vanguard of the Crusade were inevitably the Knights of St. John. It was they who held the advance-post in the Holy War, and they who were familiar with the whole area and terrain; the nature and dispositions of their enemies.

In the midsummer of 1365 the watchers on the battlements of Rhodes looked down upon a sight that must have cheered their hearts. Certainly it was a sight that would have seemed almost unbelievable to Grand Master John de Villiers who had led the shattered remnant of the Order out of Acre seventy-four years before. Moored in the commercial harbour lay transport upon transport; others rode at anchor just beyond the encircling sweep of the harbour walls. In the Mandraccio the sharklike hulls of the galleys idled in the still water while their ships' companies—anything but idle—hoisted aboard stores and weapons, and checked over details of masts, sails, rigging, oarports and oars. The armada that was designed to recoup Christian fortunes in the East numbered one hundred and sixty-five vessels in all. The bulk of them were provided by King Peter of Cyprus, the Venetians and the Hospitallers furnishing the spearhead of large fighting galleys. The destination of the armada was kept a secret, for the Moslems too had their spies operating throughout the ports of their enemies. Unlike some previous Crusades there was no division of command, for King Peter by the preponderance of Cypriot ships and men was the unquestioned leader. The Knights for their part were happy to accept this, just so long as they could fulfil their aim of chastising Islam wherever possible; the Venetians were concerned over and above all with the profit motive of the venture. King Peter, in order to fool the enemy into thinking that the attack was coming in Syria, sent word to all Cypriot citizens in Syria to return home at once and to cease all trade with that area.

The ruse succeeded. The fleet put to sea and not until they were well under way was it announced that the target was Egypt, or, more accurately, Alexandria. Alexandria, the greatest of all Moslem ports, was a sensible objective. If the crusaders could capture it they would have an excellent base for their fleet and army for a further campaign to free the Holy Land.

The fleet was off the island of Pharos and the great city by the evening of October 9th. The Alexandrians at first seem to have thought that it was no more than a large merchant fleet coming in to trade. (The Venetians conducted a large part of their eastern trade through Alexandria.) In the morning, however, the citizens saw how mistaken they had been. It was now quite clear that many of these ships—in particular the galleys of the Knights of St. John and of the Venetians—could in no way be described as merchant ships. What was more, instead of coming to anchor in the eastern harbour (the only one to which Christians were allowed access) the fleet moved into the western harbour, the Harbour of the Happy Return as it had been known in the days of the Ptolemies. The Governor of the city was away on a pilgrimage to Mecca; no attack had been anticipated; and the acting-governor failed to get his troops deployed quickly enough to prevent the crusaders from getting ashore.

Finding that the strong western walls were difficult to storm the crusaders sent the larger part of their forces round to the eastern harbour where they soon broke into the city. The inhabitants immediately began streaming out of the southern gates. Within twenty-four hours the crusaders were in possession of Alexandria. Once again, as at Antioch in 1097, Jerusalem in 1099, and Constantinople in 1204, these crusading soldiers showed that they had learned nothing from the blood-thirsty errors of their forefathers, and that they were still possessed by the maniac savagery of the *furor Normannorum*.

Making no distinction between Coptic Christians, Jews, or Moslems, they put the whole city to the sword, looting, ransacking, raping and murdering. In vain King Peter tried to restore order and discipline. In vain he pleaded with the crusaders to preserve Alexandria and put it into a state of defence so that they could hold it against the Moslem army that was certain to come against them. But by now the gates themselves had been set on fire and the whole city—once the most gracious in the Mediterranean—resembled a charnel house, illuminated by the fires of its destruction and suffocating under a rolling pall of smoke. As at Constantinople, once the crusaders laid their hands upon the fabulous treasures of the city —looting Christian churches along with mosques, private houses, as well as the great storehouses of the docks—they forgot all about the object of their mission. From the moment that the crusaders swept into Alexandria the Crusade itself was over. Before very long all the ships were down to their gunwales with loot—and not only with treasure. Some five thousand captives, Christians, Jews and Moslems, were taken away into slavery—a slavery they had not known in Egyptian Alexandria.

Although it is impossible to assign any personal blame to the Order for the atrocity that was the capture of Alexandria it cannot entirely be exculpated. (After all, members of the Order had also taken part in the rape of Constantinople.) On the other hand, the Knights were probably no more to blame than King Peter for the outrageous indiscipline and inhuman behaviour of the conquering army. They, like he, stood to gain far more by turning Alexandria into a Christian fortress from which they could have prosecuted the war, with the ultimate intention of regaining the Holy Land. It was not to be. When the overladen fleet was reunited in Cyprus any attempts to hold the army together and to make preparations for a proper long-term campaign in the following year were frustrated. The crusaders were eager to return to their homes in Europe and display their new-found wealth.

The direct result of the capture and sack of Alexandria was the re-kindling of Moslem hatred of Christians. It not only failed in its main purpose, but it provoked a response (as had the capture of Jerusalem) that was ultimately to rebound upon the victors. Sixty years later, still mindful of what had been done at Alexandria, the Moslems would invade and devastate Cyprus, sparing the Christians no more than they themselves had been spared. The fall of the last important Latin kingdom in the Eastern Mediterranean may be traced almost directly to the desire for revenge inspired by the Alexandrian massacre.

The destruction of the city, while almost certainly regretted by King Peter and the Hospitallers, came as an equal blow to Venice—though for very different reasons. The Venetians had envisaged that in acquiring it they would immensely increase their trade with the East and that, with Alexandria under Latin control, their proud City of the Waters would become even richer. Their hopes were dashed. The only people who had any cause to rejoice were the Genoese, who had carefully taken little part in the expedition. They could rejoice in the discomfiture of their great rival, as well as in the fact that their absence from the scene gave them some tolerable credit in the Moslem world. A further outcome of the campaign of 1365 was that for some years the supply of eastern luxury goods and spices to Europe practically dried up. Except for the plunder that went back to Europe from Alexandria—and no doubt also to the island of Rhodes—no real benefit accrued from this Crusade which the Pope and King Peter had so hopefully seen as the beginning of a new era in the East. All in the end, Christians and Moslems alike, were the losers.

11

The wind and the sea and the ships

THE AEGEAN SEA WAS THE BATTLEFIELD WHERE THE KNIGHTS OF ST. John were to engage the enemy for nearly two centuries. They became as familiar with it as their predecessors had been with the desert land of Syria or the mountainous peaks of the Lebanon. Battered by storms in winter the Knights knew it then only from their viewpoint on the battlemented walls of Rhodes, for the sailing season came to an abrupt end in November and sometimes a month or so beforehand. Like the ancients they brought their galleys ashore over winter for refitting and repairing, or else had them securely moored in the sheltered waters of the Mandraccio. April or May saw the galleys ready once more to creep out in search of enemy merchantmen, or to dash like aquatic insects on their oared legs at a signal from Piskopi that traffic was passing through the strait.

The sea that became part and parcel of their life, the Sea of the Kingdom as it had been called by the Greeks, was more densely studded with islands than any other area in the Mediterranean. It was this which had enabled men millennia before to develop the art of navigation, encouraged as they had been when making a departure by nearly always having another island in sight. It was also the only part of the Mediterranean that was blessed with regular winds which blew throughout the sea-going months of summer. In July and August the Etesian winds (called from the Greek *etos*, a year, because they were regular annually) blew from between north-west and north-east strong and steady, declining slightly at nightfall but picking up again shortly after sunrise and reaching their maximum in the early afternoon. It was then that the rowers at the galley benches could take their ease, while the Rhodian seamen hoisted the high-shouldered lateen sails and the galley plunged forward at top speed. Because this was the season of fair weather, *Bel Tempo*, the Etesians were also called *Beltemp* (later corrupted to Meltem, as they still are known). During the summer months, except for a little early morning mist, there were no fogs and visibility was usually crystal clear. The northerly winds broomed the atmosphere and produced that extraordinary clarity of Greek light which makes an object several miles distant as sharply defined as one a few cables away. In the spring and autumn months, when the Meltem were not blowing, the sea was often misted with calm and a haze which the Rhodians called *calina* would lie like a smoky varnish over the surface. The peaks of the islands where the Knights had their look-out points would rise up sharp above the haze, and from their viewpoints the watchmen could descry the masts and yards of merchantmen moving softly through the island channels. It was then that, alerted by a signal or a beacon fire, the waiting galley could dash forward unobserved and be at close quarters before the crew on her opponent's deck had spotted the lean bows smoking out of the mist.

Like all Mediterranean seamen they did not have to bother with tidal problems for the rise and fall was negligible, being only a matter of inches. Currents, however, were another matter and the pilots, who in any case had been familiar with the sea around the island since they were boys, had to be expert in knowing what flow might be expected in the channels between the islands. A galley under oars might make four and a half knots at full speed and about seven with a fair wind, which meant that a current of anything over half a knot was something to be reckoned with. It was upon the application of his knowledge of the direction and speed of the currents that a good pilot might help the galley-master make a capture where, on the face of it, it would have seemed that a fleeing merchantman was destined to make its escape. Up north by the Dardanelles, where the Black Sea flows into the Aegean, there was a strong surface current running south-westerly, but this was beyond the operational area of the Rhodian galleys. The overall current which interested them most was the southerly one which, driven by the Meltem, drove steadily along the islands, headlands, and inlets of the sea. Since there is a clockwise current throughout the whole Mediterranean, varying in strength but almost always present, pilots had to take this into account when working off the mainland coast. The current swirls past the island of Cyprus, turns westerly when it meets the southern coast of Turkey, and then flows northerly. In summer the current induced by the Meltem might cancel out this current or might even override it, but at other seasons of the year the pilot would have to take it into account. Similarly between individual islands, depending upon from what direction the wind was blowing, purely local currents—sometimes flowing as fast as two knots—had to be reckoned with. It was upon the Rhodian expertise in pilotage, as well as upon the excellence of their galleys and the fighting qualities of the Knights and men-at-arms, that the Order of St. John relied for its mastery of these narrow waters. Southerly gales, bringing with them thick overcast weather (although little met with in the sailing months) could negate all other currents and give a north-flowing current even as far as the Bosporus and the Dardanelles.

Around Rhodes itself the Meltem which govern all the conditions of the Aegean in summer, instead of blowing from north-west, turned towards the Asian mainland and blew hard from almost due west. This gave a good working wind under sail for running up to the northern islands like Cos and Leros or to Smyrna itself, while for cruising off the southern coastline of Anatolia, into the Bay of Anatalya, or running down to Cyprus the galleys had a fair wind from astern. In Rhodes the westerly was the prevailing wind. In midsummer it might alternate with cool northerlies but there were also times when a lowering sky over Asia would betoken the advent of the most unpleasant weather in the island—unpleasant only in the landsman's sense, for the seaman could often make good use of it. This occurred when the air over the thousands of square miles of parched mainland blew in from the east, raising the temperature and the humidity and causing the citizens of Rhodes to close their shutters and lie down in sweaty darkness on their beds. At such times galleys or merchant ships at sea could find reasonable anchorage and a lee under the south-eastern shores of the island. They could also use this summer wind to make off to the islands that lay to the west, Crete for example. Other things which the Rhodian pilots, shipmasters, and their seamen had to know about were those typical island squalls which boil up over the high limestone peaks of the Aegean. Strong winds, or gales from the north, would cause violent gusts to descend the slopes and valleys on the lee side of mountainous islands or headlands. The mariner unfamiliar with this sea, who might have hoped to find a peaceful shelter in such areas, would be hit with terrifying blasts of wind, quite sufficient to dismast his vessel.

Except at one point off Crete, where considerable depths are found, the Aegean is a comparatively shallow sea. This means that any strong winds will kick up a short and unpleasant breaking sea far more quickly than would occur in an ocean or a deep sea. Under these conditions the narrow galleys with their comparatively shallow draught would find it almost impossible to pursue a course with the swell on the beam. If there was sea room they could turn and run before the weather; if not then they must head into it, the oarsmen straining at the jumping oars to try to maintain the ship's *status quo*.

It was upon the men who manned the heavy looms of the oars that the galley depended for its speed in approach and for the run-in that preceded the action of ramming and boarding. In the days prior to the advent of guns upon ships the ram was still the principal weapon of the war galley. It could be used in two ways: either for a direct beam-on attack with the object of shattering the opponent's side, or for making a glancing blow right down the side of the enemy, shattering his oars and leaving him stationary and helpless. The final act in all these engagements was to close, secure your opponent to you with grapnels, and pour on board. As the galley ran into the attack the archers and crossbow-men would open fire, hoping to clear the decks so as to facilitate the entrance of the boarding party. The latter was composed of Knights and men-at-arms, who were stationed on a platform forward of the main mast known as the *rambades*. At a later date this area carried light cannon and anti-personnel weapons which were also used to clear the opponent's decks during the run-in.

The human machinery that toiled below decks in circumstances of almost unbelievable hardship was made up of condemned criminals and captive Moslem slaves. At a later date these were supplemented by the *buonavoglie*, usually men who to escape the jail that awaited debtors had come to an arrangement with their creditors and served a necessary number of years until their debts were cleared. These men of course were paid; they also enjoyed better living conditions than the slaves and criminals; and they were distinguished from them by a curious kind of haircut (rather like a Red Indian's) which left a plume of hair growing down the centre of the head with either side close-shaved.

The conditions of a galley slave's life have been often enough described and the expression 'working like a galley slave' has passed into the language. One of the best descriptions was given some centuries later by a Frenchman who had himself been condemned to the galleys. Despite the difference in time, the ships and the lives of the men who laboured in them had changed little.

(The galley slaves) are chained six to a bench; these are four foot wide and covered with sacking stuffed with wool, over which are laid sheepskins that reach down to the deck. The officer in charge of the galley slaves stays aft with the captain from whom he receives his orders. There are also two under-officers, one amidships and one at the prow. Both of these are armed with whips with which they flog the naked bodies of the slaves. When the captain gives the order to row, the officer gives the signal with a silver whistle which hangs on a cord round his neck; the signal is repeated by the under-officers, and very soon all fifty oars strike the water as one. Picture to yourself six men chained to a bench naked as they were born, one foot on the stretcher, the other lifted and placed against the bench in front of him, supporting in their hands a vastly heavy oar and stretching their bodies backwards while their arms are extended to push the loom of the oars clear of the backs of those in front of them . . . Sometimes the galley slaves row ten, twelve, even twenty hours at a stretch, without the slightest rest or break. On these occasions the officer will go round and put pieces of bread soaked in wine into the mouths of the wretched rowers, to prevent them from fainting. Then the captain will call upon the officers to redouble their blows, and if one of the slaves falls exhausted over his oar (which is not uncommon) he is flogged until he appears to be dead and is thrown overboard without ceremony.

It is little wonder that slave revolts aboard galleys were marked by unimaginable savagery. These would most often occur during close action and boarding work. If it appeared that their own vessel was being taken by the enemy the slaves would all rattle their chains and howl to be set free, for if it was a Moslem vessel that was being captured the rowers at the oars would almost all be Christians, and vice versa. It was the captured and defeated enemy who provided the main working power of the galley. The use of the galley slave at sea produced further problems when ships were in harbour. The slaves could not of course live permanently aboard, so elaborate prison quarters had to be constructed to house them. These also required guards and maximum security, for a slave revolt ashore might be even more disastrous than one in a ship. During the winter months when the galleys were laid up for refit the slaves were employed on harbour and defence works. Many of the great walls and fortified towers that grace the city of Rhodes were erected by slave labour working under the orders of Rhodian masons to the designs of Italian fortress engineers. It is little wonder that an Italian viewing some Turkish galley slaves could remark, 'Poor creatures! They must envy the dead.' But exactly the same fate befell any Christians who fell into Moslem hands. Many a Knight of St. John in the centuries to come would end his days on the oar bench unless, or until, his ransom was forthcoming. A hard world breeds hard men, and in the clash between Crescent and Cross that was to continue all over the Mediterranean for some five centuries these conditions of life were to be known by generation upon generation.

From the outside, however, the galley was a thing of beauty. Her lean graceful lines led up forward to her heavily decorated and painted prow and figurehead, and at the stern to her equally gilded and ornamented poop where the officers had their living quarters. In a typical galley of this period the captain would be a Knight of the Order, assisted by a professional Rhodian sailing master who was in charge of the Rhodian seamen who manned the yards and sails and did all the shipwork. The second in command was also a Knight and there would inevitably be a number of novices who were doing their year's training at sea. A galley of this period would be manned by about two hundred oarsmen, from fifty to two hundred soldiers, and up to fifty sailors. The latter would include carpenters and shipwrights, cooks, the master barber and his assistants (he was also the surgeon), as well as one or more pilots and Rhodian helmsmen. Charts existed, but the knowledge of the capes and headlands, islands, bays and anchorages, was mostly carried in the pilot's head.

The galley had evolved out of the Byzantine *dromon*, or 'racer', but for its ancestry one must go back to the days of the Phoenicians and of classical Greece and Rome. A large galley of the Venetian type might be as long as 180 feet, although the Rhodian galleys were usually shorter than this. The beam on such a galley would be only about nineteen feet and the depth of the hold eight feet. Even on an overall length of 180 feet the waterline length would probably be no more than 125 feet, for there was a very long overhang at the bow and a considerable one at the stern. She was a vessel designed for speed and mobility, not for carrying capacity or for weatherliness in anything other than the months of summer. She stepped two, and sometimes three, short masts on which were set triangular lateen sails. These had been known to the Romans and had then disappeared from the sea until brought back again by the Arabs who had preserved the usage of them in the Red Sea and in their monsoon trade with India. The lateen was, until the invention of the gaff rig centuries later, the most efficient sail for almost all purposes. It required little manpower to hoist and set, it was quite efficient for windward work while, with the two main lateens boomed out on opposing sides ('goose-winged'), it provided a well-balanced sail area for downhill work. The other principal vessel to be found upon the sea at this time—and the one upon which the Knights preyed—was the 'round ship' or merchantman.

She, like the galley, could also trace her origins back to the Phoenicians whose merchantmen had been known to them as a 'Gaulos' or 'Tub' from their shape—something like a half walnut. These of course were designed for carrying capacity above all, and were dependent almost entirely upon sails for their motive power. Beamy, high-sided, and driven by squaresails or a combination of squaresails and lateens, they were better sea-boats than the galleys, but were cumbersome to handle and, unless flying with a fair breeze astern, were no match for the galleys. Half way between these two types of vessel came the galleass, a cargo-carrying ship mainly dependent upon sail but which also had oar-power and, at a later date, was capable of mounting a fair weight of guns. It was a combination of the round ship and the galleass, evolved into a thoroughly seaworthy vessel in northern waters by English, Danes and Dutch, that was ultimately to supersede all others. For the moment though, during the centuries that the Knights were in Rhodes, the galley was the most powerful ship upon the sea. Its design was so good that, even though somewhat discredited after the seventeenth century, the galley would still be active upon these tideless waters until the nineteenth century when the advent of steam as a propulsion power changed the face of all the seas and oceans.

Quite apart from the lead and line for determining depths when in pilotage waters, the galley masters and their navigators had *portulans* or pilotage books. Their principal navigational instrument was the compass. These were in common use by the fourteenth century, and references to the magnetic compass occur as early as the twelfth century. In view of the fact that the original establishment of the Hospital derived from the merchants of Amalfi it is interesting to note that it was often claimed that the compass itself had originated there. The fact is that the Amalfitans almost certainly learned about the compass during their trade with the East, and that it was known to the Arabs a long time before it became generally used by Europeans. It is possible, however, that it was the Amalfitans who first anchored the compass needle to a marked card so as to make compass reading considerably easier. Prior to this the early method of using the magnetised needle was to rub it on a lodestone, thus magnetising the metal, and then to pierce a reed or a thin sliver of wood with the needle and float it in a bowl of water, when the needle would turn and point to magnetic north. Such a system was of course of little use unless the weather was fair, for if the vessel was rolling or heeled to a wind it was almost impossible to keep the bowl sufficiently still. Quite apart from the compass, the pilots had their knowledge of the stars to guide them at night. Polaris the North Star had been used as a navigational aid since the days of Homer—and probably long before.

When the galleys were out in company, say four of them at a time, tactics were very similar to those adopted by the cavalry, the ships advancing in line abreast against the enemy. Quite often, however, the galleys went out in twos, and they then used tactics very similar to those of the hunting lion and lioness. Hearing that a merchantman was bound through a particular channel the fastest galley would endeavour to get behind her, leaving her 'mate' lurking behind a suitable point or headland. The galley would then drive the fleeting merchantman in the required direction. At the very moment when it might have seemed that she had the legs on her pursuer and was about to make good her escape, the merchantman would find her way barred by the second galley sliding out from concealment to bar her course.

At the last stages of the run-in, or when just about to board the enemy, the Knights had another trick up their sleeves. This was Greek fire, or 'wild fire' as it was sometimes called. An invention of the Byzantines, the crusaders had come across it during their centuries in the East where it had been used in the defence of walled cities and castles. Composed of a mixture of saltpetre, pounded sulphur, pitch, unrefined ammoniacal salt, resin and turpentine (there were a number of closely guarded formulae) Greek fire was an incendiary weapon. It could be used as a liquid mixture and ejected from copper tubes so that it came out as a roaring flame, rather like a modern flame-thrower, or it could be made into a mixture designed for a hand grenade. It was poured into thin clay pots, 'of a size that would fit a man's hand and could be thrown 20 to 30 yards'. The mouths of the pots were sealed by canvas or thick paper and secured by cords dipped in sulphur which ran down inside the pot. Just prior to throwing them the cords were lit, thus ensuring that when the pot burst one or more of the fuses would explode it. On highly inflammable wooden decks, or among tangled canvas and cordage, Greek fire could be a deadly weapon, quite apart from distracting the enemy at the very moment that the boarding party was swarming over his side. There is no record of the Knights having used Greek fire as the Byzantines had done on an earlier occasion when their fleet had put to flight a Pisan fleet by the use of flame-throwers: 'On the prow of each ship he (the Byzantine admiral) had a head of a lion or other land animal fixed, made in brass or iron with the mouth open, and gilded over so that the mere aspect was terrifying. And the fire which was to be directed against the enemy through tubes he made to pass through the mouths of the beasts, so that it seemed as if the lions and other monsters were vomiting fire.'

It is more likely that the Knights confined themselves to less elaborate methods such as the incendiary hand grenade (from which in any case there was no danger of a 'flash back' into one's own vessel). Sea-fighting was still essentially land-fighting afloat, the object being to board and overwhelm the enemy. It was not for a long time after the general use of cannon ashore that ships would be constructed which could win their battles by accurate and heavy gunfire. Arrows, crossbow quarrels, and incendiaries only served to soften up the enemy. It was the armoured knight and the mail-jerkined man-at-arms, swinging themselves over the gunwales and beating down their opponents, that finally determined the course of an action at sea.

12

From fire comes fire

IT WAS NOT TO BE EXPECTED THAT THE ORDER OF ST. JOHN WOULD BE allowed to remain safe for ever in their fortress-island when they were so regularly harassing the Moslems. If their fighting record had been inadequate, as their enemies in Europe were prone to maintain, then they might have been allowed to remain masters of Rhodes. But it was because they were so active that they were bound to provoke retribution. Their record over the fourteenth and fifteenth centuries speaks for itself. Two years after the sack of Alexandria the galleys sailed south from Rhodes and attacked the coastline of Syria, raiding and looting throughout the whole area. As a commando-type raid it was eminently successful. But it also revealed the inability of the Knights to achieve anything more than such hit-and-run operations. They did not have the men to secure a real foothold in the area.

In 1396, in an effort to check the increasing power of the Turks, yet another Crusade was launched and a great international army assembled under the leadership of the Duke of Burgundy's eldest son. The force, of about 100,000 men, was composed mainly of French, Burgundians, and Germans, together with an English contingent led by the Earl of Huntingdon, the half-brother of King Richard. The objective was the Turkish dominated territory beyond the Danube. The crusaders hoped that, once the Turkish army had been defeated, they would be able to march through Anatolia and repeat the successes of the First Crusade, culminating once more in the liberation of Jerusalem. The Hospitallers in company with the Genoese and the Venetians were to provide the ships, and a fleet under the command of Grand Master Philibert de Naillac sailed north into the Black Sea and lay at readiness off the mouth of the Danube. After some early successes the army moved on to Nicopolis, an important fortified stronghold on the Danube. The army encamped round the city in an effort to starve it into surrender. Meanwhile the fleet moved up stream to prevent any supplies reaching Nicopolis by water.

The crusaders had learned little over the centuries, and they had not even brought with them adequate siege engines to breach the walls. While they were encamped in relative idleness, hoping that the city would fall into their hands without further effort, the Turkish Sultan moved up rapidly with his army. This was largely composed of light cavalry, who were to prove more than a match for the old-fashioned tactics of the armoured Knights on their heavy horses. The result was almost inevitable, and in the ensuing battle the Turks were left masters of the field. Few Knights survived the slaughter, the only exceptions being those who could afford to pay the enormous ransoms demanded by the victorious Sultan. The Hospitallers themselves, although they did not suffer as badly as many of the others, were nevertheless involved in the defeat; a defeat which finally and forever turned the western Europeans against any further crusading adventures. As Sir Steven Runciman has commented: 'The Crusade of Nicopolis was the largest and last of the great international Crusades. The pattern of its sorry history followed with melancholy accuracy that of the great disastrous Crusades of the past . . .'

There was one salient difference however: the last of the Crusades was essentially a defensive one. Instead of being launched at the heart of the Moslem enemy in their own territories, it was designed to prevent that enemy from advancing any further into Europe. The same inadequacy in military preparation, the same dissensions between rival leaders, and the same rash impetuosity on the field led to disaster. The principal lesson that the Hospitallers learned from the campaign was that they were now on their own. There would be no more major expeditions from Europe. They learned also that, just as the sea gave them their mobility to attack the enemy, so it gave them the mobility to withdraw rather than be captured or cut down like the land-bound soldier. It confirmed what they had learned during their sea-going years in Rhodes. Except on a very few occasions—and these more in the category of seaborne raids than land campaigns—the Knights were now wedded to the sea for almost four centuries.

Despite a number of minor engagements the history of the next few years was comparatively quiet. This was largely due to the fact that the Turks were engaged in fighting the Tartars under Timur the Lame, who had also overrun much of the East and in 1392 had even captured Baghdad. The whole Moslem world was far too much preoccupied with the onslaught of the Tartars to worry about the relatively unimportant gadfly of a handful of Christians in Rhodes. The Knights were also to suffer from Timur's conquering hordes when, in 1402, he swung north and captured Smyrna. It was the general confusion in the Moslem world that helped the Order to pull off a diplomatic coup a year later, and conclude a most successful treaty with the Egyptian Mamelukes. This gave them the right to maintain a consulate in Jerusalem as well as to open consulates at Damietta and Ramleh. Even more important than these diplomatic concessions was the fact that the Knights were to be allowed to rebuild their old hospital in Jerusalem. A clause in the agreement, designed to make the Rhodians happy, secured for them preferential trading rights in Alexandria, Beirut, Damascus, Damietta, and Tripoli. During the thirty-eight years that this truce lasted the Order and the island it administered enjoyed a prosperous period. But the fortifications were not neglected, and the galleys continued to sweep out from the Mandraccio on their caravans.

In Anatolia the main effect of Timur's invasion was to introduce a further influx of hardy horsemen and warriors almost indistinguishable from the Turks. If Timur's sons had not fought between one another over the succession there can be little doubt that Constantinople would have come under attack earlier than it did. During the breathing space afforded by this civil war the Byzantines managed to acquire a number of coastal cities that had formerly been theirs, while the Order of St. John built a powerful fortress on the narrow peninsula that juts out from the mainland opposite the island of Cos. They now had the Cos channel securely in their grasp. The fortress called St. Peter the Liberator still stands, its name corrupted into Budrum (from *Bedros*, Peter). It provided a refuge point for Christians fleeing from slavery throughout Anatolia, a place from which they could be ferried to the security of Rhodes.

In 1440 Pope Eugenius IV preached a new Crusade. Only the Albanian chieftain Skanderberg, the Prince of Serbia, and the Hungarians came forward to declare war on the Turks and, after a few indecisive skirmishes, they were to sign a ten-year truce with the enemy. No western European powers paid any attention to the Pope's call; they were far too engaged in their own affairs and national rivalries. As far as the West was concerned the Crusades were over. But the Knights, in the same year that the Crusade was preached, secured a notable victory. Their treaty with the Mamelukes had broken down and a fleet of seventeen ships had been despatched from Egypt to blockade Kastellorizo, that strongpoint held by the Order on the Turkish coast due east of Rhodes. The Order's operational fleet at this time seems to have consisted of four sailing vessels—presumably 'round ships' designed for carrying troops and stores—and eight galleys. Coming up with the blockading force they soon proved their immense superiority over the Egyptians, capturing twelve of their vessels along with all their crews. This in itself was profitable enough, but they went on to put a party of Knights and soldiers ashore, engaging the Mamelukes who had landed from the Egyptian ships. In the ensuing battle 700 Mamelukes were killed while the rest, unable to escape by the sea since their fleet was destroyed, were all captured. If the Pope's call to arms had fallen on deaf ears the Order had shown that it was still as active as ever in its war against Islam.

Four years later, in 1444, the Egyptians once more tried their hand against the Knights, landing on Rhodes itself and laying siege to the city. Their efforts were frustrated by their own inefficiency in siege warfare and by the strength of the city's fortifications. Defeated yet again at sea, the Egyptians withdrew after a siege lasting forty days and returned to Alexandria. They were never again to trouble the Order of St. John. Within a few years they themselves were to find the Turks at their gates, and their country was ultimately destined to become part of the Ottoman empire. Over the centuries since they had first established their hospital in Jerusalem and had evolved the military branch of their Order the Knights had been in conflict with almost every Moslem power in the East, as well as pagans like the Tartars. Their hardest task now lay ahead, for the Turks and Turcomans who embraced Islam were to combine the religious fanaticism of the Saracens with the hardiness and violence of the Asiatic steppe peoples.

The activities of the Knights during the years since they had firmly established themselves in Rhodes, right up to the moment when the first major attack was launched against them (while ill-acknowledged in

Europe) had been largely responsible for the fact that the Turks had never made much of a showing as a naval power. Like the Arabs long before them they feared and distrusted the sea. They might have echoed the remark of 'Amr, the great Arab conqueror of Alexandria: 'If a ship lies still it rends the heart; if it moves it terrifies the imagination. Upon it a man's power ever diminishes and calamity increases. Those within it are like worms in a log, and if it rolls over they are drowned.' But the Turks, again like the Arabs, were to prove that within a comparatively short time they too could learn to be seamen. In this, and in their shipbuilding techniques, they were to be aided by Greek subjects from Asia Minor and by the knowledge and expertise of the shipbuilders of Constantinople. For, in 1453, the great city that had been founded by Constantine the Great, that had been captured by the Latins in the Fourth Crusade, and later retaken by the Byzantines, fell for the last time to the victorious Sultan Mehmet II.

Mehmet, son of the Sultan Murad, was one of the most distinguished men in Turkish history and he was to make himself the terror of Europe. Although he was to advance Turkish arms into Europe itself, and to be revered ever after by his people as the conqueror of Constantinople and the founder of Turkey-in-Europe, he was far from being of pure Turkish descent. He himself liked to claim that his mother was a Frank, and he certainly had Greek and Armenian blood in his veins. His appearance was more European than Turkish, as is borne out by the famous painting of him by Gentile Bellini. A good looking man, with piercing eyes under curved eyebrows, he had a thin Semitic nose above full red lips. An intellectual, he had an extensive knowledge of Greek literature as well as Islamic, and he was well read in science and philosophy. A brilliant linguist, he spoke Turkish, Arabic, Greek, Latin, Hebrew and Persian. It was said of him that his greatest desire was to emulate Alexander the Great. Unlike Alexander, however, he was a man of monstrous cruelty, with all the implacability of the Oriental despot. When, on the death of his father, the latter's widow came to condole with Mehmet and congratulate him on his succession her young son was at that very moment being drowned in his bath on Mehmet's orders. Yet, like many a tyrant, he enjoyed the company of artists and scholars. His first words as he rode through conquered Constantinople were the lines from the Persian poet Sa'di:

Now the spider weaves the curtains in the palace
Of the Caesars,
Now the owl calls the night watches in the
Towers of Afrasiab.

Contrary to the code of Islam he was a notorious wine-bibber, happiest perhaps when in his cups. He was also, in common with many Turks, a paederast, and among his many acquisitions after the fall of Constantinople were a number of handsome Greek youths. A strange compendium of virtues and vices, this was the man who was to look south from his new capital and plan the destruction of Rhodes and the end of the Knights Hospitaller.

The man who was to meet this challenge as Grand Master of the Order was a Frenchman of the Langue of Auvergne, Pierre d'Aubusson. Born in 1423, he was fifty-seven at the time that Mehmet launched his attack on the island. He had first come to Rhodes as a novice at the age of twenty-one and had risen rapidly in the Order, being chosen in 1454 by Grand Master de Lastic for the delicate mission of going to Europe and securing money and armaments against the impending Turkish attack. Later, appointed to the post of Captain General, he had personally supervised the extension and modernisation of the defences. As Prior of Auvergne, and virtually head of the Order since the then Grand Master was old and ill, d'Aubusson had pressed on with the task of making the city as impregnable as he could with the funds at his disposal. A large curtain wall had been raised to protect the seaward approaches to the city, three new towers were built, the ditch on the landward side was everywhere widened and deepened, and a boom-defence was constructed to protect the somewhat vulnerable commercial harbour. D'Aubusson appears to have been a man of humour, sensitivity and intelligence: he was a very fine example of the '*chevalier sans peur et sans reproche*'.

By 1479 it was clear to the Grand Master and the Council that they might expect the blow to fall at any moment. D'Aubusson had already declined to pay tribute to the Sultan or to refrain from molesting his shipping. The Sultan for his part was encouraged in his plans by information given him by a small group of Rhodian renegades in Constantinople that the city of Rhodes was weak and would fall easily to his arms. That same winter he sent his commander-in-chief, Misac, south through the

Aegean with a number of galleys to reconnoitre the island. This reconnaisance force achieved nothing apart from burning a number of hamlets, and it was finally driven off with heavy losses. Misac Pasha retired to Marmarice on the mainland, just eighteen miles from Rhodes. Here he sat down to winter and to await the arrival of the Sultan's fleet and army in the spring of the following year. At long last the great trial between Cross and Crescent was to be made—the first of any real consequence since the thirteenth century.

13

Siege

IN THE SPRING OF 1480 THE TROOPS MARCHED OVERLAND FROM THE
Hellespont and assembled under the Sultan's standard at Marmarice. All
was ready for the assault upon Rhodes, 'that abode of the Sons of Satan'.
Despite attempts by Mehmet to conceal the object of the expedition
(among them the carefully promoted rumour that the army and the fleet
were designed for the capture of Alexandria), Pierre d'Aubusson was far
too well informed ever to be deceived. The Knights and the Rhodians all
had their instructions. As many of the former as could possibly arrive in
time were to report to the Convent, while the Rhodians, as soon as the
armada was sighted, were to burn and destroy the land behind them and
retire with their families, property, and animals, either into the fortified
points around the island or into the city itself.

The force that had been assembled against the Knights has been put at
about 70,000 men. As always, when dealing with estimates made of the
enemy at this or almost any period in history, allowance must be made for
exaggeration. Nevertheless, it was an immense army for its time, and the
fleet which transported it and escorted it—some fifty ships or more—
suggests that the figures were not far from accurate. Against the might of
the Turkish Empire the Knights opposed about 600 members of the
Order, including servants-at-arms, and between 1,500 and 2,000 paid
foreign troops and local militia. In addition, of course, there were the
townsfolk themselves, nearly all of whom were capable of lending some
kind of hand in the defence. There is no record of the number of slaves at
that time held in the city but they too could be used under strict super-
veillance for rebuilding defences and for other manual work.

The siege of Rhodes was marked by the extensive use of cannon, something that had been foreshadowed by the siege of Constantinople where the cannon constructed for Mehmet by a Hungarian engineer had been largely instrumental in the city's fall. Cannon had been used in European wars for a century, but mainly as field pieces for dispersing troops. Generally speaking they had not reached the size that could carry enough weight of ball seriously to damage city walls. The Sultan, however, with his keen interest in the sciences, had long been a believer in the efficacy of cannon for reducing cities and from early in his reign had ordered his foundries to experiment in the production of larger and more efficient weapons. At Constantinople, for instance, the largest cannon used against the walls had a barrel length of over twenty-six feet and fired a ball weighing twelve hundredweight. At Rhodes we hear of one heavy battery consisting of three 'basilisks', seventeen feet long, which fired cannon balls nearly seven feet in circumference. There was one drawback to these massive early cannons: the rate of fire was very slow because the barrel had to cool after each round before a fresh charge could be inserted. This gave them a rate of fire of little more than one round an hour.

At dawn on May 23rd the fleet was sighted coming down towards Akra Milos, the most north-westerly point of the island. The ships then turned and made their way towards Marmarice where the embarkation began. The first landings were made shortly after sunset that night in the pleasant Bay of Trianda, with its shelving beach and its swiftly-running streams. The attack began next morning with a bombardment of the Tower of St. Nicholas. This was the large fort, with walls twenty-four feet thick, which stood at the end of the long mole that divided the Mandraccio from the commercial port. If it could be reduced both harbours would immediately become vulnerable. Meanwhile innumerable other cannons of varying weight began to bombard the city itself, hurling their projectiles high over the walls with the object of demoralising the townsfolk, none of whom had ever before experienced the violence of modern war. D'Aubusson, however, with his usual foresight had already organised shelters in cellars throughout the city where the women and children, and the old and the sick, could take refuge.

Strong though it was, St. Nicholas began to crumble before the weight of the gunfire. D'Aubusson, realising that almost everything hinged upon its preservation from the enemy, immediately set about converting its ruins into an even stronger fortress. (Now that its profile was reduced its actual thickness was almost doubled.) He knew that if it fell not only would the harbours become untenable, but the Turks would be able to storm along the mole and attack the two city gates at its landward end. During the days and nights that followed gangs of slaves, soldiers and townspeople laboured continually to maintain the structure of the tower and at the same time convert the whole mole into a walled rampart facing the Turks across the waters of the Mandraccio.

On May 28th the Grand Master sent off an urgent despatch to all members of the Order in Europe. He implored their help and angrily pointed out that many of the brethren had already turned a deaf ear to his previous pleas and exhortations. The situation, he said, was critical, and no member who failed to do all in his power to come to the Order's assistance could ever be excused. 'What is more sacred than to defend the Faith?' he concluded. 'What is happier than to fight for Christ?' But the fact was that in those days of poor communications and worse travel facilities Rhodes was just too far away for many members of the Order ever to reach it on short notice. Even if they were to band together and equip a ship, by the time they had done so and reached the island all would be over one way or another. There was the likelihood too that if the island was as closely invested by a large fleet as it appeared to be, then a relief force would have no chance of getting through. Surprisingly enough, only a few days later a relief vessel did get through and make its way into the commercial port. This was a Sicilian carrack, laden with grain and a number of reinforcements—very helpful to morale at this stage in the siege.

On the same day that d'Aubusson wrote his letter to the absent brethren a very strange defector made his way over from the Turkish lines and asked to be let into the city. This was none other than Master George, the great German artillery expert, regarded as the main brains behind the siting of the cannon and the conduct of the bombardment. Like so many who served in the Turkish ranks he was a Christian by birth. As he told d'Aubusson when he was interviewed, his heart had been moved by the plight of his co-religionists and he wished to join them and give his services to the Holy Religion. D'Aubusson received him courteously enough and accepted the offer. At the same time he detailed six Knights to form a permanent bodyguard for the master-gunner, telling them never

The capture of Damietta by St. Louis, 1248, with the ships of the Order in the background.

The fall of Acre in 1291. The Knights of St. John form the rearguard and hold back the Mamelukes while the Christian survivors of the siege embark.

A Crusader Castle at Safita, Syria. (*Ronald Sheridan*)

A Knight of the English Tongue. From the Grand Master's Palace, Valetta.

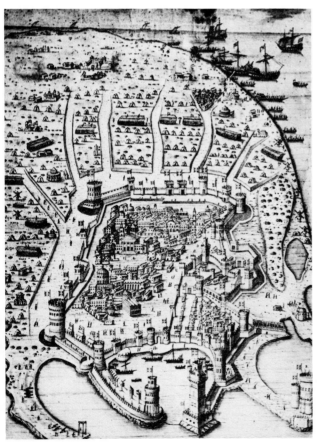

The city of Rhodes in the time of the Knights. Fort St. Nicholas lower right.

Rhodes. The Street of the Knights. (*A. F. Kersting*)
Rhodes. The western gate with the Palace of the Grand Masters behind. (*A. F. Kersting*)

L' ASSEDIO E BATTERIA DELL ISOLA DI S·MICHELE A DI XXVIII DI GIVGNO. F·VI

Dopo la preca di Santermo fuggirno molti rinegati dalli quali se intese che il Bassa voleua battere le fortezze con 6 o pezzi imaginandosi in pochi giorni ridurle isate in poluere. Quella Isola di S Michele e posta dalla lingua de Italia nella quale era superiore l Armiraglio Fra Pietro de Monti et Fra Pietro Giustiniani.

A Castello S Angelo. — F L Isoletto. — K La Fronte dell Isola di S Michele. — N Sanbuchieri alla scarpa del fosso. — R Margheria doue stauano 6 cannoni un bombaiso.
B Il Borgo. — G Le spronte dell Isola e le molina. — K Il Galeone che su pigliato ai Turchi. — O L Artegliaria che conducono da Santermo. — che battuano lasfronte dis Michele e Prouenza.
C Posta di Prouenza. — G L sprone dell Isola e le molina. — L Il Ponte che su passata dall Borgo all isola. — P Batteria de 5 canoni che battuano il Borgo e S Angelo. — S Il Curadiso doue stauano 17 cannoni che battuano.
D Il Palauespo. — H L saltemo e a preso da Turchi. — M Catena di antena salta del maglio. — Q Posta di Draguti doue stauano 4 canoni che battuano Santermo. — S Michele 1565 la coffoni

T La Burmula doue stauano 2 cannoni che tirauano a S Angelo et al Borgo. V La Mandra con 4 canoni che battivano S Michele. X Barcha cedone piena g Mori d affalto al operat. Batteria di 5 canoni che tirauano al operand isola S Ermolo

IOANNES DE VALETA MAGNVS MAGISTER
HOSPITALIS HIEROSOLIMITANI·
VERA EFFIGIES·A·DIL·GRAN·MAGISTRO EFFIGVRATA
Abconterfetung des grosen Maisters zu Malta S Die 3 vstung wie so na ch der belegnug erhalten

The siege of Malta, 1565.
The peninsula of Senglea
is in the centre, Birgu
with Fort St. Angelo at
the tip, on the right.

La Valette. A German
engraving of 1557, the
year that he became Grand
Master.

Senglea Point with Fort St. Angelo behind. (*Bill Smeaton-Russell*)

The State Galley of Grand Master Cotoner.

The city of Valetta from Marsamuscetto harbour. Attributed to Canaletto.

INFIRMIS SERVIRE FIRMISSIMVM REGNARE.

The Sacred Infirmary in Valetta, with the Knights tending the patients.

The 77th Grand Master, Fra Angelo de Mojana di Cologna at the tomb of La Valette.

to let him out of their sight, and to watch and report on everything he said and did. D'Aubusson was no man's fool and the defection, particularly of so important a figure in the Sultan's camp, seemed a little too easy. Meanwhile the main weight of the bombardment continued to fall upon the Tower of St. Nicholas and it was clear that before very long the Turk would come to the attack.

The blow fell early one June morning, when specially modified Turkish triremes were seen rounding Akra Milos from their base at Trianda and heading across the misty sea for the fortress. The vessels had had their masts, spars and rigging removed, and were fitted with special fighting platforms in the bows. Manned by Sipahi troops, professionals second only to the crack Janissaries, they came onward towards their objective to the usual clamour of cymbals, drums, pipes and ululating cries with which the Turks always went into battle. The Knights and men-at-arms were waiting for them. While the advancing ships kept up a steady fire on the fort, all the guns that could be brought to bear opened fire upon them, from the fort itself and from the Post of France, that part of the city wall which faced the mole. The attackers were brave enough, hurling themselves off the bow-platforms into the sea and swarming ashore. But they were committing the unforgivable mistake of attempting a landing right in the face of a strongly fortified and strongly held position. (If the Turkish command had over-estimated the damage that their bombardment had done and had reckoned that the defence must be almost non-existent, they were to be sadly disillusioned.) Even as the first wave of Sipahis attempted to come ashore they were met by a withering fire from crossbows, arquebuses and long bows, while for those who actually managed to reach the palisades erected round the fort there waited the sizzle of Greek fire. And at the palisades themselves stood the long line of armoured men—a curtain-wall of steel—swinging above their heads those great two-handed swords that could split a man from head to crotch in a single blow. Many were drowned, others killed on the spot, and the attack was foredoomed from the start. The survivors turned, splashed back through the shoals, and made for the safety of their ships. But even here no safety existed, for the fort's guns and small arms once again came into play. One vessel blew up, and most of the others sustained such damage that it took the carpenters and shipwrights days to put them into service again.

But by mid-June so weighty and sustained was the general bombardment (nearly a thousand cannon balls a day, d'Aubusson calculated) that
certain parts of the city walls were on the point of collapse. The worst
area was to the south of the commercial port, the curtain wall surrounding
the Jews' Quarter of the city which was held by the Langues of Auvergne
and Italy. All the time the Turks were snaking forward their trenches,
advancing them night after night towards the counterscarp of the great
ditch that surrounded the city. On the night of June 18th a second major
assault was launched against St. Nicholas, this time by the cream of the
Sultan's troops, the fearsome Janissaries. The Turks had constructed a
large floating pontoon on to which the Janissaries were marched, the
pontoon then being towed under cover of darkness up to the threatened
tower. Brave though the attempt was, and this time better thought out
than the previous daylight operation, the Turks were not to find the
defenders asleep at their posts. Every gun that could be brought to bear
swept the crowded pontoon and the galleys and other escorts that had
moved up for the kill. The night was dark no longer. Flares, bursting
grenades, and liquid fire illuminated a scene reminiscent of hell. In the
waters the bodies of hundreds of Janissaries testified to the firepower of
the garrison and of the city. By daylight next morning all was over. Once
again the fort, that all-important defence work, had held out against the
arms of Islam.

As in any city under siege there were always some who felt that it would
be better to save their skins than to die in the crumbling, smoking ruins.
Two such plots against the Order were exposed and the men concerned
were put to death. One of the schemes involved poisoning the Grand
Master himself. The renegade, a Dalmatian or Italian, who had conceived
it, was torn to pieces by the townspeople on his way to the place of
execution. But, despite these and other attempts to suborn the Rhodians
or betray the city, d'Aubusson kept his eye all the time on the mysterious
German, Master George. Like so many spies Master George finally betrayed his purpose by the fact that the information he gave the Grand
Master about the Turkish dispositions or the siting of the city's guns was
always shown to be either inaccurate or ineffectual. At length d'Aubusson
had had enough. The German was put to torture, admitting at last that he
had been true to his Turkish masters from the very beginning. There seems
little doubt, despite the inevitable mistrust which must always hang

around answers elicited under torture, that Master George was guilty. He was publicly hanged and a message to the effect that their master-spy and master-gunner was dead was shot into the Turkish lines.

By the third week of July it was quite clear to the defenders that the first great mass assault must soon fall upon the city. The wall surrounding the Jews' Quarter was a crumbling ruin and, despite the fact that the defenders had built another wall and ditch behind it, there was little that could be done about the point just seaward of the tower of Italy where only a narrow and largely destroyed curtain-wall protected the city between it and the commercial port. On July 27th following upon not days and nights but week after week of constant bombardment (during which time the whole city of Rhodes seemed like a ship sailing over a sea of smoke and fire) the great attack was launched. In the first wave came the Bashi-Bazouks, irregulars, many of them of Christian birth. Violent, predatory, the scum of the eastern earth, they fought under the Turkish banner only for plunder. Brave though many of them undoubtedly were, they were an undisciplined crew, and their Turkish masters made sure that their enthusiasm did not wane too rapidly in the teeth of resistance. Behind them they sent a line of Turks armed with whips and maces— working on the principle that if they feared their officers more than the enemy then all would be well. The Bashi-Bazouks were expendable. Their bodies would fill the ditch and provide the stepping stone for those who came after them. And these were the Janissaries.

Yeni-Cheri, 'New Soldiers', was the Turkish word for them and it was accurate enough since they were a completely novel concept. They were all Christians by birth, who had been selected on account of their physique during a five yearly inspection made throughout the Turkish empire for healthy young males aged seven. Destined for the army, they were taken away from their parents, trained as strict Moslems, and instructed in the arts of war. As W. H. Prescott wrote of them: 'Those giving the greatest promise of strength and endurance were sent to places prepared for them in Asia Minor. Here they were subjected to a severe training, to abstinence, to privations of every kind, and to the strictest discipline . . . Their whole life may be said to have been passed in war or in the preparation for it. Forbidden to marry, they had no families to engage their affections, which, as with the monks and the friars of Christian countries, were concentrated in their own order.' They were the Moslem equivalent of the

Knights of St. John. It was often said by both sides over the centuries that if the Knights were only Moslems, or the Janissaries were only Christians, either would be happy to fight alongside the other. Their mutual respect was founded on an equal bravery, an equal fanaticism, and an equal belief in the righteousness of their respective causes.

Misac Pasha, the commander-in-chief, had ordered a devastating fire to be opened upon the whole area around the tower of Italy just before the main advance was made. This was not so much to destroy the walls any further—they were already in ruins—but to drive the defenders off the walkaways and send them under cover. The minute the fire ceased, the Bashi-Bazouks rolled forward like a wave and thundered over the storm-beaten rocks of the city walls. Behind them came the Janissaries. It was not long before the Grand Master saw that terrible omen of defeat, the standard of Islam, flying above the shattered tower of Italy. It burned there in the blue summer air as it had done above so many other cities from Constantinople to Baghdad.

Although lame from an earlier arrow wound in the thigh, d'Aubusson was the first to lead the defenders into the breach. Followed by about a dozen Knights and three standard bearers he mounted one of the ladders leading to the top of the wall. It was now that the armoured man came into his own. Standing on the narrow walkaway, almost invulnerable in their armour to anything but an arquebusier's lead bullet, the plate-armour of the fifteenth century gave a single man an advantage over dozens of opponents. Even so it was inevitable at close quarters that some thrusts should pierce through 'the chinks in the armour'. D'Aubusson received three or four wounds before finally a Janissary 'of gigantic structure' hurled a spear clean through his breastplate and punctured his lung. This moment, when he was being dragged back out of the affray, might well have seemed to signal the end of Rhodes. The enemy were in the breach, the tower of Italy was in their hands, and the attackers swarmed onwards thicker and thicker, like bees driven by some strange urge in their nature to found a new colony in this remote and stony outpost. It was the very density of the onrushing enemy that proved their downfall. Once the first men were closely engaged 'breast to breast', those behind 'cried forward, and those in front cried back'.

One is inevitably reminded of Macaulay's 'Lays of Ancient Rome', for the style of warfare had changed little over the centuries. Warfare was still entirely personal, and in such close engagements individual morale counted for more than anything else. The Bashi-Bazouks, driven forward by the fear of their officers behind them, and yet again by fear of the Janissaries behind *them*, did not relish the punishment that even a small group of dedicated armoured men could inflict upon them. For them, as indeed in a different way for the Christians, it was an age of superstition. Omens and portents were everywhere and—just as in ancient, classical warfare—the hands of the gods were seen as spread in involvement over scenes of carnage and battle. Somehow, the banners of d'Aubusson's standard bearers, shining bright against the sky above the smoke and turmoil of the struggle, were interpreted by the Moslems as the figures of strange Christian divinities come down to protect those who believed in them. (It must be remembered that almost all were illiterate and that, because of the requirements of their religion, all images were foreign and indeed incomprehensible to the Moslem mind.) A sudden wave of panic overtook the foremost Bashi-Bazouks. They turned to flee along the narrow, spilling wall from these strange men encased in metal—behind whom shone colourful and curious images that twisted and lifted in the wind of battle. The banner of St. John the Baptist, the Banner of the Holy Virgin, and the Cross of the Order of St. John became converted in the eyes of their opponents into terrifying djinns, devils from the abyss.

That is one explanation of the sudden flight of the leading Turks, who had gained a seemingly impregnable position on the ramparts—with all the city of Rhodes laid out before them. There are others. The Christian version was that a Cross of gold appeared in the sky accompanied by the figures of the Virgin Herself, and by St. John clad in goat skins and followed by a dazzling band of heavenly warriors. The more simple and prosaic explanation is that it was the very mass of the Turkish soldiers all piled together in so narrow a space that caused their ruin. When the leading Bashi-Bazouks met the small group that opposed them they turned in undisciplined fear, to be cut down by the officers and Janissaries behind them. As men spilled off the crumbling parapet, causing others to fall in their own ruin, no one knew what had caused the original panic. No one could make themselves heard above the din, smoke and confusion of battle, to restore order and to secure the advantage that they had won. In any case, in such encounters the advantage nearly always lies with the defenders. It is they who see ruin staring them in the face and they who, aware that only desolation and death await them, fight with the fury of the hopeless.

Unbelievably, so it seemed, the tide of battle turned. It was now the Turks who fled helter-skelter before the advancing tide of Knights and men-at-arms. Meanwhile the sharpshooters in the city below picked them off as they fled, silhouetted above the ruined walls of the Langue of Italy. 'We cut them down like swine' reads one account. Flying in panic confusion the Turks were chased back as far as their main camp at the foot of Mount St. Stephen to the west of the city. Here the ultimate disgrace befell them: the Sultan's standard, the Banner of the Grande Turke, was captured by the victorious Christians.

Estimates of the number of Turks slaughtered on this day vary from 3,500 to 5,000. The figures are probably exaggerated, but there is no doubt that the Turkish losses were severe, quite sufficient to make them lose heart in the whole campaign. Among those who fell were 300 Janissaries, who had stormed into the Jews' Quarter and were cut off and killed to a man when the rest of their forces turned and fled. Caoursin in his description of the siege, which was printed in Venice in the same year, describes how the city was heaped with Turkish corpses, and how the defenders had to burn them to prevent a plague breaking out. The defenders' losses were comparatively small, although one chronicler says that ten Knights were killed in the battle in the Jews' Quarter alone. Whatever the true figures, the fact remains that the general engagement on July 27th marked the end of the Turkish attempt to destroy Rhodes. Within ten days their army had struck camp and was assembling on the beach at Trianda, that pleasant anchorage where they had landed in expectation of a quick campaign and easy plunder just three months before. Even now Misac Pasha did not give the order to embark, and the army remained in Rhodes for a further eleven days. No doubt he feared the Sultan's anger: unsuccessful generals and unsuccessful politicians were not retired with honours at the Sublime Porte but had their heads divorced from their shoulders. In the event he was lucky and, upon his return, although threatened with execution, the Sultan relented and exiled him to Gallipoli.

Grand Master d'Aubusson, although his life was at first despaired of, recovered from his wounds. He was fortunate, as were the other Knights and all those who fought for the Order in this and other sieges, that the Order possessed the finest physicians and medical equipment in Europe.

With a knowledge of hygiene, proper sanitation, and pure drinking water, the Order and its defenders always had the advantage over an enemy encamped under canvas, in insanitary conditions, and with only the most elementary medical care. Then, as in later centuries, an army in the field almost invariably suffered more losses from sickness and disease than from battle.

Rhodes and the Order of St. John had survived, but the toll was a terribly heavy one. The fertile island looked as if clouds of locusts had passed over it, while ruined farms and houses, slaughtered animals and scorched grapevines, showed that the Turk in his passing was as great a destroyer as the Tartar or the Mongol. It would take years before the evidence of the siege of 1480 was effaced from the landscape, and many months before the ruined walls and towers could be restored. Had Mehmet himself returned with a fresh army the following year there can be no doubt what the result would have been. Rhodes at that moment could not have endured another siege. In the spring of 1481 the great conqueror himself led out his army to achieve what Misac Pasha had failed to do—the expulsion of the Knights and the destruction of 'their damnable Religion'. On his way south through Asia Minor he fell ill of dysentery, or a fever, and died. The Order was spared by the will of God.

14

Peace and power

THE MAIN RESULT OF THE SIEGE OF 1480 WAS TO RESTORE THE KNIGHTS to a prominence in Europe which had largely escaped them ever since the loss of *Outremer*. Their raiding parties into Asia Minor, their successful galley actions against Egyptians and Turks, all these had seemed very peripheral activities to the powers of Europe, concerned with their own internal affairs and their external rivalries. But ever since the fall of Constantinople and the steady encroachment of the Turks upon European territory the eyes of Popes, rulers and princes had been increasingly turned towards the eastern frontiers of the continent. Out there, far away in the Aegean, so close to Asia Minor as almost to be part of Turkey itself, the island of Rhodes was Europe's last hope in the East. The news that Mehmet II, the unconquerable Sultan, had sustained a major reverse at Rhodes, and that his army and fleet had been decimated and forced to turn tail, brought a new surge of hope. Perhaps Turkish fortunes were not irreversible? Perhaps this strange crusading Order, which for a long time had seemed an anachronism, was the potential instrument that might breach the main gate of the Turkish empire? Rhodes and the Knights who defended it were now seen as standing in the front rank holding back the hostile tide—unconquerable swords laying waste the infidel.

The outcome of 1480 was that gifts of money and munitions poured into the island from all over Europe. As one of the last secure ports of trade with the East, Rhodes attracted merchants and tradesmen, artisans and ship captains, as well as plain freebooters eager to operate under license against the rich shipping routes of the Moslem world. D'Aubusson was not slow to catch on to the advantages to be gained for his island-state by this new and favourable light in which it was now held. He needed in any case as much money as he could get to repair the ravages of the Turkish occupation and siege. The towers and walls must rise again, but twice as powerful as before, and constructed to the designs of the best military architects of the period. Among those who were sent on diplomatic missions was the Rhodian Vice-Chancellor, Caoursin, the author of the eyewitness account of the siege. As ambassador to the papal court he would make sure that the Pope and his Cardinals, and everyone of importance who came within the papal circle, heard from his own lips of the gallantry of the Knights, of the terrible reverses of the Turks—and of the necessity to aid Rhodes in every possible way.

For forty years the Order of St. John enjoyed an unprecedented period of prosperity, their reputation higher than ever before. Quite apart from the successful outcome of the siege there were other reasons for this. One was that there was a new feeling of optimism in the air since the opening up of the Atlantic trade routes to the New World gave western Europe the access to immense wealth which could not be denied them by the Turk. True, the old trade routes to the Far East were barred by the Ottoman Empire lying like a scimitar across all Asia Minor and the Near East, but the Knights had now inspired the hope that these two could in time be restored and Turkish power broken. (Perhaps, indeed, it could have been if the European powers had been prepared to support the Knights with men, as well as money and materials.) The other heady influence during this period emanated from Italy and spread like wild fire throughout Europe—the Renaissance. The fuse for this had been lit as long ago as 1204 when the Latin conquest of Constantinople had unleashed innumerable works of art, as well as artists and craftsmen, into the victorious city of Venice. Among the loot from Constantinople were the bronze horses that now adorn St. Mark's in Venice, the Byzantine enamels that decorate the famous Pala d'Oro in which rests the body of St. Mark, and the finest Byzantine ivory casket in the world, the Veroli casket. Ever since then the influence of the ancient world had been gradually permeating Europe, and by the fifteenth century there came the flowering summer of speculation in science and philosophy, of technical and artistic achievement, and in the whole concept of man as the measure of the universe. In Rhodes these things will have had comparatively little impact, for the Knights were bound to a system of ideas and a way of life that was at complete variance with the new thought. Nevertheless even here the influence of the Renaissance was to be felt, particularly in the scientific study of military architecture; in the great advances that had been made in cannon-foundry and weapon design; and in the elaboration of the galley into a work of art as well as a more efficient weapon of war.

But what above all gave the Order of St. John during these years the opportunity to turn their small state into an almost model kingdom of efficiency and prosperity was the dispute over the Ottoman succession that followed upon the death of Mehmet II. The Sultan had had three sons, the eldest of whom had been strangled on his father's orders for seducing a wife of his chief Vizir. (Fornication, adultery and sodomy were common enough in Turkey, but even a son must be sacrificed if it meant retaining the good will and loyal service of a senior administrative official.) The two sons who disputed the imperial throne were Bajazet, the second son, and Djem the youngest. At first glance it might seem that Djem had no claim to the throne, but his and his supporters' contention was that he had been born when his father was already Sultan, whereas Bajazet had been born before he had ascended the throne. This conception of being 'born in the purple' was a Byzantine inheritance, and might casuistically just be held to refer to the throne of Constantinople. It could hardly be considered as applying to all the lands of the Ottoman Empire, where the Moslem writ held good that the eldest son must succeed. Nevertheless it was upon Djem's claim, and the dispute between the two brothers, that d'Aubusson, as skilful in the wiles of diplomacy as in the arts of war, managed to secure the Order a long breathing space during which to put its house in order.

Defeated by his elder brother in 1482 in a battle at Bursa, the ancient capital of the Ottomans before their acquisition of Constantinople, Djem had fled to Egypt where he failed to arouse the support of the ruling Mamelukes. After a further attempt against his brother, in which he was yet again defeated, Djem in his search for an ally and protector turned to the Grand Master of the Order of St. John. The choice may seem incongruous, but the fact was that he had had a close and friendly relationship with d'Aubusson since he had been employed by his father as an ambassador to the Order. The Knights in any case were the principal enemies of the Sultan, and the Sultan was now Bajazet. If Djem could enlist their help and have himself made Sultan he would be quite agreeable to coming to such terms with them as would guarantee their security in Rhodes, while at the same time guaranteeing his own upon the throne. Pretenders and contenders for thrones have commonly looked towards their country's enemies for succour and support.

So, in the midsummer of 1482, the youngest son of Mehmet II sailed into the harbour of Rhodes in the Order's flagship, with an escort specially provided for him by the Knights of St. John. He received a reception worthy of a reigning monarch, the whole city *en fête*, the balconies dense with Rhodian beauties eager to behold the son of the man who had tried to destroy their city, and the pavements thronged with citizens, sailors and foreign visitors. The Grand Master himself accompanied by the Council waited on their mounts to receive their guest. Djem himself was ugly, he squinted, he was short—though immensely broad—and had physically little to commend him except the bravery of his robes and his jewelled turban. But the fact remained that he was symbolic of the might of his father, and of that great empire which Mehmet had everywhere led to victory—except at Rhodes itself.

Djem became d'Aubusson's personal guest and the Grand Master showered upon him all the entertainment of which the island was capable, from feasts and banquets where—like his father before him—he showed, contrary to the edict of the Prophet, a considerable fondness for wine. But although treated with every mark of favour and consideration he was a prisoner none the less, watched always by a detail of Knights: as much for his own protection as for anything else, for the spies and poisoners of the Sultan had a way of infiltrating into the cities of their enemies. It was probably on this account that d'Aubusson came to the conclusion that Djem was too much of a liability to be allowed to remain in the island. Enemies of d'Aubusson and of the Order have maintained that the unfortunate Djem was used quite cynically as a pawn on the chessboard, and that the decision to send him away to Europe was only made because d'Aubusson envisaged that he could be more useful there in any subsequent dealings with the Sultan Bajazet.

The true facts are unlikely ever to be known, but on the face of it it seems reasonable enough to have sent him to a place of greater security than Rhodes. In the autumn of 1482 Djem was accordingly despatched in the Order's flagship, destined for France and for the mother house of d'Aubusson's Langue, Auvergne. Documents which Djem left behind for custody in the Order's archives included one which gave the Order his authority to treat with Bajazet and secure from him a guarantee that the necessary funds would be made available to pay for Djem's maintenance in the style that befitted a son of Mehmet, and a further document declaring that he left Rhodes of his own free will. A third, contingent on Djem's ever regaining the throne, bound him, his heirs, and even his future successors to lasting friendship with the Order of St. John.

If Djem could indeed be restored, then d'Aubusson would have secured a diplomatic triumph. If, on the other hand, as seemed likely, Bajazet was too firmly entrenched upon the throne ever to be shifted then a second line of policy must be adopted designed to secure his good will towards the Order. In the winter of 1482 a treaty was signed between Bajazet and the Order in which the former proclaimed that he would pay a large annual compensation to make good for the damage caused to the island during his father's reign, and that he would also pay an even larger annual sum to the Order for his brother's subsistence while in Europe.

Djem's subsequent history—while tragic enough—has little bearing upon the Order in Rhodes. Having failed to secure any promises from the king of France for action against Bajazet, Djem, after a lot of tortuous correspondence between d'Aubusson and Pope Innocent, finally arrived in Rome as the Pope's guest. Here he remained, even after the accession of the Borgia Pope, Alexander VI, a prisoner, but well treated and accorded all the respect due to his rank. After further intrigue he was handed over as a hostage for the good behaviour of Pope Alexander to Charles VIII of France who had invaded Italy. He died at Terracina in Italy in 1495.

As usual, since the Borgias were involved, it was widely reported that he had been poisoned. This seems highly unlikely, for no one had anything to gain by his death—least of all d'Aubusson, who was also rumoured to have been privy to the plot. While Djem was alive the Hospitallers, the Pope, and the European powers had a powerful hostage in their hands, and one who could always serve as a useful figurehead if any opportunity arose to unseat his brother Bajazet. If d'Aubusson can be censured it is not for despatching him from Rhodes to France in the first place, but for having allowed him to be transferred to Rome which brought him into the hands of Alexander VI, and then of King Charles VIII. The charge of poisoning was common enough in those days when medicine was so little understood, and Terracina in the vicinity of the Pontine marshes was hardly the healthiest of places. Djem is just as likely to have died of malaria or of ordinary food poisoning as by any machinations of the Borgias.

The Order itself had nothing to gain by Djem's death. Alive, he was valuable in any bargaining that might take place between Rhodes and Constantinople. Dead he was worthless. Some of the censures that have been directed against d'Aubusson derive from the fact that the Grand Master is seen to have been playing international politics with Djem as a pawn. But d'Aubusson of course, like all Grand Masters of any consequence, was a political animal. He had to be. He was head of a sovereign state, and one which, small though it was, was of extraordinary complexity. Because of its international character the Order was a microcosm of all Europe. Its Grand Master, indeed, was the only European to rule over a composite of nations which reflected the interests and concerns of some of the richest and most powerful families in many nations. Furthermore he could never afford to break with the papacy—whoever might be Pope. This fact almost certainly accounts for d'Aubusson's original, if reluctant, agreement to hand Djem over to Innocent VIII. It is clear, at any rate, that d'Aubusson saw the death of Djem as the beginning of new difficulties for the Order. Within a year we find the Grand Master writing off to Sicily to enlist help from any shipowners or sea captains who might be prepared to bring their vessels to Rhodes and assist in the war against the infidel. He was, in effect, offering letters of marque to any privateers who cared to come and avail themselves of the rich pickings to be had on the Moslem trade routes.

Had it not been for the general deterioration of relations between the Turks and the Mamelukes of Egypt there can be little doubt that Bajazet, despite all the assurances of good wishes and friendship that had passed between himself and the Order, would soon have come to the attack. But the breathing-space afforded first by the 'affaire de Djem', and then by open warfare between the Sultan and Egypt, gave d'Aubusson a chance to improve the defences of his island, and to build new galleys for the Order's fleet. In the last year of his reign the Order, in company with a papal squadron, had a notable success over the Turks near the island of Chios, capturing a number of large and richly laden vessels. Shortly afterwards, on their sweep back to the south, they ran into a Turkish squadron off Samos, all of whom surrendered to the Standard of the Holy Religion. Laden with years and with honours, Pierre d'Aubusson died aged eighty in June 1503. One of the most remarkable of all Grand Masters he had successfully repulsed the massive invasion sent by Sultan Mehmet II. He had also restored the Order's finances as well as the fortifications of Rhodes, while by diplomatic negotiations (whether Machiavellian or not) he had secured a much-needed breathing space for his island kingdom.

15

By order of the Sultan

THE YEARS FOLLOWING UPON THE DEATH OF GRAND MASTER d'Aubusson and his succession by Emeric d'Amboise of the Langue of France were marked by the same steady progress in the Order's fortunes. In 1503, when the Turks sent a force of sixteen galleys to Rhodes and put ashore raiding parties, their galleys were brought to action by the small fleet of the Knights, and despite the difference in numbers, the Turks were soundly trounced, eight of their ships being sunk and two captured. The only damage to the Order was caused by the explosion of a powder keg which blew the bows off one of the galleys, killing eight Knights and a number of sailors in the forward position on the rambades. Other actions over the years confirmed that the navy of the Order was immeasurably the superior of the Turkish, both in seamanship and in firepower.

The flagship of the Holy Religion, a carrack of about 2,000 tons, proved that it was not only in her galleys that the Order was more efficient. Coming up with a large Egyptian ship off Candia in Crete the carrack successfully engaged the Egyptian and captured her intact. She was the richest single prize that had so far fallen to the Order, being laden with treasure and valuable merchandise, as well as having among her passengers a number of distinguished Mamelukes whose ransom value was almost as great as her contents. Successes such as these, when reported throughout Europe, naturally increased the esteem in which the Knights were held by the European powers and, coming upon their triumphant defence of Rhodes in 1480, promoted the feeling that the Knights were invincible. This led in due course to a dangerous disregard of the Order's true situation: a Christian outpost in the heart of the ever-growing Turkish empire, and an outpost moreover which was out-flanked by the Turkish occupation of the Greek mainland.

A remarkable victory at sea in 1510 was taken as even further proof that the Order was quite capable of looking after itself. The action took place off Laiazzo on the Turkish mainland just north of Cyprus, where the Sultan Bajazet and the Mameluke Sultan Qansuh al-Guri had pooled their resources and were combining to build a large fleet in the Red Sea designed to drive out the Portuguese who had infiltrated into the Indian Ocean and were seriously disrupting the Moslem spice trade from the East Indies. Laiazzo's importance was that it was the main port for the great timber areas that lay behind it in Asia Minor, and it was here that the wood for the new fleet was being seasoned and stored. Upon a report reaching Rhodes that a large convoy was on its way from Egypt to Laiazzo, under the command of the Mameluke Sultan's nephew, the Order's fleet was immediately sent to sea with orders to intercept. The sailing vessels were under the command of a Frenchman subsequently to become one of the Order's greatest Grand Masters, Philippe Villiers de L'Isle Adam, and the oared galleys under a Portuguese, Andrea d'Amaral.

The great problem in the Mediterranean, in the days when fleets were composed of two such completely different types of vessel, was that while one part was efficient under canvas (provided that the wind came from abaft the beam) the other was only really efficient in calm or light weather conditions. On this occasion when the fleet came up to Laiazzo, where the Mameluke ships were at anchor in the harbour, the weather was light—ideal for galleys to slip in like wolves among the sheep-like merchantmen, but dangerous for the wind-dependent 'round ships' which might well get becalmed and end up being blown to pieces by the shore batteries. L'Isle Adam accordingly was in favour of staying outside and enticing the Mamelukes into open water, while d'Amaral was all for using the speed and mobility of his galleys to get in among the prey. Fortunately for the Order the wise restraint of L'Isle Adams prevailed over the impetuosity of the 'destroyer captain' d'Amaral, and the fleet was dangled like an enticing bait off the harbour mouth. The Egyptians, trusting as had the Turks on previous occasions to the fact that they far outnumbered their opponents, were rash enough to come out from the security of their defended haven and engage. Once again the seamanship and tactics of the Knights and their Rhodian sailors proved superior to that of the Moslems. It was the old conflict between quality and quantity and, as the Knights had learned long ago, it is axiomatic at sea that it is quality which prevails. (On land, on the other hand, the Turks as they so often showed achieved their victories by sheer weight of manpower, the 'steamroller principle' which was to make them master of so many towns and countries.) In the battle that followed, the Order captured fifteen ships, eleven of them large sailing vessels—the pride of the Egyptian fleet. The standard of the Order waved triumphantly over the ruin of the Turkish-Egyptian armada, while the raiding parties which they put ashore drove the garrison inland. They then set fire to the immense piles of timber that had been destined for a Red Sea fleet that would now never take the water. So great a triumph, and one of such importance to a Europe that had grown to rely on the Portuguese supply of spices rather than—as in the past—having to buy it from Moslem traders, raised the Knights' prestige to a point where it seemed that the Cross of St. John was indeed protected by heavenly powers. This reputation for invincibility was in the end to prove of fatal consequence to the Order. In another matter, the dispute between L'Isle Adam and d'Amaral (in which the former had been shown to have been tactically correct), lay the seeds of discord that would one day have a sinister impact upon the Order's future.

In 1520 the Ottoman Sultan Selim the Grim, who had succeeded Bajazet, and who had vastly enlarged his empire by annexing Egypt, died just as he was assembling an army designed to destroy the 'Christian nest of vipers'. He was succeeded by his only son, Suleiman, destined to become the greatest ruler in Turkish history; to be revered by his own people as 'The Lawgiver', for his reformation and codification of Turkish law, and to be feared and at the same time honoured throughout Europe as Suleiman 'The Magnificent'. He was twenty-six when he ascended the throne, his birth having coincided with the opening year of the tenth century of Moslem chronology (Anno Hegirae 900). He initiated a period which has been described as 'the most glorious in the history of Islam'. In his day Turkey attained the summit of her political and military power, for Suleiman was a brilliant statesman as well as an excellent general. A poet in his own right, he was no simple Turkish warlord but—like Mehmet II—a man of culture and intelligence. This was the man, 'Allah's deputy on Earth, Lord of the Lords of this World, Possessor of Mens' Necks, King of Believers and Unbelievers, King of Kings, Emperor of the East and West' who looked south from his palace above the Golden Horn and decided that, before all else, the Standard of the Holy Religion should be removed from his seas.

In 1521, one year after Suleiman ascended the throne, Philippe Villiers de L'Isle Adam became Grand Master of the Order. He succeeded an able Italian Grand Master, Fabrizio del Carretto, who had spent most of the years in which he was head of the Order in renewing the defences of Rhodes and in preparing for that second siege which was clearly inevitable. He had employed one of the most able military engineers of the time, a fellow Italian, to bring the fortifications of Rhodes into line with the conditions now obtaining in a warfare that was dominated by the use of cannon and of mining. The old days of high curtain-walls were long gone and battlements now had to be massive. Huge angled towers provided covering fire along the exposed sections of the walls through gun ports that were splayed so as to give the guns a wide angle of fire. The city of Rhodes that L'Isle Adam inherited was as strong as any fortified place on earth.

His election to the office came about while he was away in France, and it was unfortunate that among the contenders for the post was the Portuguese d'Amaral who had disputed L'Isle Adam's decision at Laiazzo. D'Amaral held the post of Chancellor and was somewhat over-confident that he was destined to be the next Grand Master. The election of L'Isle Adam undoubtedly came as a blow to d'Amaral, a man who was noted for his pride. L'Isle Adam, the new Grand Master, was fifty-seven, an aristocrat to his fingertips, an experienced seaman, a devout Christian and—as he was later to prove—a diplomat who never lost his nerve even when everything seemed lost. His family was one of the noblest in France; among his relatives was the premier Duke and Constable of France, Anne de Montmorency. Curiously enough, and a portent of which much was to be made in later years, during his voyage back to Rhodes the great carrack in which he was travelling was struck by lightning in the Malta Channel. A number of the ship's company were killed, and L'Isle Adam's sword is said to have been reduced to ashes. As it was unlikely that he would have been wearing his sword at sea during a storm, and not in conflict with any enemy—one may perhaps read into this story the reflections of a later historian determined to introduce the name of Malta into the annals of L'Isle Adam. Malta—it was to prove an historic connection . . .

Hardly had the Grand Master taken over the reins of office than he received the first intimation of Sultan Suleiman's intentions. A letter from Constantinople, signed by the Sultan himself, informed him of the latter's conquests during the year 1521. It was what was known as 'A Letter of Victory', and could certainly only be construed by L'Isle Adam as a definite threat directed at his kingdom. After referring to his capture of Belgrade, Suleiman went on to say that he had taken 'many other fine and well-fortified cities, killing most of the inhabitants, and reducing the rest to slavery'. Snidely the Sultan asked him as 'a most cherished friend to rejoice with me over my triumphs'. The Grand Master replied in terms which were certainly more direct than diplomatic, that he had 'fully understood the meaning of your letter', and went on to boast of his own success over a notorious Moslem pirate, Cortoglu, who had attempted to capture him (almost certainly on Suleiman's orders) during his voyage from France to Rhodes. L'Isle Adam was not the victim of any illusions. As he showed in another letter to Francis I of France he knew full well that the Sultan had Rhodes next on the list of Christian cities destined to fall to his all-conquering sword.

In the summer of the following year, 1522, the Grand Master received the message that he had been anticipating ever since he had taken over his office: '. . . I order you to surrender your island to me at once . . . What is more, I give you permission to leave it in safety with your most valued goods.' Suleiman also offered him the chance of remaining in Rhodes—even without homage or tribute—provided that the Order was prepared to accept the overall sovereignty of the Sublime Porte. L'Isle Adam did not even deign to answer.

So, after forty-two years, the point had yet again been reached where the Order of St. John had been declared *persona non grata* in the Aegean world—a world that had now become an appendage of the Ottoman Empire. There was little hope of any reinforcements from a Europe where almost all the powers were locked in conflict with one another, while in England Henry VIII was already casting his eyes on the rich properties of the Order. It is an interesting sidelight upon the structure of the Order of St. John that, while France and Spain were at war with one another, and Italy was being devastated in the process, the Knights from the Langues of these various countries could work together in unity. There were some dissensions of course, but amid the fierce nationalistic rivalries of the sixteenth century the Knights still managed to preserve the international ideals that had once sent all the nations of western Europe in company together against the Moslem enemy.

Throughout 1521, as the Sultan's plans were being implemented for the great assault designed for the following year, the espionage systems of both sides were in full operation. It was not too difficult for the Knights to obtain their information, for the whole of Asia Minor, Turkey-in-Europe, and the Levant were clearly being geared for war. It was less easy for the Sultan, but he too had his successes. He even managed to get one of his spies, a Jewish doctor converted to Christianity, working in the Hospital itself. The preparations for defence could hardly be concealed. Ditches were being widened, the new bastion of Auvergne was being completed, and the harbour was full of ships coming and going with stores, supplies and armaments. So, as the new year drew on into the spring, the Order girded its loins. It waited to receive the wind of the Sultan's sword.

16

The end of a dream

By June 1522 Sultan Suleiman was ready. A large part of his fleet was gathered in Constantinople (700 ships according to one account), while his armies were already on the march through Asia Minor. Marmarice was once again destined to be the main base for the embarkation of the troops. Soon those outriders of the Knights' defensive system, the Dodecanese islands with their fortified watchtowers and their fast escorts, were beginning to bring in reports. One advance force made an attempt on the island of Cos and received a severe rebuff, but nothing could stem the march of the main force that was on its way with the Sultan and his brother-in-law Mustapha Pasha. On June 26th the advance force of the Turkish fleet, about thirty in all, were sighted cruising past Rhodes. Some way behind them, scattered out of sight over the blue Aegean, the main body came inexorably on, to the sound of tambours and the shrill piping of bosun's whistles and the crack of the overseers' whips. The chief of staff of the navy was the corsair Cortoglu, the very man who had tried to take L'Isle Adam on his passage from France to Rhodes. Meanwhile another fleet was on its way from Syria.

The total number of men that the Sultan assembled for his attack on Rhodes was estimated at about 200,000, but (as in the figures given for the previous siege) allowance must be made for natural exaggeration. In any case it was an immense force to send against an island so small. The Knights, for their part, had probably no more than 1,500 trained mercenary and Rhodian troops, commanded by some 500 Knights and Servants-at-Arms. They had of course all the able-bodied people of Rhodes to assist them. The odds against them seemed wildly disproportionate, but they were balanced by those bastions and ditches, scarps and counterscarps, angled towers and massive walls. It was reckoned that the Order had enough stores, provisions and munitions to hold out in Rhodes for a year. If they could endure until the winter it might well be that the cold and the rain would cause sickness and disease among the Sultan's troops, and the Aegean gales wreak havoc among his ships.

The Sultan had brought an immense variety and weight of cannon and, even more formidable perhaps, thousands of trained miners. If Rhodes did not fall to his guns it might well fall to the sappers working under its walls.

The main force began to come ashore in Kalitheas Bay, below Mount Phileremos and a little to the south of the City. On July 28th the Sultan himself landed, accompanied by a picked battalion of Janissaries. The thunder of the salutes, the cries and shouting, and the noise of the Janissaries' band told the garrison and all the citizens of Rhodes that the real siege was about to begin. Prior to this there had been a number of minor encounters, and a heavy but somewhat ineffectual bombardment of the posts of England, Provence and Aragon. The Turks now settled around the city, spanning it from one side to the other like the Crescent of Islam. More cannon were brought up, vast bombards capable of firing balls nine feet in circumference, double cannon, mortars, and a wide assortment of smaller pieces. Under cover of a devastating bombardment the Turks began to throw up a great earthwork facing the tower of Aragon, the purpose being to drag cannon on to the top from which they could fire into the city itself. The tower of St. Nicholas at the end of the mole had borne the brunt of the attack during the earlier siege. It again came under heavy fire, but it had been completely reconstructed and was now practically impregnable. Throughout the whole of August, while besieged and besiegers alike sweltered under the sun, the artillery duels kept up, thousands of cannon balls being expended by the Turks in their determination to crush those frowning walls above which waved the Standard of St. John.

Casualties were heavy on both sides, but heavier by far among the Turks in their more exposed positions. The gunners of Rhodes, behind their splayed gun-ports, wrought havoc among the Turkish batteries and the men that manned them.

Nevertheless, towards the close of August, breeches were beginning to appear in the walls in a number of places. The science of fortification had improved tremendously since 1480, but so too had the skill of the cannon-founder and the whole art of gunnery. Meanwhile, despite the blockade maintained by Cortoglu, a ship managed to slip in from Europe with supplies, a few soldiers, and four Knights. The Sultan, enraged at the failure of the corsair, had Cortoglu bastinadoed aboard his own flagship. It was never wise to fail when in the service of the Grande Turke.

Throughout the siege L'Isle Adam was helped by the fact that he had been able to secure in his service one of the foremost fighting men in Europe, and one of the most brilliant military engineers of his time, Gabriele Tadini. It was Tadini who was largely responsible for building the retrenchments within the walls and, above all, for supervising the tunnelling and countermining—for all the time the Turkish sappers and miners were probing in to try to sink their shafts and charges beneath the walls and towers. Early in September they did have a notable success, set-ting off a mine under the bastion of England and blowing a gap in it over thirty feet wide. They immediately came to the attack, surged up the smoking ruins, and planted their standards on the wall itself. The English counter-attacked, the Grand Master himself as well as Tadini joining in the mêlée. Gradually the Turks began to yield. Mustapha Pasha, who had come up with the second wave, by the force of his personality, rank, and liberal use of his scimitar on the fugitives, forced them back into the breach. The struggle raged around the crumbling bastion for two hours until the Turks had finally spent their force. They fled for their trenches, leaving their dead and wounded in heaps along the wall. The Knights too had their casualties, three dead, and an unrecorded number of dead and wounded soldiers. It had been the most dangerous moment in the siege so far.

Throughout September the cannonading, the mining and counter-mining never ceased. Rhodes seemed to rise like some smoking mountain above the shot-whipped Aegean Sea. The skill and ingenuity of Tadini time and again foiled the enemy, who were blown up in the dark ruins of their tunnels as his countermines exploded against them. Among numer-ous other inventions and new techniques used by Tadini was one designed for detecting the presence of enemy miners. It was a listening device which, by means of a taut parchment diaphragm, could detect the slightest sound or movement beneath the ground and, when this occurred, it immediately caused a number of miniature bells to chime. It was during this period, when the siege was well into its second month, that a spy in the midst of the city was revealed. The Christianised Jewish doctor in the Hospital was caught in the act of firing a message into the Turkish lines. Put to torture, he confessed that he had been steadily giving information to the Turks, even before the siege had opened. He was hung, drawn, and quartered.

At dawn on September 24th the first great general assault was launched against the posts of Aragon, England, Italy and Provence. Preceded by the heaviest continuous bombardment of the siege the greater part of the Turkish forces were hurled at this semi-circle of the Rhodian defences. The first part to fall was the bastion of Aragon, which had been selected as the point at which the main weight of the Janissaries was to be hurled. Led by Bali Agha, their commander, they stormed the defences and soon their banners waved in the smoke-dense air. The men who boasted that 'the body of a Janissary is but the stepping stone for his brother into the breach' had proved—as they had on so many other battlefields—that they deserved to be called 'The Sons of the Sultan'. But, for all their fanatical bravery, the guns of Auvergne mowed them down, and they were then taken in the rear by a picked band led by the Knight Jacques de Bourbon. (His chronicle of the siege was published four years later.)

Suleiman, like Xerxes at Salamis centuries before him, had had a conqueror's throne set on a raised platform so that he could witness his day of triumph. Again like Xerxes he was doomed to disappointment. The tide of battle which had roared all along the selected points of the walls began to recede before Greek fire, shot and shell, and the indomitable armoured men who gleamed like beacons at every point where the fighting was thickest. L'Isle Adam himself was prominent wherever it seemed that the flood was making up against the defenders. Behind him his standard bearer carried the banner of the Crucifixion. Although it only served to draw the Turks' attention to the one man whom above all they wished to see dead, it did indeed seem that there was some special protection attached to the Grand Master. The attack wavered and then gradually the advancing hordes began to fall back towards their trenches.

Suleiman in his rage at the failure of the day condemned Mustapha Pasha to death. The senior of his Vizirs pleaded with him to spare Mustapha—and he in his turn was condemned. It was only the pleas of all the Pashas, pointing out that such an action could only help the Christians by depriving the army of two of its leaders that caused Suleiman to relent. The losses on both sides that day were considerable but, if the Turkish by far outnumbered the Christians they could afford the toll. The Knights could not. Already the Turkish steamroller tactics were beginning to exhaust them. Some 200 of the defenders were dead and an equal number seriously wounded. They had little or no expectation of any relief from Europe. Indeed, although they were not to know it, a short while later the only relief ship to leave for Rhodes foundered and sank in the Bay of Biscay, taking all her men with her. Despatched from England in October under the command of Frà Thomas Newport, she might well have played an important part—had she arrived.

Two important events marked the month of October, a month in which the Turks carried on with their continual wearing-down of the garrison and its defences. The first, and the most serious for the defenders, was the disablement of Gabriele Tadini. He was shot in the head and, although not mortally wounded, was confined to the Hospital for some six weeks. Happening as it did at a moment when the Turks were redoubling mining beneath the defences, Tadini's disablement was a tragic blow. The second and far more sinister event was the discovery of treachery within the ranks of the Knights themselves. A Portuguese in the service of the Chancellor, Andrea d'Amaral, was caught firing a message into the enemy lines. The message contained information that the condition of the defenders was desperate, and that if the Turks only kept up the siege for a little longer Rhodes must certainly fall. Under torture the man came out with the further confession that this was not the first time that he had communicated with the enemy, but that he had been doing so constantly throughout the siege and even before. He then produced the most terrible piece of information of all. He had done so, he said, not for himself, but at the instigation of his master. Andrea d'Amaral, the Pilier of Castile, the Grand Chancellor!

The trial and subsequent execution of Andrea d'Amaral have given rise to endless controversy among students and historians of the Order. D'Amaral was an arrogant and extremely unpopular man. He was known to dislike L'Isle Adam not only because of their dispute at Laiazzo, but because L'Isle Adam, and not he, had become Grand Master. This had undoubtedly embittered him, but could it have done so to such an extent that he would actually have betrayed the Order? The truth will never be known. D'Amaral was tried and racked. He said nothing—either in his defence or in confession. A number of Knights brought charges against him, one of them being that, after the election of L'Isle Adam, d'Amaral had been heard to say that 'He will be the last Grand Master of Rhodes.' This in itself might mean nothing more than that d'Amaral had come to the pessimistic conclusion that Rhodes was certain to fall one day to the Sultan. Proud to the last, he said nothing when carried to the place of execution, disdaining even the comforts of religion. L'Isle Adam himself was certainly convinced by the evidence that was brought against the Grand Chancellor. As he wrote to his nephew, the Marshal of France: ' . . . I must tell you, nephew, that I have been at war not only with the Turks, but with one of the most important members of our Council who, out of envy and lust for power, had for a long time conspired to bring the Turk here and to surrender the city to him.'

The weather was now wet and cold and the shattered ramparts were slimy with mud. Ruin and desolation stalked the streets of what had once been the jewel-city of Rhodes. But the Turks under canvas and in the trenches were in as bad a condition as the besieged. There still seemed a hope that if Rhodes could hold out a little longer the enemy would withdraw. The arrival of one or two supply ships bringing a small number of men, but a fair amount of fresh victuals and wine, emboldened their hopes. Then, during the month of December, a number of offers were made to the Knights giving them fair and honourable terms if they would surrender their city. The news of these offers gave rise to much dissension; many of the Rhodians being by now exhausted with this seemingly eternal siege; even some of the Knights being in favour of accepting the terms so long as honour was satisfied.

L'Isle Adam was adamant. He represented the old crusading spirit: he would rather they all died buried in the ruins than that the Order of St. John should compromise with the Moslem. But the fact was that the Order had often compromised, had traded with the Moslems, and had quite often established reasonable relationships with them. In the end, with the Rhodians saying that they would make their own terms if the Knights would not, it was the peace party that won the day.

On Christmas Eve Sultan Suleiman made it quite clear to the Grand Master that he was offering peace with honour. The Knights and any

Rhodians who cared to accompany them might leave the city freely. He paid tribute to the astonishing resistance that they had put up, and said that he would even supply them with ships if their own were not sufficient or too badly damaged to put to sea.

On December 26th, L'Isle Adam, who had already had two previous conversations with the Sultan, went to make his formal submission. Suleiman is said to have treated him with courtesy and respect, and there is no reason to believe that he would not have done so. Indeed, turning to his Grand Vizir, Ibrahim Pasha, he is reported to have said: 'It saddens me to be compelled to force this brave old man to leave his home.' The remark is not unlikely. In those days, as indeed in the days of Saladin, a spirit of chivalry and courtesy could still veneer the harsh canvas of war.

'Nothing in the world was ever so well lost as Rhodes,' said the Emperor Charles V when they told him the story of its fall. It was indeed astounding that a handful of men could have held out so long against an army of the size that the Sultan had brought against them. Tribute must also go to the military engineers who had designed those walls and ramparts, the remains of which are still one of the architectural wonders of the Mediterranean. The Rhodians themselves (as they had shown in that other famous siege when they had defeated the Macedonian king Demetrius Poliorcetes in the fourth century B.C.), were as brave on land as they were at sea.

The fact remained that, however grand the resistance, however brave the men, the Knights no longer had a home. For over two centuries they had lived in Rhodes. They had embellished the island not only with the beauty and grandeur of their city but with villas and hunting lodges, gardens, roads, harbours and high towers. All these were now the Sultan's as he and his triumphant soldiers occupied what had been the city and the island of the Holy Religion.

17

'Two fine, large harbours'

ON A COLD WINTER'S EVENING ON JANUARY 1ST, 1523, THE PEAKS OF the Carian mountains across the strait white with snow, and the sea darkening as the sun went down behind Rhodes, the survivors of the siege left their island home for ever. Their destination was the port of Khania in Crete where they intended to water and victual, as well as give the wounded some respite from the rolling and pitching of the ships before setting course for Messina. L'Isle Adam was in the great carrack *Santa Maria* which was commanded by an Englishman, Sir William Weston. Accompanying him were two galleys, *San Giovanni* and *Santa Caterina*, together with a barque, the *Perla*. It was a small enough fleet to represent all those years in Rhodes and all those triumphs at sea, and little enough that they had with them. They had, however, been allowed to take their arms, with the exception of the bronze cannons. They took also along with their personal belongings those relics so dear to the Religion, including the Right Hand of St. John in its jewelled reliquary, as well as the precious archives of the Order. (These records of their history over the centuries, together with relics of the True Cross, the Holy Thorn, the Body of St. Euphemia, and the Ikon of Our Lady of Phileremos, were all to accompany them to their next island home.) It is interesting to reflect that, as Eric Brockman observes, 'Amongst the survivors who embarked with the Grand Master was a young Provençal called Jean Parisot de la Valette. Forty-three years later, when the remnants of his armies came back to Constantinople from the siege of Malta, beaten and shamed by the Grand Master La Valette, Suleiman was to regret his youthful act of chivalry in letting these accursed Kuffar escape alive.'

It was not until April that the ships reached Messina, the port from which, if those in Europe had honoured their obligations, a relief force should have sailed for Rhodes many months ago. The fate of the Order now rested very largely on L'Isle Adam, and on his ability to use his skill in diplomacy. This fortunately was almost as remarkable as his skill in warfare. Nevertheless, he had as hard a task ahead of him as he had ever known—even in the siege of Rhodes. Europe was in its usual troubled state, the Order seemed something of an anachronism, and the spectre of Martin Luther and his followers had appeared to haunt the security of the papacy; a papacy indeed which was so far from secure that in 1527 Rome itself was to be sacked by the German Lutheran troops of Charles V. It was very largely the forceful personality of L'Isle Adam that kept the Order from collapsing altogether. The Knights thought constantly of Rhodes. Its memory haunted them; their gracious city, the street of Auberges, the view across the strait to the land whence their enemy had come, the pleasant vineyards, wooded slopes, and butterfly-bright valleys.

During these years of exile the Knights had two homes, the first at Viterbo north of Rome, and the second at Nice. L'Isle Adam travelled constantly through the courts of Europe endeavouring to solicit help, but even his diplomatic charm could achieve little in that troubled age. The Renaissance, the New Thought, the questioning of all authority, the struggles of nationalism, these were real enough. The Order, it was said, was medieval. It belonged to a dead and forgotten world. Curiously enough, one of the few rulers to respond to L'Isle Adam was Henry VIII of England, who gave him a number of valuable bronze cannon to replace those that had been lost, together with a considerable quantity of weapons and armour. Within a few years, in his search for money and his conflict with the Pope, Henry would forget his earlier sympathy, and would seize all the possessions of the Order within his realm. But before that happened the Order would have acquired a new home.

They had asked for peninsulas in Sicily, Corsica and Sardinia, and even the island of Elba; anywhere indeed where they could recreate on a narrow strip of land the fortified home that they had lost. But rulers felt suspicious of them, for might they not turn from their avowed obligation to fight only the infidel, and allow their fleet to be used by one European power against another? Then, in 1530, Charles V of Spain was crowned Emperor by Pope Clement VII at Bologna. Now among the immense areas that came under his rule there were the three small islands of the Maltese archipelago. These had in fact already been discussed by the Order, but the three French Langues had been fervently against the idea (possibly because the islands were sterile, unfertile, and did not look like good wine country). The German Langue and the two Spanish Langues, however, had considered them quite favourably. They were largely influenced by the fact that the main island, Malta, had a number of extremely fine natural harbours. Admittedly the feelings of the French can be understood when one reads the report on the islands that had been made by eight commissioners in 1524.

The island of Malta [they said] is merely a rock of a soft sandstone, called tufa, [it was, in fact, limestone] about six or seven leagues long and three or four broad; the surface of the rock is barely covered by more than three or four feet of earth. This also is stony, and most unsuited for growing corn or other cereals. It does, however, produce plenty of figs, melons and other fruits. The principal trade of the island consists of honey, cotton, and cummin seed. These the inhabitants exchange for grain. Except for a few springs in the centre of the island there is no running water, nor even wells, so the inhabitants catch the rainwater in cisterns. Wood is so scarce as to be sold by the pound and the inhabitants have to use either sun-dried cow-dung or thistles for cooking their food.

It hardly sounded encouraging! They went on:

The capital, Città Notabile, is situated on rising ground in the centre of the island. Most of the houses are uninhabited . . . On the west coast there are no harbours, coves or bays, and the shore is extremely rocky. In the east coast, however, there are many capes, bays and coves, and two particularly fine, large harbours, big enough to accommodate any size of fleet.

It was this that turned the scales. First-class harbours were rare enough in the Mediterranean and, since the Knights' business was upon the sea, it was natural that they should want adequate and sheltered accommodation for their ships. Ambassadors were accordingly sent by the Order of St. John asking the Emperor if he would graciously consider giving the Knights Malta. Charles V and his advisers considered the question carefully and came to the conclusion that it would be generally convenient for the protection of his dominions, and in particular Sicily, to have the Knights in Malta. In the same way that the Knights had used little Dodecanese islands like Leros and Cos as bastions and outriders to their home in Rhodes, so Malta might provide a useful defence and listening post against the Turks and the corsairs of the North African coast. Charles agreed to the gift—in return for an annual nominal rent of one falcon—but added the uncomfortable rider that in return for Malta the Knights should also agree to garrison the town of Tripoli due south of the islands on the North African coast. This was indeed a left-handed gift, for Tripoli was in the middle of hostile Moslem states, nearly 200 miles away from Malta, and would be difficult enough to garrison let alone maintain. It is indicative of the desperate straits to which the Order had been reduced that they agreed to the Emperor's offer.

In the autumn of 1530 the Knights of St. John of Jerusalem (and now of Rhodes) sailed south from Sicily across 'The Canal', or Malta Channel, headed for their new island home. They were not at all happy with what they found. The commissioners had indeed warned them that Malta was rocky and barren, but they had hardly envisaged the harsh North African face that the islands present at the end of summer, before the first rains have fallen and the land has become alive again. Everywhere they looked as they coasted along, first past the rugged little island of Gozo, then past the islet of Comino, and then down Malta itself, they saw only a barren moon-landscape of harsh limestone crags and rocks. Only here and there a patch of green glowed dully where some dusty carob tree provided a patch of shade. Hostile and inimical, the islands glowered back at their new owners.

The local inhabitants, as the commissioners had reported, spoke a dialect of Arabic, and only a few merchants, coupled with the local aristocracy, spoke any French, Spanish or Italian. The aristocracy, related to the principal families in Aragon and Sicily, certainly had no cause to feel any affection for these newcomers who had been granted the over-lordship of the islands, out of which they themselves had been accustomed to drawing their rents and accepting the tributes of the peasantry. The Knights for their part were dismayed and indeed horrified by all that they saw: a peasant population of some 12,000, illiterate and unskilled compared with the quick-witted and intelligent Rhodian Greeks. Città Notabile, or Mdina as the natives called it, was indeed well-situated but almost desolate. Only the harbours could console them, and in particular the great harbour on the east coast known to this day as Grand Harbour. Here, indeed, there was room for a fleet immeasurably greater than even the resources of any European monarch could afford to maintain. But again the doubts came back—the harbour was so ill-defended. It was clear at once that there would have to be an immense amount of building before they could consider it even moderately defensible against a corsair raid, let alone a seaborne attack by the fleet of Suleiman.

To the considerable relief of the ancient nobility the Knights decided to settle on a narrow peninsula of land which jutted out on the south side of Grand Harbour. Here they found a miserable fishing village known as Birgu (the Borg or Township), and at the head of it a small dilapidated fort. Unattractive it all might be, but somehow or other the sight of that harbour with its numerous creeks and inlets lying off it to the south and west contrived to make the gift of Malta seem acceptable. Nevertheless, for months and even years to come, there was always to be a predominant party in the Order which maintained that they must in due course re-capture Rhodes. Malta would do for the moment—a last resort as it were —but looking at the island under the late sun of that autumn day 'they wept remembering Rhodes'.

The ordinary Maltese people for their part regarded the Knights rather as if they were visitors from another planet. Their lives of back-breaking toil on a hard soil under the sun's hot eye had little accustomed them to these armoured men with their airs and graces, their colourful trappings and standards, their pages and squires, men-at-arms, Greek artisans, pilots and seamen; let alone their elaborate sailing ships and galleys with their decorated bows and sterns. And then there was the unfamiliar sight of the lines of manacled Moslem slaves being ushered under guard into contemporary quarters ashore. The last sight must at any rate have brought the Maltese some comfort, for it was the fate of the Maltese and their Gozitan fellows in the northern island to be constantly subjected to the raids of pirates and slavers from the Barbary coast to the south of them. At any rate these new masters, these Knights of St. John, were as good Catho-lic Christians as themselves. It was clear that they were enemies of the Moors for they used them as galley slaves—a fate hitherto, they had thought, reserved for those Maltese who were captured and sold in the great market of Tunis.

On other counts the Maltese were not so happy at the arrival of the

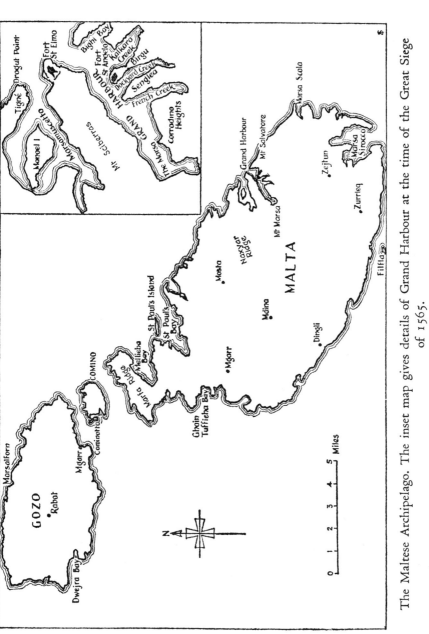

The Maltese Archipelago. The inset map gives details of Grand Harbour at the time of the Great Siege of 1565.

Knights. Here is a Maltese historian, Sir Themistocles Zammit, on the
subject:

> By the time the Knights came to Malta, the religious element in their founda-
> tion had fallen into decay. Their monastic vows were usually regarded as mere
> form, and they were remarkable for their haughty bearing and worldly aspirations.
> The Maltese, on the other hand, accustomed to being treated as freemen greatly
> resented the loss of the political liberties which had been conceded to them . . . It
> is not, therefore, surprising that there was little love lost between the Maltese
> and their new rulers.

There is some exaggeration here, for this portrait of the Knights, while it
may well have been true in the seventeenth and eighteenth centuries, was
hardly the case when they first settled in Malta in 1530. The outlook of
the nobility, however, settled in their old palaces in Mdina has been
accurately portrayed by Elizabeth Schermerhorn. Reporting on the comments of some of their modern descendants, she goes on:

> To the educated and aristocratic Maltese, well-informed on local history, the
> memory of the imperious Order that took away their parliament and free institu-
> tions, interfered with the sacred privileges of their bishopric, snobbishly refused
> membership to the sons of families whose titles of nobility ante-dated the occupa-
> tion of Rhodes . . . is simply not to be discussed or defended in any well-bred
> circles.

The 'imperious Order', however, had its own problems. The first of
these was to transform Birgu into something that, however remotely,
might resemble their former home in Rhodes. Over two centuries of
living a rigidly patterned life within the walls of Rhodes had conditioned
the Knights to such a degree that they could not imagine that there was
any other way of living except on, or hard by, the water; with a view of
their ships and galleys immediately beneath them, and a prospect of the
open sea beyond. Birgu met these requirements. Its transformation was not
to be achieved by L'Isle Adam however. He had led the Order through
the siege of Rhodes, he had held it together during the years of exile, and
now he had found it a new home. As Quentin Hughes comments:

> To the meagre defences [of Birgu] L'Isle Adam added detached works wherever
> the nature of the ground permitted, repaired the existing walls of Fort St.

Angelo [at the seaward tip of the peninsula] . . . but otherwise held his hand; for in his mind he planned to reconquer Rhodes, and considered the sojourn in Malta as no more than a temporary expedient. To this end the fleet of the Order was set in battle array and, as a preparatory move, dispatched to capture Modon in southern Greece. In this attempt the ships suffered a serious defeat, and all further idea of reoccupying Rhodes had to be abandoned.

L'Isle Adam's later years were troubled by dissensions and even insubordination among a number of the young Knights. They found Malta boring and unattractive and were too young to realise how lucky the Order was to have a home at all. L'Isle Adam died in the ancient capital of Mdina in 1534, four years after he had first set foot on Malta: a brilliant and enterprising Grand Master, and one of the greatest in all the Order's long centuries of history.

Among his immediate successors the most important was the Spanish Grand Master Juan de Homedes, who reigned from 1536 to 1553. It was under Homedes that the defences of Birgu began to assume a realistic form. An Italian military engineer, Antonio Ferramolino, was sent to Malta by Charles V to advise on the reconstruction of the old fishing village and in particular to improve its fortifications. Farramolino immediately pointed out—as others were to do after him—that the whole area was low-lying and was dominated by the gaunt limestone ridge of Mount Sciberras which formed the northern arm of the entrance to Grand Harbour. Ferramolino counselled Homedes to shift the Convent to those rugged heights and build there a completely new city.

The Grand Master undoubtedly recognised the wisdom of his words but there was little or nothing that he could do to act upon them, for the cost of building a new fortified city was, at that moment, completely beyond the finances of the Order. He had to content himself with getting Ferramolino to strengthen the existing works around Birgu. Principal of these was the fort at the head of the peninsula. St. Angelo was now transformed into a formidable strong point, Ferramolino erecting over and above it a large cavalier from which guns could be brought to bear upon the entrance to Grand Harbour as well as upon the extreme point where Mount Sciberras plunged into the sea. Another radical improvement was to cut a great ditch through the peninsula, so that the fortress was cut off from the township of Birgu behind it. Access to St. Angelo was now only by means of a drawbridge. The moat thus created between the fortress and Birgu was also useful in providing a galley port, somewhat reminiscent of Mandraccio in miniature. Later developments to the fortifications protecting Grand Harbour were initiated by a Spanish engineer Pietro Pardo and by Count Strozzi, the Prior of Capua. These included a star-shaped foot at the sea-ward end of the neighbouring peninsula, called L'Isla (the Island) and later Senglea, after Grand Master de la Sengle. This fort named after St. Michael provided additional covering fire over the waters of Grand Harbour and reinforced the fire of St. Angelo.

The most important development during these years was the construc-tion of another star-shaped fort at the very end of Mount Sciberras. This dominated the entrance to Grand Harbour as well as the entrance to the other large harbour, Marsamuscetto, that lay to the north of the peninsula. The fort, called St. Elmo after the patron saint of sailors, was sited where a small watchtower had formerly stood, and where there had probably been some form of a beacon ever since Greek and Roman times. (The Maltese name for the peninsula, Sciberras, means literally 'The Light on the Point'.) In the course of all the new works that were initiated during their first twenty years on the island the Knights discovered one major asset hitherto unlooked for among the islanders—their remarkable skill as stone masons. Although the fortifications that arose were designed by specialist military engineers, and a lot of the back-breaking stone-shifting was done by the slaves from the galleys, the bulk of the work was done by the Maltese themselves. Living for centuries in their barren islands where wood-construction was unthinkable they had developed into some of the finest masons and stone carvers in the world. They were helped in this by the softness of most of the island's limestone, which could be quite easily cut into blocks but which, after a few years exposure to the briny air, developed a thick, hard crust. Yet another variety of Maltese limestone was immensely hard. This produced an excellent material for facing battle-ments so as to provide a glancing surface against cannon balls.

Naturally enough, in view of their depleted finances, the Knights very quickly reinstituted their sea-going 'caravans'. They found to their delight that even if the Moslem shipping routes were somewhat further afield than they had been at Rhodes, they were immensely rich. Furthermore, they had for so long been immune to attack that their merchantmen were little prepared for the sudden hawk-like arrival of the Order's galleys.

Working out of Malta and Tripoli together—but principally out of Malta—they were soon bringing back fine rich prizes with which to help the exchequer, thus speeding the work of building not only the fortifications but the new Hospital and the Auberges of the different Langues.

Although small, the Order's navy was still, as it had been at Rhodes, the most efficient in the Mediterranean. The Knights were also lucky in the fact that, although they had been accompanied by some Rhodian pilots and a number of seamen, they soon found trainable replacements in the Maltese themselves. The latter were familiar with the lateen sail from the Arabs who had dominated their islands for two centuries, and they were excellent small-boat sailors, having long been dependent on coastal fishing to supplement the inadequate amount of meat to be found in Malta and Gozo. Short-legged, barrel-chested, hardy and enduring, the Maltese were in due course to prove as great an asset to the Order's navy and military arm as the Rhodians had been in previous centuries.

The fleet was also reinforced by the *Great Carrack*, one of the most powerful vessels of its time and probably the largest warship in the Mediterranean. This had been built at Nice and, since it foreshadowed the end of the galley and the coming of the man-of-war dependent solely upon canvas (and the weight of metal which the guns could throw from so large and stable a platform), it is worth describing in some detail. The following account of the *Carrack* is given by J. Taafe in his *History of the Order* (1852):

It rivalled with our lifeboats in this, that, however pierced with multitudinous holes, no water could sink it. When the plague was at Nice, and the mortality so frightfully huge that the stench of the corrupted air made the birds of the sky drop dead, not a man was ever sick aboard it, which is chiefly attributed to the great quantity of fires kept by the workmen to supply the requisite screws, nails, and other irons . . . (It) had eight docks or floors, and such space for warehouses and stores, that it could keep at sea for six months without once having occasion to touch land for any sort of provisions, not even water; for it had a monstrous supply for all that time of water, the freshest and most limpid; nor did the crew eat biscuit, but excellent white bread, baked every day, the corn being ground by a multitude of handmills, and an oven so capacious, that it baked two thousand large loaves at a time. That ship was sheathed with six several sheathings of metal, two of which underwater, were lead with bronze screws (which do not consume the lead like iron screws), and with such consummate art was it built that it could never sink, no human power could submerge it. Magnificent rooms, an armoury for five hundred men; but of the quantity of cannon of every kind, no need to say anything, save that fifty of them were of extraordinary dimensions; but what crowned all is that the enormous vessel was of incomparable swiftness and agility, and that its sails were astonishingly manageable; that it required little toil to reef or veer, and perform all nautical evolutions; not to speak of fighting people, but the mere mariners amounted to three hundred; as likewise two galleys of fifteen benches each, one galley lying in tow off the stern, and the other galley drawn aboard; not to mention various boats of divers sizes, also drawn aboard; and truly of such strength her sides, that though she had often been in action, and perforated by many cannon balls, not one of them ever went directly through her, or even passed her deadworks.

The Moslems were soon to find out that, with such a 'battleship' as the core of the Order's fleet and with the lean galleys streaking down on their shipping lines, the sea along the Barbary coast—for so long exclusively their preserve—was to become a dangerous one into which to venture. Malta, situated at the crossroads of the Mediterranean, deserved the Homeric epithet 'the navel of the sea'. The Knights of St. John were soon to find that their new island home, although it could never replace Rhodes in their hearts, was to be the ideal base for their eternal warfare against the enemies of the Cross.

18

Knights and corsairs

FOR THE FIRST THIRTY YEARS THAT THE KNIGHTS WERE IN MALTA THEY inevitably found themselves in constant conflict with the corsairs of the Barbary coast, that whole area ranging from modern Libya, to Algiers and the strait of Gibraltar. The main founders of these groups of states, or semi-states, were two remarkable brothers, Kheir-ed-Din and Aruj, 'Barbarossa' (or 'Red Beard' as they were known to the Christians). Although ardent Moslems, both brothers were the sons of a Christian Greek woman married to a Janissary who had been settled on the island of Lesbos by the Sultan as a reward for his service in its capture. It is unlikely that either of the brothers had any Turkish blood in their veins.

Operating principally out of Tunis they had made themselves the terror of the central Mediterranean shipping routes, and had often come into conflict with the ships and men of the Spanish monarch. The elder brother Aruj died quite early in 1518 in an action against the Spaniards in the neighbourhood of Oran. He was immediately succeeded as leader of the North African Moslems by his brother Kheir-ed-Din (Protector of the Faith), who was to prove himself as able politically as he was as a commander at sea or ashore. Kheir-ed-Din, to whom the sobriquet of 'Barbarossa' was to be exclusively applied by Europeans, was an enemy of all Christians—and a worthy enemy at that.

So famous had Barbarossa become as a naval leader that he was summoned to Constantinople by the Sultan shortly after his brother's death, and was appointed High Admiral of the Turkish fleet by Suleiman himself. It was he who set in train the prodigious ship-building expansion of the Ottomans and he who, by introducing into the ranks of the Sultan's sea-captains a number of men of his own calibre, raised it to the point when it was, to all intents and purposes, the most efficient navy in the whole Mediterranean. Barbarossa soon secured Tunis and its surrounding area for the Sultan, and it was against this former pirate that the forces of the Spanish emperor were constantly engaged in warfare over the next decades.

Some idea of the conditions in the Mediterranean during the years when Barbarossa was supreme in North Africa, and the Knights were busy establishing themselves in Malta, can be gained from the account of Abbot Diego de Haedo in his *History of Algiers* (1612). Although written at a much later date, it was based on the Abbot's own experience of Algiers, and of his acquaintance with a number of Moslems who had known Kheir-ed-Din Barbarossa when they were young. The Mediterranean, it becomes immediately clear, had become a completely lawless sea, where no Christian ship or coastal town was safe—the Sea of the Corsairs. Over the centuries to come, the Order of St. John was to be constantly engaged in sweeping the sea-lanes and in doing their best to eradicate the menace of these pirates.

While the Christians with their galleys are at repose, [the Abbot writes] sounding their trumpets in the harbours, and very much at their ease regaling themselves, passing the day and night in banqueting, cards, and dice, the Corsairs at pleasure are traversing the east and west seas, without the least fear or apprehension, as free and absolute sovereigns thereof. Nay, they roam them up and down no otherwise than do such as go in chase of hares for their diversion. They here snap up a ship laden with gold and silver from India, and then gain another richly fraught from Flanders; now they make prize of a vessel from England, then of another from Portugal. Here they board and lead away one from Venice, then one from Sicily, and a little further on they swoop down upon others from Naples, Livorno, or Genoa, all of them abundantly crammed with great and wonderful riches. And at other times carrying with them as guides renegadoes (of which there are in Algiers vast numbers of all Christian nations, nay, the generality of the Corsairs are not other than renegadoes, and all of them exceedingly well acquainted with the coasts of Christendom, and even with the land), they very deliberately, even at noon-day, or just when they please, leap ashore, and walk on without the least dread, and advance into the country, ten, twelve, or fifteen leagues or more; and the poor Christians, thinking themselves secure, are surprised unawares; many towns, villages and farms sacked; and infinite numbers of souls, men, women, children, and infants at the breast dragged away into a wretched captivity. With these miserable ruined people, loaded with their own valuable substance, they retreat leisurely, with eyes full of laughter and content, to their vessels. In this manner, as is too well known, they have utterly ruined and destroyed Sardinia, Corsica, Sicily, Calabria, the neighbourhoods of Naples, Rome and Genoa, all the Balearic Islands, and the whole coast of Spain: in which last they feast it as they think fit, on account of the Moriscos who inhabit there; who being all more zealous Mohammedans than are the very Moors born in Barbary, they receive and caress the Corsairs, and give them notice of whatever they desire to be informed of. Insomuch that before these Corsairs have been absent from their abodes much longer than perhaps twenty or thirty days, they return home rich, with their vessels crowded with captives, and ready to sink with wealth; in one instant, and with scarce any trouble, reaping all the fruits that the avaricious Mexican and greedy Peruvian have been digging from the bowels of the earth with such toil and sweat, and the thirsty merchant with such manifest perils has for so long been scraping together, and has been so many thousand leagues to fetch away, either from the east or west, with inexpressible danger and fatigue. Thus they have crammed most of the houses, the magazines, and all the shops of this Den of Thieves with gold, silver, pearls, amber, spices, drugs, silks, cloths, velvets &c., whereby they have rendered this city [Algiers] the most opulent in the world: insomuch that the Turks call it, not without reason, their India, their Mexico, their Peru.

Later critics of the Order, contemplating its decline in the seventeenth and eighteenth centuries, have not been slow to brand them as no better than the Moslem Corsairs. The truth is quite different. The Order of St. John, while it certainly preyed on Moslem shipping, was basically concerned with stabilising the trade routes in the central Mediterranean, and with imposing some form of law and order upon a sea that had become utterly lawless.

Determined to eradicate the Moslem threat to his kingdom, Charles V finally managed to drive Barbarossa and his men out of Tunis. Inflated by his success, he next attempted to capture the city of Algiers, even nearer the Spanish homeland, and an even greater threat to Spain's communications with her possessions in the New World. An additional reason for Charles' desire to clear the corsairs out of Algiers was that, with Tunis now safely in his hands, it was possible to envisage a North African coast in which all the principal harbours from Algiers to Tripoli would be held by Christians. And the condition of Tripoli was a very unhappy one, as Grand

Master Homedes kept reminding him. Built upon shifting sand, and surrounded by hostile tribes, the city was proving a drain upon the Order's resources which they could not possibly meet at a time when they were diverting all the money they could into making Malta secure. To a further request that Charles V either provide additional resources for strengthening the city, or else permit the Knights to abandon it, he replied that he was already preparing an expedition against Algiers. If the Knights would lend him their assistance in getting rid of the main root of the trouble, he was confident that Tripoli could be held.

The expedition which was mounted in 1519, the first year of Barbarossa's rule in Algiers, was a remarkable example of European co-operation in what almost amounted to an international armada. With the exception of France, a country which 'led an uneasy life with most of its Christian neighbours', nearly all the states with any interest in the Mediterranean contributed all or part of their naval forces. The attack was to be spearheaded by fifty war galleys, while somewhere between 300 to 400 transports were available for the troops. The Pope provided a squadron of galleys, as did Naples, Monaco and Spain, while Fernando de Gonzaga and Andrea Doria also brought twenty ships between them. The Order sent a contingent of 500 Knights, each with two attendants, a *corps d'élite* designed to form the vanguard in the attack on the city. Unfortunately, as so often happened in those days when the problems of logistics were imperfectly understood, the armada did not get under way until much later than had been planned, and it was not until August 24th, St. Bartholomew's Day, that the fleet came to anchor in the Bay of Algiers.

What followed was a disaster of the first magnitude. Two days after the army had landed, a heavy swell, nearly always the forerunner of bad weather in that part of the world, was succeeded by a terrible northerly of the type for which this coast has always been notorious, and which has made it the graveyard of ships ever since the Phoenicians first opened up the trade routes to the west.

Charles V, unfortunately, did not have the meteorological knowledge available to modern navigators:

Off the coast of Algeria [with the passage of a depression], the winds set in from westward as a rule, increasing to gale force with the passage of the cold front of the depression and the accompanying shift to north-westerly or north-

north-westerly; in those parts the gales are frequently preceded by a heavy swell from northward, and their onset is accompanied by characteristic cold-front cloud and thunderstorms, with heavy rain. From time to time, after the gale has moderated, the north-westerly winds back again towards westerly with the approach of secondary cold fronts, and the gale is renewed . . .

Charles' fleet and army—and all his hopes—were ruined by just such a classic weather situation. Anchors dragged, ships drove ashore, ships collided as cables broke, and the heavy transports—difficult to manage even at the best of times—were either wrecked or scattered up and down the coast miles distant from one another. Over twenty ships were totally wrecked and many hundreds of men were drowned. The Knights of St. John, who had been promised the honour of the vanguard and who had hoped to see their eight-pointed Cross waving above the battlements of Algiers, were now assigned an equally honourable, but far less happy, position—that of forming the rearguard to cover the army's retreat. Their losses during the retreat were immensely heavy, and it has been estimated that less than half the Knights who had set out for Algiers ever returned to Malta.

The disaster at Algiers, coupled with the loss of life that the Order had sustained, meant that the situation at Tripoli became more acute than ever. It could only be a matter of time before the city fell, and it was quite clear that, after his failure at Algiers, Charles V would be in no position to render the Knights any effective help in garrisoning this isolated outpost in the near future. Tripoli, however, was not destined to fall for some years yet, years in which, while the Knights consolidated themselves in Malta, the power of the Ottoman fleet under Barbarossa practically turned the Mediterranean Sea into a Turkish lake.

In the autumn of 1538 a sea battle took place which marked the high tide of Ottoman fortunes in the Mediterranean. After 1538, and up until the siege of Malta in 1565, the Crescent of Islam was dominant over the Cross from one end of the sea to the other. It is true that in isolated pockets, such as Malta under the Knights and Crete under the Venetians, the Moslems had to navigate with caution. Elsewhere, throughout the length and breadth of that sea (which had never been unified since the fall of the Roman Empire), sheer anarchy reigned. It was in an attempt to clear the sea of the pirates, and to secure the safety of the Christian territories in the west, that Charles V appointed that outstanding seaman and *condottiere*, Andrea Doria, to overall command of the imperial navy. The Venetians, concerned more than any other for the safety of Crete and for their trade route with the East, provided eighty-one vessels—both galleys and sailing ships, while thirty galleys came from Spain, together with a papal squadron and the small navy of the Order of St. John. The object was to check Barbarossa, to shatter the Turkish fleet once and for all or, at the very least, to administer such a drubbing upon him, that the Turks would henceforth confine their operations to the Aegean and the East.

The action took place off Preveza Strait, just north of the island of Levkas in the Ionian, at the very place—Actium Point—where the forces of Antony and Cleopatra had been defeated by Octavian in 31 B.C. Barbarossa, who had been engaged in harrying the islands of the Aegean for slaves and loot, hurried northwards on hearing that the Christian fleet was assembling in the port and roadstead of Corfu. Like Antony all those centuries before, he was determined that his enemy should not be allowed to strike unhindered at the west coast of Greece, so he took his fleet up to Preveza and anchored in the Ambracian Gulf, just as Antony had done. But Barbarossa was a far abler sea captain than his famous predecessor, and he had no intention of being bottled up in his retreat. He merely waited there to see what his enemy intended to do and—if they headed south—to sweep out and engage them before they could attack the Sultan's territory.

The action that followed, spread over three days from September 25th to 28th, was mainly inconclusive, although, if anything, it must be said that the advantage lay with Barbarossa. (Certainly it was later celebrated in Constantinople as a triumph of the first magnitude.)

The main reason for the inconclusive showing of the Christian forces under Andrea Doria was the fact that his fleet was almost equally divided between large sailing galleons and typical Mediterranean galleys. As L'Isle Adam had discovered at Laiazzo some years before, a mixed fleet was extremely awkward to handle—the one part being at its best in windy weather and the other under conditions of calm. After an ineffectual engagement off Preveza Strait, Doria's fleet headed south past the island of Levkas, clearly bent on raiding or making a landing in the Sultan's Grecian territory. Barbarossa immediately came out of his lair and gave chase.

The main action took place in the vicinity of Levkas, where Barbarossa succeeded in capturing two Venetian galleys, one papal galley, and five

Spanish sailing ships. As against this Doria's forces could not claim a single Turkish ship captured or sunk. A number of Barbarossa's galleys had, however, been disabled and compelled to withdraw from the action by the gunfire of the great *Galleon of Venice*, the flagship of the Venetian fleet, under the command of the most able Venetian seaman of her time, Alessandro Condalmeiro. Built somewhat on the lines of the *Great Carrack of Rhodes*, she was very heavily constructed, metal-sheathed below, and carried a great weight of cannon. With her, and with the *Great Carrack*, was sounded the death-knell of the galley.

Although galleys would still be used until the close of the eighteenth century, and the Order itself would still have one or two galleys in commission until the end of their days in Malta, the coming of the large stable fighting platform that could accommodate a heavy weight of guns meant that the lean greyhounds which had dominated these tideless waters since the dawn of naval history were at an end. The Battle of Lepanto in 1571 was to be the last naval action in history in which the oared galley predominated. Although the galley remained, until the Age of Steam, the most efficient vessel for the long calms of the Mediterranean, it was impossible—because of the limitations laid upon it by its method of propulsion—to build galleys of sufficient size to provide large floating gun-platforms. The Knights in their windy island of Rhodes had been among the first to perceive this. Although they long continued to build galleys for their 'caravans' against the Moslems, sailing frigates and galleons became increasingly the main arm of their fleet.

Twelve years after the battle of Preveza, a battle which, inconclusive though it may have seemed to the European powers, was in fact a Turkish victory (for it left the Ottomans and their allies still dominant in the Mediterranean) Charles V determined upon another action to erase the memory of his failure at Algiers and to help the Order maintain its hold upon Tripoli. The target this time was to be the town of Mahdia, often referred to by contemporary chroniclers as Africa, a port half way between Tunis on the one hand and Tripoli on the other. Situated in the dangerous Gulf of Gabes, where every northerly piled up mountainous seas, and protected by shifting sandbanks and by variable and tricky currents, Mahdia was an ideal home for the corsairs. From it they posed a threat to both Tunis and Tripoli, and from it they could launch themselves northward towards Sicily and the main current of east–west trade flowing through the central Mediterranean. It was immediately apparent to Grand Master Homedes and to his Council that, unless Mahdia was reduced, they could do comparatively little to protect Christian shipping from Malta, let alone maintain an effective supply route between Malta and Tripoli.

Once again the overall command was put in the hands of Andrea Doria, the Order of St. John sending a picked force of Knights, brethren-at-arms, and hired soldiers. The attack against Mahdia was launched in the summer of 1550. Despite the awkward nature of the place, it was entirely successful. Dragut—Barbarossa's successor (for the latter had died at Constantinople in 1546)—had relied too much on the inaccessibility of his chosen base. Mahdia was captured and, since it was impossible to garrison it adequately, the city and port were reduced to ruins. In the siege and the sacking of the town the Knights had the lion's share. Their part in the expedition—while it seemed for the moment to secure for them their tenure of Tripoli—was in fact to lead to the loss of that city. It was a loss which, though the Knights may openly have bewailed it, was in fact the very best thing that could have happened.

One year later, in July 1551, Dragut, bent on revenge, brought up the fleet under his command to Malta, anchored in the southern harbour of Marsamuscetto, and prepared to lay waste the island. Surprised by the apparent strength of the Knights' two townships, Birgu and Senglea, he reconnoitred the whole position round Grand Harbour and came to the conclusion that the Knights could certainly be driven out—but only by a far greater number of men than he had under his command. Moving north, he laid siege to the old city of Mdina but even here he was frustrated. Weak though the defences were, he found that the city's position on its angled peak of rock required more men and more armaments to storm than he could bring against it. At the same time, alarmed by a completely false report that Andrea Doria was preparing to sail for the relief of the island, Dragut decided to abandon Mdina and the rest of Malta for a future occasion. He crossed the narrow strait to Gozo and ransacked the small island. Ill-defended, and ill-prepared for anything other than a casual corsair raid, Gozo fell easily to Dragut, nearly all its inhabitants being carried off to slavery.

Not content with this minor success, and aware that the Knights of St. John were fully preoccupied with strengthening their defences in Malta, Dragut turned back to Tripoli. If the Christians had deprived him of his base at Mahdia he was determined to secure another upon the North African coast—and one from which he could cause the maximum amount of harm to the Order of St. John. The Governor of Tripoli at this time was the Marshal of the Order, a Frenchman, Gaspard la Vallier, who, despite the inadequacy of the defences and the forces under his command, was certainly not prepared to treat with this Turkish 'Pirate'. He might well have saved himself the trouble of his heroic attitude. Once Tripoli was invested by a powerful naval force (with no hope of assistance reaching the city from Malta) its fate was a foregone conclusion. Tripoli fell to Dragut and the Moslem power was now firmly entrenched to the south of Malta. The survivors of the siege, who were accorded honourable terms of withdrawal, looked their last on the pale sandy coast, home of the scorpion and the hateful south wind of spring and autumn. They made their way northward to the last home in the Mediterranean that still remained to the Holy Religion, to the Order of St. John and of Rhodes—so soon to be known as the home of the Knights of Malta.

19

Opponents

JEAN PARISOT DE LA VALETTE WHO BECAME GRAND MASTER IN 1557 was worthy of L'Isle Adam and d'Aubusson before him. 'Entirely French and a Gascon,' as he was described by the Abbé de Brantôme, 'he was a very handsome man, speaking several languages fluently—including Italian, Spanish, Greek, Arabic and Turkish.' Born in 1494 he had been twenty-eight when he had served throughout the last siege of Rhodes. He was twenty when he had first joined the Convent, and from that day to the end of his life he stayed entirely devoted to the Order, never as far as is known revisiting his family estates in Toulouse, even during the period when the Order was in exile at Nice. A totally dedicated man, a Christian of the old crusader breed, he would allow no backsliding among his Knights. He was as ardent in his religious practices as he was upon the field of battle. He had for a time been Admiral of the Order's fleet. This was a distinction in itself, since most Admirals came from the Langue of Italy—something which had been among the terms required by Charles V when he had granted Malta to the Knights.

For a whole year La Valette had served as a galley slave, after the Order's galley in which he was serving had been captured by a Turkish corsair (it was a myth that the Knights were always successful in their actions against the Turks). Enslavement was a fate that often befell men in the Mediterranean in those days—the wheel came full circle and victor became vanquished and vice versa within a matter of hours. Usually the only way in which a man could escape from the benches was by having his family or friends raise his ransom, although sometimes the ship in which he was imprisoned might later be taken by his own side or, as on occasions happened, there was a large-scale exchange of prisoners between Christians and Moslems. La Valette was sixty-three when he became Grand Master, a man of iron frame and resolution. Both of these he would have need of when the great test came, and when the Sultan Suleiman designed to rid the Mediterranean for ever of 'Those sons of dogs whom I have already conquered and who were spared only by my clemency at Rhodes forty-three years ago!' By that time both La Valette and the great Sultan would be men of seventy. But, whereas the Sultan would be sitting in the scented gardens of Constantinople, La Valette would be fighting in the breach.

Dragut's raid in 1551 had shown which way the wind was blowing. Although the enslavement of the people of Gozo had for him at least justified his failure to do anything of consequence in Malta, yet his reconnaissance in depth of Malta and its defences had probably been of more value to the Sultan. Dragut had seen and reported on the shape that Birgu now presented; the enlarged fortifications of St. Angelo; the new fort of St. Michael's; and the unexpected star-fort that had sprung up on Mount Sciberras overlooking the entrance to the harbour.

La Valette for his part was under no illusion that, just as at Rhodes when he had been young, the blow was not soon destined to fall upon this new and almost certainly last island-home of the Order of St. John. The man of whom it was said that 'He was capable of converting a Protestant or governing a kingdom' was well suited to the task that lay ahead. Like d'Aubusson before him he had to ensure as far as possible within the limits of the Order's resources that all the defences of the island were made good. Fort St. Elmo, for instance, needed to be further strengthened, especially on the northern side towards the harbour of Marsamuscetto. A new ravelin (a detached work beyond the fort itself) needed to be thrown up. Because of the shortage of time, this had to be done not with stone but with earth and fascines, the latter being bundles of sticks bound together to strengthen an earthwork. Indicative of the paucity of earth and wood in Malta is the fact that both these materials had to be specially imported from Sicily. This ravelin was in fact scarcely completed by 1565 when the Turks made their great attack on Malta.

What had finally provoked Suleiman to besiege the island was the capture by the Knights of a large merchant ship which belonged to the chief eunuch of the seraglio, Kustir-Aga. In the boudoir politics of

Constantinople the chief eunuch was one of the most important figures in the court, and it happened that in the case of this vessel he had prevailed upon a number of ladies in the harem to invest in the project. (The Spanish soldier of fortune, Balbi, who served throughout the subsequent siege estimated that the merchandise aboard the vessel was worth 80,000 ducats alone.) Among other notables who were captured aboard it was the old nurse of Suleiman's daughter, Mirmah, who was the child of his favourite wife, the Russian-born Roxellane. Among other distinguished captives was the Sanjak of Alexandria, and the Sultan was reminded that 'the island of Malta is swollen with slaves, the true believers!'

The Sultan was growing old and, like most men in their declining years, he valued some elements of peace and tranquillity in his life. But now he found that he was beset on all sides with crying women and imploring courtiers, all insisting that he should never let these 'Christian dogs' continue to make mock of the greatest empire on earth and its greatest ruler, 'The Peacock of the World'. Finally even the Imam of the Great Mosque added his voice (prompted no doubt by Kustir-Aga and others). He reminded the Sultan of the fate that was being suffered by his subjects, held in slave quarters in Malta or lashed to work on the benches of the Christian galleys. 'It is only thy unconquerable sword,' the Imam cried, 'that can break the chains of these poor creatures, subjects of thine, whose cries rise to Heaven and afflict even the ears of the Prophet himself. The son cries for his father, the wife for her husband and children, and all of them wait upon thee—upon thy justice, and power, and thy vengeance upon their enemies—their implacable enemies who are thine also!'

In the autumn of 1564 Sultan Suleiman the Magnificent presided over a Divan, or formal council, in his palace overlooking the Golden Horn. The subject for discussion was the forthcoming year, and what military or naval projects were envisaged for which the general staff and their subordinates must make provision during the dead months of winter. Malta was debated, but many were against it on the ground that it was an unimportant rock. 'A great many more victories,' it was pointed out, 'have fallen to the Sultan's scimitar than the capture of a handful of men on a small and scarcely fortified island.' The Sultan took the opposite view. His armies were already on the threshhold of western Europe and he was astute enough to see that Malta with its magificent harbours provided the ideal springboard from which to attack Sicily and then Italy. From 'that not unpleasant rock' he could spring the trap and effect a pincer movement upon Italy, his armies sweeping down from the north while his fleet moved up from the south. His edict went forth: 'Those sons of Satan shall, for their continual piracy and insolence, be forever crushed and destroyed!'

Even without the excellent espionage system that the Order maintained in Constantinople La Valette and his Council could have hardly failed to learn from visiting merchantmen of the activity that was now taking place in the great dockyards of the city. Messages were accordingly sent off to the brethren in Europe, and all arrangements were made for the transport of additional grain from Sicily and munitions and armaments from wherever they could be secured. La Valette had one distinct advantage over his great predecessor L'Isle Adam. He *knew* that the Order could be defeated—because it had happened once in his lifetime—and he knew also that this time no monarch in Europe would be forthcoming with any further gift of territory. Malta was literally the last ditch, and it was here that the ultimate battle between Cross and Crescent—the Armageddon of the Crusades—must take place.

Throughout the winter, while the North-East Gregale winds hurled themselves over the limestone island, and while in sudden but heavy thunderstorms the life-giving rain fell like a blanket causing the cisterns beneath private houses and fortresses to gurgle with its coming, the people of Malta, the Turkish slaves, the Knights and the men-at-arms toiled at their various tasks. So much was to be done in so short a time. They had been in Malta little over thirty years, whereas in Rhodes they had had 200 years to prepare for a major invasion and siege.

One great advantage they had in their favour, and something that the Council no doubt (which had earlier regretted it) now regarded with approval, was the barrenness of the islands. At Rhodes, while the Turks had been able to victual themselves easily from Marmarice on the mainland, they had also had the fertile island itself on which to feed and water their troops. In Malta all would be different. There was little enough grain, and that would have been cut in the spring before any attack was likely to develop. Water was extremely scarce, and the nearest supply of any consequence was to be found in the Marsa, a low-lying area at the far end of Grand Harbour fed by the rain catchment on the limestone hills behind it. The Grand Master gave orders that, as soon as an attack was imminent, the Marsa waters were to be rendered foul and poisonous with ordure, dead animals and bitter herbs—anything that might induce sickness among the enemy.

Quite apart from the nature of the terrain, so unsuitable for a large investing army, the very geographical position of Malta gave it an enormous advantage over Rhodes. Nearly 500 miles from the Greek Peloponnese, and as much again from the Sultan's capital, the fleet would be extended across 1,000 miles of sea. True, some supplies and provisions could be brought up from North Africa and from now Moslem-dominated Tripoli, but the main lifeline stretched all the way across the Ionian Sea and then across the windy Aegean. The Turks would need to bring practically everything they needed with them, not only guns and gunpowder and men, but materials for mending sails and making tents, and even—as the Knights had found out—such elementary supplies as wood for cooking, and rods or saplings for building into any trenches they might throw up on that harsh and intractable soil. Malta, although it had not had the benefit of centuries of industrious toil upon its fortifications, was of its very nature a fortress in itself.

Philip II was now the ruler of Spain and, since Malta was a Spanish gift and in effect a dependency of Spanish Sicily, it was he who was first informed of the imminence of the attack by La Valette through the medium of Don Garcia de Toledo, the Sicilian Viceroy. In April 1565 the latter sailed down to Malta with a fleet of twenty-seven galleys, but if the Order hoped that these were to provide substantial reinforcements they were to be sadly disappointed. The Viceroy brought promises but little else. He had, after all, his own and far more important island to worry about. Malta, like the advance defence post that it was, must hold out as long as possible while Sicily—clearly the next target of the Sultan's ambitions—had time to put itself into a state of readiness. Don Garcia's actions, or lack of them, in the months that followed have nearly always been construed by historians of the Order as those of a weak or even evil man, eager to see the Order reduced to insignificance. The truth was that he was constrained by the very nature of his position to think of Sicily first. He had in fact already asked Philip II for 25,000 infantry. That those were never forthcoming was hardly Don Garcia's fault.

At the beginning of the siege the Order of St. John had about 540 Knights and servants-at-arms distributed throughout the three main positions—Birgu and St. Angelo, Senglea and St. Michael's, and Fort

St. Elmo. La Valette also had under his command about 1,000 Spanish foot soldiers and arquebusiers, as well as 3,000 to 4,000 Maltese militia and irregulars. The latter were to form the core of the resistance and, aided by the townsfolk and the peasants (who flocked within the walls as soon as the siege began), must deservedly claim a large part in the victory that was to make their island famous above all others in the Mediterranean. 'Nothing,' as Voltaire was later to write, 'is better known than the siege of Malta.' The fact that this was so was because Malta, so near to Europe, seemed—and was—of far more consequence to the European powers than distant Rhodes, which was not even 'European' in the first place. The Aegean was an area which had long ago been written off as belonging to the Byzantine Empire, then temporarily Latinised, and then lost to the Turk. But Malta, adjacent to Sicily and commanding the main trade routes of the Middle Sea, was another thing altogether. Western Europe, despite all its internal dissensions, was united in fear of the Ottoman Empire which was now at the zenith of its power. The Sultan's kingdoms stretched from the Persian Gulf to Austria, and it was plain, even in the limited strategical concepts of the sixteenth century, that the loss of Malta might well entail the loss of Italy. And after that, what was to prevent a Turkish occupation of the whole of Europe? For these reasons, then, the siege that was to follow became famous in history, ballad, song and folklore long after other sieges were forgotten.

The army which the aging Sultan was prepared to throw against the remote island of Malta has been variously estimated as between 30,000 and 40,000 men, the bulk of whom were formed of Sipahis and Janissaries. A further formidable corps was composed of some 4,000 Iayalars, religious fanatics who sought death rather than life, and who were used as a spearhead in advance of the regulars. The whole was transported to Malta in an armada consisting of well over 200 ships, one hundred and thirty of them being galleys, thirty galleases, eleven of the largest type of merchant ships, and a host of smaller sailing vessels, frigates, barques and the like. On the fringe of the armada, like jackals skirting a pride of lions, came innumerable small privately-equipped vessels, fitted out by pirates, renegades and merchants on the make. Not until the Spanish Armada sent against England in 1588 was anything comparable in numbers and power to be seen upon the high seas. The greatest force that the Ottoman Empire could raise—that empire which was 'built upon an ever-extending conquest'—was moving in the calm April weather southward through the Aegean, destined for Malta.

Mustapha Pasha (the same who had failed against the Knights at Rhodes) was in command of the army. He had redeemed his earlier failure by successes in the Hungarian and Persian wars, and it was no doubt thought fitting by the Sultan that he should now have the opportunity to take his vengeance on the Knights. Piali Pasha, famous for his capture of the North African island of Djerba from the Spaniards, and the son-in-law of the Sultan, was Admiral of the Fleet. Other outstanding commanders included the Governor of Alexandria, the Governor of Algiers, and a notorious pirate and renegade, Ali Fartax, a former Dominican brother who—until he had entered the Sultan's service—had been the most ruthless corsair in the Aegean. Later to follow was Dragut, or Torghoud Rais, the greatest Moslem seaman of his time and one of whom a French admiral was later to write:

Dragut was superior to Barbarossa. A living chart of the Mediterranean, he combined science with audacity. There was not a creek unknown to him, not a channel that he had not sailed. Ingenious in devising ways and means, when all around him despaired, he excelled above all in escaping by unexpected methods from situations of great peril. An incomparable pilot . . . he had known the hardship of captivity and he showed himself humane to his own captives. Under every aspect he was a character, and no one was more worthy than he to bear the name of 'King'.

Sultan Suleiman had summoned out of the length and breadth of his vast empire the finest ships and seamen, and the finest troops and commanders, that he could muster. All these were to be sent against an island eighteen miles long by nine miles wide, which was almost as inadequately garrisoned as it was hastily fortified.

20

Attack

ON FRIDAY, MAY 18TH, 1565, THE FLEET OF THE GRANDE TURKE WAS sighted by the watchmen in Fort St. Elmo and St. Angelo moving in a forest of spars, bound for the south of the island. La Valette sent out the Chevalier de Romégas, the Admiral of the Galleys, with four ships to reconnoitre. There could be no question of the Order's vessels attempting to engage the immense fleet that was now passing down the coast of the island—even though Romégas, one of the greatest sailors the Order ever possessed, would undoubtedly have liked to try to cut out a few stragglers. At first it was naturally assumed that the Turks intended to come to anchor in the excellent harbour in the south of the island, Marsasirocco, 'South Wind Harbour'. They carried on, however, passed up the west coast, and anchored in a small bay beneath the village of Mġarr at the north-western end of Malta. This may have been no more than a ruse, or —more probably—the Turks were anxious to establish whether there were any other suitable harbours that they did not know about on the iron-bound coast to the west. The Grand Master immediately sent a small boat up to Sicily with the message: 'The Siege has begun. The Turkish fleet numbers about 200 vessels. We await your help.' It would be many months before he received it.

Within twelve hours it was clear that the Turks had come to the conclusion that the southern harbour would best suit their purpose, for squadron after squadron began to move back again, passing the rocky offshore islet of Filfla and turning to the east until they came within the great sheltering arms of Marsasirocco—following, though little they knew it, the practice of the Phoenician mariners who, 2,000 years before them, had made this their principal base on their voyages north to Sicily. The harbour, as its name suggested, was open to the south and—since the south wind or *sirocco* was rare in summer—would have proved perfectly adequate as the main base for the Turkish fleet throughout the whole of the campaign that was to follow. But it was upon the desirability of a harbour that seemed to be sheltered from almost every direction that the Turkish High Command was to become divided.

Within a matter of days the main body of the army was ashore, and the first clashes had occurred between mounted scouting parties of the Knights and the advance, foraging parties of the Sultan's army. Just as in the two sieges of Rhodes no attempt was made to hold the invaders at the beach-head and prevent them coming ashore. Some later historians have wondered at this, but the simple fact of the matter was that with the limited numbers at their disposal the Knights and their cavalry and men-at-arms could never possibly have managed to do so. They would always have found themselves outflanked. Their small disciplined force was designed to fight within the fortifications, causing the enemy to expend themselves in their thousands in their efforts to breach the walls. This was, and had always been, the whole reason for castle building, and the theory of the defence of fortified places against infinitely superior numbers.

Unlike Rhodes, which had only presented one fortified city as a target for attack, Malta caused the Turks to diversify their efforts. Not only was there Fort St. Elmo on the point of Mount Sciberras, but there were also the peninsulas of Birgu and Senglea and, some miles away to the north, rising in ancient splendour on its crested hillock, the old capital of Mdina. Not one of these objectives presented in any way the same strength of fortification that had been built over centuries into the city of Rhodes. At the same time there was an unlooked for strength in the very fact that they were situated in different parts of the island—only Birgu and Senglea being adjacent to each other within the space of half a mile.

The great mistake of the Turkish High Command which became increasingly apparent during the course of the siege, was that they failed to concentrate first of all on the old and ill-fortified city of Mdina. This was weakly garrisoned and, indeed, was mostly used by the Knights as a post for their cavalry, from which they sallied out to cut off Turkish foraging parties. Had the Turks concentrated upon Mdina they would have cut off

the main positions in Grand Harbour from any contact with the north—
and the north meant communications with Sicily. As it was, throughout
the course of the siege, La Valette managed to get messengers past Mdina
and up to Gozo, whence they proceeded in small open boats to the harbour
of Syracuse, only seventy miles away. This constant contact with their
friends, although for a long time it elicited little more than one small
relief force, served nevertheless as an immense source of morale. Unlike
Rhodes, where Europe and their friends had seemed a world away, the
Knights were always conscious that potential help was only a few sailing
hours distant. Furthermore, there were natural springs in the area of
Mdina and the land around the citadel was among the most fertile in
Malta—two things which the attackers could well have made use of.

The weight of the first Turkish attack fell upon the Post of Castile, on
the landward end of Birgu. Because of its exposed position it had been
designed as one of the strongest points in all the defences. The reason that
Mustapha Pasha decided to make his first probe at this point was due
entirely to the bravery of a Knight who had been captured during one of
the early clashes. He was Adrien de la Rivière, of the French Langue, who,
when put to torture, cried out that if Mustapha was seeking for a quick
victory he should attack Castile first, since it was the weakest point in the
defences. After the abysmal failure of this first attack, in which many
hundreds of his best Turkish troops were lost, it was patently clear to
Mustapha that Rivière had been lying. He was taken from confinement
and beaten to death. The attack on Castile was called off and the Turks
withdrew to their tents while their commanders debated how best to
prosecute the siege.

Since the two low-lying headlands of Birgu and Senglea could both be
commanded from the higher land that lay just to the south of them, while
Birgu itself could also have been brought under fire from the adjacent
peninsula to the east (where the hill of Santa Margherita dominated the
whole of the area), it would have been logical to concentrate all the army's
firepower and all its weight of men upon these two areas. After all, it was
here that the Knights had their main positions, and here only that they
could finally be defeated. The reason why the Turks did not adopt this plan
of action—quite the most sensible once they had failed to adopt the best
of all, the capture of Mdina and the occupation of all the island to the
north—was a marked divergence of views, and indeed an open hostility,

between the two principal commanders, Mustapha Pasha of the army and Piali Pasha of the fleet.

Mustapha was determined that Malta should be seen as his own personal triumph, a vindication of his abilities as army commander, and a personal revenge for all those years ago when he failed at Rhodes and incurred the Sultan's displeasure. Piali on the other hand, a younger man, and entrusted by the Sultan with the pride of his whole empire, the greatest fleet that had ever sailed out of the Golden Horn, was determined that it should be berthed in a harbour where he felt confident that it could never come to harm. Since Grand Harbour itself, dominated by the guns of Fort St. Elmo and of St. Angelo, was clearly impossible he had decided that Marsamuscetto to the north of Sciberras peninsula was the place where the fleet must lie during the course of the campaign. His motives were sensible, but his reasoning was unsound. Having no knowledge of the weather conditions obtaining in the central Mediterranean during the summer months he looked always for weather conditions similar to those that might be expected in the Aegean. Had he but known it was extremely unlikely that anything stronger than moderate winds from north or north-west would blow until September, he would have been content to let his fleet rest where it was. But—to the great good fortune of the Knights and of the Maltese—he insisted that the Sultan's fleet must be berthed in Marsamuscetto. This meant that first of all Fort St. Elmo must be captured.

The Turkish base camp was now established in the Marsa area at the very end of Grand Harbour, where there was a supply of fresh water (which had already been contaminated on La Valette's orders). The Marsa, being about equidistant between the townships of Senglea and Birgu to the south, and Fort St. Elmo at the head of Sciberras, seemed the most sensible place from which to operate against divided objectives. From the slopes hard by the Marsa the whole of Grand Harbour could be kept under surveillance. Mustapha Pasha now sent forward his engineers to bring him back an 'on the spot' report as to the situation and defences of St. Elmo. He was heartened by what he heard. 'It is a star fort,' he was told, 'and there are four main salients. The front which we shall have to storm is broken into a bastioned form. The cavalier which rises to sea-ward is separated from the fort by a ditch. There is also a small ravelin. Both of these outworks are connected to the main fort, the one by a drawbridge, and the other by a fixed bridge.' It was a simple and old-fashioned type of fort similar to many which the Sultan's troops had captured in other parts of Europe.

Preparations were immediately made for the transport of the major part of the artillery up the long stony peninsula, so that they could be sited on the crest of Sciberras (where the city of Valetta now stands). The greatest difficulty that beset the Turks during this phase of the operation was digging trenches for the protection of their troops and sites for their guns. There was hardly any earth on the peninsula's spine and a steady train of men moved like ants from the Marsa bringing with them earth and fascines to construct protective barriers for the attackers. This diversion of the main part of the Turkish forces for the attack on Fort St. Elmo gave La Valette time to make additional improvements to the defences, to carry on with the preparation of the Greek fire bombs, and the tightening up of every security aspect of the two fortified townships. He must have known that St. Elmo could not possibly hold out for very long against the massive firepower of the Turkish gunners and the weight of their army. But the Turkish High Command, by turning to the attack of isolated St. Elmo, had given all the other defenders of the island a more than useful breathing space. An additional high rampart was now built on top of the cavalier of Fort St. Angelo so that two extra heavy cannon could be mounted there to command the Turkish positions on the top of Mount Sciberras. Night and day the slaves, soldiers, and Maltese citizens toiled at reinforcing the weaker places in the ramparts, while out of sight in the underground cellars the powder mills worked ceaselessly, and the cannon balls were hauled up and sited around their gun positions. St. Elmo was the key to Malta. The longer it could hold out the more chance there was of the island and the garrison surviving.

It was now the end of May and the summer heats were beginning. The thunder of the guns as they relentlessly bombarded that small star fort, beyond which glittered the Mediterranean sea, never stopped. All night long the flicker of flares ascending and descending the slopes from the Marsa showed where the ammunition parties kept up their continuous supply, and where the diggers of trenches and the sappers and miners prepared for the gradual encirclement of the fort and for the demolition of its walls. The Turkish gunners operated with a mathematical accuracy, interspersing balls of iron, marble and stone, and concentrating on one point or salient at a time. The indiscriminate gunfire of earlier days had been replaced by precision and accuracy.

It was hardly surprising that by the end of May parts of St. Elmo's landward walls were beginning to crumble. It was at this moment that La Valette received one night in his Council Chamber in St. Angelo a most surprising and unwelcome delegation. A number of the Knights from St. Elmo had slipped across to tell him that the position was untenable. La Valette remembered Rhodes. He must have felt (as have so many both before him and since) that the younger generation was not worthy of its fathers. Under his icy scorn the mood of dissent began to turn to one of shame. When he said that they need not go back to St. Elmo but that he and a picked band would personally relieve them, they begged to be allowed to return to their post. After they had gone the Grand Master told the Council that he knew perfectly well that the fort was doomed, but that the longer it held out so much the longer was there hope for the Order in Malta. In order to keep the battered and depleted garrison up to a working strength he had fresh troops ferried across every night in small boats, which also took out the wounded and brought them back to the Hospital in Birgu. Had it not been for this regular nightly blood-transfusion St. Elmo would have fallen long before it did.

Smoking under the hot midday sun or ringed with fire at night, St. Elmo looked like a volcano rising out of the parched limestone rock. It seemed incredible that so small a fort manned by so few defenders could hold out for so long. Its end was signalled by the arrival of the great Dragut, master of Tripoli, who brought with him a further squadron of ships and a number of picked fighting men. Like all professionals he believed in quality rather than quantity. Dragut's appearance upon the scene changed the entire Turkish course of action. For one thing both Mustapha Pasha and Piali had been instructed by the Sultan to heed Dragut's advice in all things. He was, in fact, though never so nominated, overall commander. He had another advantage over Mustapha and Piali, he already knew Malta well. He knew the central Mediterranean like the back of his hand, and he had an unweaning contempt for 'staff college' soldiers who directed operations from the sherbet and shade of silk-lined tents. He made no secret of his feelings about the conduct of the whole campaign to date. They should have secured the north of the island first, and then concentrated on the two main fortified places—Birgu and

Senglea. They should have ignored St. Elmo altogether. However, since they had now committed themselves to this totally unnecessary siege it would be bad for morale to withdraw. He himself immediately took charge of the whole operation, making his quarters among the soldiers and gunners on Mount Sciberras, and directing the mounting of further batteries on the points north and south of St. Elmo. The fort was soon under attack on three sides at the same time.

The effect of Dragut's arrival was electric. Within a matter of days it was plain that the fort must soon fall. Early in June the ravelin and the counterscarp were in Turkish hands, and already the Janissaries had probed the main defences and, despite heavy losses, had established that the walls would soon be sufficiently breached for a general assault. Nevertheless the heroism of the defenders and the strength of the fort were still sufficient to preserve intact for a further three weeks a position which even Dragut, with all his expertise, had presumed doomed within a matter of days. Its end was hastened not only by Dragut's resiting of the batteries that were enfilading it but also because it was he who discerned that it was the nightly transfusion of troops from St. Angelo that was enabling St. Elmo to hold out. On Dragut's orders Turkish patrol boats now thronged the waters of Grand Harbour by night, and the supply of fresh men and materials was cut off at source.

On June 21st, the Knights of St. John celebrated the Feast of Corpus Christi as they had always done, a solemn procession through the streets of Birgu to the Conventual Church. Dressed in their formal robes, 'The Grand Master and all available Knights . . . participated with lay and ecclesiastical dignitaries in escorting the Holy Host through streets lined by a devout population . . . On their return procession they all knelt and implored the Lord of Mercies not to allow their brothers in St. Elmo to perish utterly by the merciless sword of the Infidel.'

The following day the Turks launched a mass assault against the fort, the Iayalars preceding the Janissaries, and the whole preceded by so heavy a bombardment that the whole island seemed to shake. St. Elmo itself disappeared under a swirling cloud of dust and smoke. Yet still, to the astonishment of the watchers in St. Angelo and St. Michael's as much as to that of the Turks, the fort emerged once more after hours of bombardment and assault with the Cross of St. John still flying above the crumbling ruins. So moved was La Valette at the astonishing endurance of the besieged that he endeavoured even at this last hour, and even though he knew it was hopeless, to send a last relief across under cover of darkness. But the Turks now held the waters of Grand Harbour firmly in their grasp and the boats despatched from St. Angelo were reluctantly compelled to turn back. St. Elmo was now abandoned to its fate.

On June 23rd, in the small hours of dawn, the Turkish fleet closed in around the base of the peninsula, while the first of their ships began to make their way into the harbour of Marsamuscetto—that harbour for the sake of which the whole of the Turkish army had been diverted to St. Elmo for the length of a month. At a prearranged signal the ships opened up with their bowchasers on the fort, at the same moment as the main batteries, which had been daily drawing nearer and nearer to the walls, commenced the last and fatal cannonade. Then, in the awesome silence that followed this man-made thunderstorm, the voices of the Imams could be heard, calling upon the Faithful to conquer or die for Islam. By now there were no more than 100 defenders left in the fort, nearly all of them wounded, and some too weak to stand. Two of these crippled Knights, De Guaras and Miranda, had themselves carried in chairs into the breach so that they could confront the enemy to the last. Wave after wave of the finest troops in the Sultan's army now hurled themselves against this 'small star fort which it should not take the army more than a few days to capture'. It fell of course at last. But to the astonishment of Mustapha Pasha even now St. Elmo took an hour to die.

When all was over, when one of the last of the Knights had lit the signal beacon that told La Valette that the Turk was within the walls, Mustapha and his staff, their turbans bright with gems and the hilts of their jewel-encrusted scimitars shining in the early sunlight, crossed the blood-soaked walls to view their conquest. A few of the Knights and men-at-arms were still alive—despite Mustapha's orders to the contrary—and were being bound prisoners by corsairs from the Barbary coast who were more eager for ransom than for valueless bodies. St. Elmo had cost the lives of thousands, including many of the army's leaders, the master gunner, the Aga of the Janissaries, and even Dragut himself. The latter had been struck on the head by a splinter of rock thrown up by a cannon shot from St. Angelo. He is said to have survived until this dramatic moment when, the news of the fall of St. Elmo being brought to him, 'he raised his eyes to heaven as if in thankfulness and immediately expired'.

For all these losses, what had the army of the Grande Turke gained? A ruined fort, and the access to the long sheltering arm of Marsamuscetto, into which Piali's ships were already gliding. Even at that moment of victory it seems to have occurred to Mustapha Pasha that their whole strategy had been wrong, and that St. Elmo had been bought too dear. He looked across the waters of Grand Harbour at the daunting bulk of Fort St. Angelo, whose guns were still thundering into the ranks of his advancing troops. 'Allah!' he is reported to have cried as he gazed round the limited perimeter of St. Elmo. 'If so small a son has cost so dear, what price shall we have to pay for so large a father?'

21

The territory of the Knights

ALTHOUGH IT WAS NOT OBVIOUS AT THE TIME, EITHER TO BESIEGERS OR besieged, St. Elmo had proved the key point in the defence. During the thirty-one days that the small fortress had held out, the Turks had incurred immense losses, their morale had suffered, and it was now high summer—the last days of June when the island of Malta becomes brazen with heat. Now the whole army had to transfer from the headland of Sciberras right round Grand Harbour to lay siege to the two principal defence points, each of them immeasurably larger than St. Elmo since they were not only fortresses but townships. Before he left, as a gesture to the Knights in St. Angelo of his unspeakable contempt for the Christian Faith, and as an indication of what kind of treatment they too might expect to incur at his hands, Mustapha had the bodies of the Knights decapitated. They were then nailed to improvised wooden crosses in mockery of the crucifixion, and were launched into Grand Harbour just opposite St. Angelo.

Next day, impelled by the gentle current that washes the southern shores of the harbour when the midsummer northerlies are blowing, the bodies of four of the Knights were washed up on the limestone shelf at the foot of St. Angelo. Two of them were recognised by their own brothers who were serving in the fort, but the other two remained unidentified. La Valette read Mustapha Pasha's meaning clearly enough. This was a *guerre à l'outrance*, a war with no quarter given. In that case he would make it quite clear that he had understood the message—and let them receive his in return. He ordered the execution of all the Turkish prisoners in the dungeons of St. Angelo and had their heads placed in the two large cannon on the top of the cavalier and fired into the Turkish lines across the harbour. 'From this day on,' we also read in the account of an eyewitness, 'they hanged one Turkish prisoner every morning from the ramparts of Mdina.' All this was a far call from Rhodes forty-three years before, and from the chivalrous exchanges that had taken place between L'Isle Adam and the young Suleiman. The atmosphere had hardened over the years and, while Mustapha was warning the defenders that they might expect no quarter, La Valette by his action was also saying to them, 'You see, there can be no turning back. We either survive in Malta or we all perish to a man!'

While the Turkish army, hampered by the unwieldy gun carriages and the weight of shot, ammunition, and supplies which they had to transport round the harbour over difficult terrain (with nothing but cart-track roads), was gradually moving into position opposite Senglea and Birgu, La Valette received some more than welcome news. Unknown to him, on the very day that St. Elmo fell a small relief force had made its way down from Sicily and had arrived off Gozo. There were not more than 1,000 of them all told, but at this stage in the siege the arrival of any reinforcements was an immense boost to morale. Forty-two were Knights, there were also a number of gentlemen volunteers (two of them from England), fifty-six trained gunners, and about 600 Spanish troops. On the night of June 29th, the leader of the force, Chevalier de Robles, a member of the Order and a distinguished soldier, managed to bring his troops down through the enemy occupied countryside and reached the head of the creek where the fishing village of Kalkara now stands, opposite the fortifications of Birgu. The safe passage of the relief force was aided by the fact that it was a damp and misty night—rare in late June—and, by dint of taking small bypaths and tracks known only to the Maltese peasants who guided them, not a man was lost and the relief force was soon within the walls. Next morning the Knights did nothing to conceal their presence, and the triumphal sound of church bells, the laughter and the shouting from the ramparts, told the Turks that the besieged had received reinforcements.

Possibly Mustapha overestimated the amount of men that had managed to slip through his lines overnight, or possibly—after his losses at St. Elmo—he disliked the prospect of investing these two major positions. At any rate, he now offered the Grand Master the same terms that L'Isle

Adam had accepted at Rhodes—a safe passage for the Order and their followers, with all the honours of war.

La Valette listened to the messenger and then had his eyes bandaged. The man was led out to a position between the bastions of Provence and Auvergne where his eyes were uncovered and he was asked to look up at the height of the defences above him and the depth of the great ditch below. 'The Turks will never take this place!' he cried. La Valette gave him his reply to take back to Mustapha Pasha: 'Tell your master this is the only territory that I will give him. There lies the land which he may have for his own—provided always that he fills it with the bodies of his Janissaries.'

Mustapha's reaction to this arrogant dismissal of his generous offer was to redouble his efforts to make sure that the two peninsulas were entirely sealed off both by land and sea from any contact with the outside world. Already his troops were spread all round the Margherita Heights, the high ground that lay to the south, and he now set about ensuring that even the waters of Grand Harbour came under Turkish control. A small fleet of galleys was dragged from Marsamuscetto across the narrow neck of land that separated the two harbours and was launched into the sea at the Marsa end of Grand Harbour. It was an action that the Knights could not oppose, for their own vessels were laid up for security in the sea-moat between Fort St. Angelo and Birgu. They would undoubtedly have been blown to pieces if they had ventured out under the Turkish guns that were mounted on Sciberras and Mount Corradino to the north of them.

During the first week of July the combined batteries opened a heavy crossfire on both the main positions. Mustapha's aim was to attack the landward end of Senglea as soon as it had been sufficiently reduced, at the same time making a seaborne attack from the Marsa on the tip of the peninsula. He was to some extent thwarted in this plan by the activity of the Maltese, nearly all of whom were excellent swimmers. Under the orders of their Militia officers, they now erected a palisade of stakes and underwater obstructions all along the side of the peninsula where it was shallow enough for boats to be run ashore. On July 15th a massive attack was launched by land and sea, and a great battle took place around the palisades, where the invading Turkish boats either plunged into the stakes or were caught up on chains that had been strung between them all along the shore. While the gunners and the arquebusiers opened up a withering fire as the boats approached, the trained Maltese swimmers waited for the moment when they reached the palisades. Then they swam out to encounter the Turks as they tried to cut down the defences, and a savage hand-to-hand battle developed in the sea. As the Spanish soldier Balbi wrote: 'They attacked the Turks with such spirit that I do not say for Maltese, but for men of any nation, it would have been impossible to be more courageous.'

Despite the fact that part of the wall was breached by the explosion of a powder magazine—which enabled some of the attackers to secure a foothold on the wall itself—the seaborne attack against Senglea proved a failure. For days afterwards the water was full of lolling bodies, which were stripped of their fine robes, their jewelled scimitars and turbans by the very men who had killed them. During the latter stages of this encounter a number of the Turks, who had been left behind as their boats withdrew, attempted to surrender. But the message of St. Elmo had been well understood by the local people. 'St. Elmo's pay!' they cried as they slit their throats.

While the battle had been raging at both ends of the peninsula an attempt had been made by Mustapha Pasha to create a diversion by sending ten large boats laden with Janissaries to attack the other side of Senglea and storm the low walls which it might well be expected would be undefended when all the troops were otherwise engaged. The Janissaries set off from the shore below Mount Sciberras, passing between the tips of the headlands of Senglea and Birgu. Now at the very foot of Fort St. Angelo there was a concealed battery, sited right down on the water's edge, and designed for just such an action—to prevent any enemy ships from entering the creek. The French commander of the battery, de Guiral, could hardly believe his luck when he saw that these boats, laden with their heron-plumed Janissaries, were drawing out from the shore opposite and heading straight beneath the muzzles of his guns. He waited until they were all in the mouth of the creek, a range of about 200 yards, and then gave the order to open fire. It was a massacre. Nine of the boats were sunk and at least 800 of the Sultan's crack troops were hurled into the water. Only the tenth boat managed to struggle back to the safety of the farther shore. 'This day,' as Balbi wrote, 'Commander de Guiral's battery was undoubtedly the salvation of Senglea. There can be no doubt that if these boats had managed to put their troops ashore we would not have been able to hold out any longer.'

After the failure of this first major assault on Senglea Mustapha decided to proceed with more caution. He realised that against these fortified positions, which were fortified also by the sea that surrounded them, the traditional 'steamroller' tactics could not be applied with any real prospect of success. While he himself undertook the conduct of the campaign against Senglea he put Piali in charge of that against neighbouring Birgu, the headquarters of the Order and the centre from which Grand Master La Valette conducted the whole campaign. At dawn on August 2nd all the encircling guns from Mount Salvatore above Birgu to the east, to the heights of Mount Margherita south of Senglea, opened up with a roar, a continuous roar that lasted until the sun was high in the sky. So great was the noise that it was reported that 'In Syracuse and Catania, the one 70 and the other 100 miles from Malta, the inhabitants heard the sound, and likened it to the distant rumble of thunder.'

Fifty major pieces of artillery alone directed their fire against the two main positions, and these included 60-pound culverins, ten 80-pounders, and one or two immense 'basilisks' which fired solid shot weighing 60 pounds. Under the brilliant sky of high midsummer the island shook with heat-haze, and now to this was added the trembling of the ground itself, and the lazily spiralling clouds of limestone dust that rose above the embattled walls. Even before the guns had silenced to a trumpet call, the Turkish soldiers were swarming down the slopes, tearing up and against the walls that stood like storm-lashed rocks above the white tide of attackers. For six hours the battle raged around the walls of Senglea and Birgu and, although on several occasions the Turks had even managed to establish themselves in a breach of the walls, their force was finally spent. Tearing his beard with mortification, Mustapha Pasha finally called off his troops. He had underestimated the strength of the walls and the obstinate endurance of the defenders.

The ensuing bombardment, designed to soften up the defences finally and forever, went on for five days. Then, on August 7th, the assault was once again renewed. The main blow fell this time upon Birgu and was directed against the Post of Castile, that Post which had mocked Mustapha's men in their first trial of the fortifications many weeks ago. Behind the main walls the defenders had built inner defensive walls (as had been done at Rhodes), so that even if the enemy breached the main wall they found themselves with a second one, usually designed so that they could be met with a steady fire from more than one angle at a time. This was exactly what happened at Birgu. The advancing troops, victorious as they thought when they poured through the breach, found themselves under a murderous crossfire. They broke and ran, back to the safety of their trenches. Mustapha Pasha was being more successful at Senglea, and his men had actually established themselves inside the defences and had gained a footing in the citadel itself. For the besieged this was by far the most dangerous moment in the whole siege. Although La Valette had had a bridge of boats laid across the creek between Birgu and Senglea so that help could swiftly be transferred from one quarter to another, at this moment, hard pressed as he was himself, he had no reinforcements to send to his threatened brethren. For the Turks victory seemed to hang suspended in the air, a golden dream of the fields of Paradise for those who died, and a vision of loot, rapine and plunder for those who survived.

At that very moment, when all seemed lost in Senglea, a trumpet call rang out—to be repeated throughout the long lines of the army. It was the Retreat! Almost unbelievably, it seemed, when the citadel itself was within their grasp, the advance troops found themselves being ordered back by their officers and under-officers. To the amazement of the defenders, who felt quite sure that their last hour had come, the whole of the Turkish army was soon seen in full-scale retreat, headed back for their base camp at the Marsa. For a moment the defenders must have thought that the long-promised relief force had at last reached the island. This was exactly what Mustapha himself had been told. A messenger had brought him word that troops of Christian horsemen were harrying and burning the camp and slaying all the inhabitants. (These were mainly the sick and wounded who had been left with their attendants and a few guards while the army was engaged on the major assault.)

When Mustapha Pasha heard what had really happened—and realised that he had called off the attack when victory was within his grasp, his rage knew no bounds. The so-called 'relief force' was no more than a detachment of the cavalry stationed at Mdina, who, hearing the noise from Senglea and Birgu, had realised that a major assault was in process and had decided to create a diversion by cutting to pieces the Turkish base camp while the army was otherwise engaged. They succeeded admirably in their project, killing most of the inhabitants of the camp, firing tents and supplies of stores, hamstringing or leading off the horses, and disappearing back to

Mdina before the army could catch up with them. If they had only made a havoc of the Turkish base their raid would have been worthy of praise, but the fact that they had caused the Turks to withdraw at a moment when victory was almost within Mustapha's grasp was the salvation of the Knights and the Order of St. John. Like de Guiral's concealed battery, which had decimated the Janissary attack, they had struck where no blow had been expected. And their blow had been devastating.

As August drew on and the Turks redoubled their artillery attacks, and their sapping and mining beneath the outward-spilling walls of Senglea and the Post of Castile in Birgu, it seemed to many of the Knights as well as to members of the Council that it could only be a short matter of time before one or other, or indeed both, positions must fall. The suggestion was put to the Grand Master at a Council meeting that the township of Birgu should be abandoned, and that all the able-bodied Knights, brethren-at-arms and soldiery should withdraw into the fortress of St. Angelo. There, they said, they could surely hold out until either relief arrived, or the rains and storms of winter forced the Turk to withdraw and call off his attack. La Valette was adamant—on no account would there be any such withdrawal. He knew perfectly well that it would be difficult if not impossible for the Turk to winter in Malta, with their supplies and sea-communications spread out across the Ionian and Aegean seas (notoriously one of the stormiest areas in the Mediterranean). But he was of the opinion that they could hold out perfectly well where they were—better indeed than being cooped up in one fortress which, however strong, must inevit-ably come under an overwhelming fire from every point of the compass. Besides, as he pointed out, he had absolutely no intention of abandoning the brave Maltese people, the men, women and children, who had daily suffered with the garrison and who had taken as able a part in the defence as any of the trained soldiery, or militia.

The Grand Master next received a further despatch from Don Garcia in Sicily, saying that before the end of August he would be bringing a relief force down to Malta of at least 16,000 men. The Grand Master did not put his 'trust in princes'. As he said to his good friend Sir John Starkey, his Latin secretary and the head of the Langue of England, 'we can rely no further upon his promises. When the Council meets next they must be told that they must in no way expect a relief force. Only we ourselves can save ourselves.' As an earnest of his decision that there should be no more retreat, he had the bridge between St. Angelo and Birgu blown up. The garrison in St. Angelo were on their own, and so were the garrisons of Senglea and Birgu. By thus forcing the enemy to continue diversifying his fire the Grand Master undoubtedly made the right decision—the decision that saved both Malta and the Order of St. John.

'. . . And all day and all night the enemy's guns did not cease.' Such entries are common enough in Balbi's diary for this period. Mustapha and his staff, aware that within a few weeks the autumn would be upon them, redoubled their efforts to shatter the walls and the morale of the defenders before the summer was over. As at Rhodes, where sapping and mining had contributed so largely to the success of the Sultan's arms, specially trained teams of Egyptian miners were now busy beneath the outspill of the crumbling walls and underneath the hot basic limestone rock itself, driving their tunnels forward to blow wide the main points of the defences. Siege engines which could overtop the walls were also brought into play, but these on more than one occasion proved of more trouble than they were worth. A sudden determined sally by the defenders—often through secret passageways cut through their own walls—would leave these grim monsters an easy target for fire and the axe.

On August 18th a mine was exploded at the head of a tunnel which had been slowly probing forward beneath the all-important Post of Castile. With a rumbling crash a vast section of the main bastion came tumbling down, leaving for the moment an undefended gap towards which the white-robed hordes of the enemy were already pouring in a flood. The defenders hesitated, there was danger of panic spreading, and then the Grand Master himself was seen leading a countercharge into the breach itself. Seventy years old, 'this intrepid old man, placing only a light helmet on his head, and without even waiting to put on his cuirass, rushed boldly to meet the infidels'. His example heartened the Knights, men-at-arms, and townsfolk, and soon they had taken the breached wall at a run and were at hand-to-hand grips with the enemy. A grenade burst alongside La Valette and he was wounded in the leg, but he knew too well the value of his presence in the hour of need. Urged to withdraw by a member of his staff, who pointed out that the position was secured and the Turks on the run, La Valette obstinately refused. He pointed with his sword to some Turkish standards which had been planted in the breach. 'Never will I withdraw,' he said, 'so long as those banners wave in the wind.'

There was a further attack that night, reinforced for the first time by fire from some of the Turkish galleys which had already begun to occupy the waters of Grand Harbour, as if confident that the siege was at an end. The third week of August was the most crucial of the whole siege. There was not a single bed unoccupied in the great Hospital, ammunition although not running short had to be carefully husbanded, and it was said that 'no one in those days was considered wounded if he could even walk'. Burnt by wildfire, torn by rock splinters, wounded by bullets, arrows and the iron quarrels of cross-bows, the defenders dragged themselves about the ruins of their fortified townships like horrifying visions risen from the depths of Dante's Inferno. The condition of the Turks was better only in so far as they could retire at night out of range of their enemy to the comparative peace of camp or trench. But even they were suffering badly from their exposure to the blistering heat of midsummer Malta, from inadequate food and, far more important, from the inevitable dysentery and disease that haunted large armies in the field in those days when the principles of hygiene were unknown. In their desperation to achieve a major breakthrough the Turks redoubled their efforts against the garrisons. Mines and petards, towers laden with arquebusiers, infernal machines that were pushed down the slopes to roll against the quaking walls and there explode (sometimes blowing up their inventors in the process), all and every device known to the military science of the time was tried out in the final phases of the siege of Malta.

Dissensions meanwhile increased between the two Turkish commanders, Piali keeping an anxious eye seaward for the advent of bad weather, and Mustapha calculating whether he could manage to secure enough victuals from Tripoli, Greece, or Constantinople to keep the army in the field throughout the winter. He was confident that if only he could maintain the siege and the blockade into the winter he would triumph just as Suleiman himself had done at Rhodes. But neither he nor his staff could inject sufficient enthusiasm into an army whose morale was already flagging. The fact is that the Knights and their soldiers and the Maltese people had already defeated the besiegers before relief finally did reach them.

It came at long last on the evening of September 6th, 1565, when Don Garcia's fleet, which had earlier been dispersed by storms, finally reached the safety of Mellieha Bay in the north-east of the island. Their numbers were small enough, little more than 8,000 men, and the Turks—however great their losses—must still have had at least 20,000 troops in the field. But the news of the landing of the relief force (whose numbers were inevitably exaggerated both by Turkish scouts and by peasants who had seen them pass on their way to Mdina) was sufficient to cause both Mustapha and Piali to agree to abandon the siege. The latter, indeed, could not be gone quick enough, for now as always he was worrying about the precious fleet that Suleiman had placed in his hands. It seemed like a miracle, an act of God, something quite unbelievable to the defenders, when they looked out from their gap-toothed bastions one morning and saw the great army melting away like smoke, pouring along the dusty roads around Grand Harbour and heading for their base camp. Tents were being struck, slaves and animals were being harnessed to gun carriages, and the whole complicated apparatus of siege warfare—trenches and earth ramps and leather-shielded towers—was either being dismantled or abandoned.

On September 8th, the Feast of the Nativity of the Virgin, the siege was raised. The bells of the Conventual church of Saint Lawrence rang out over the ruins of Birgu, their clangour to be caught up and repeated by the bells in the Church of Our Lady in Senglea. 'I do not believe that ever did music sound so sweet to human ear. It was three months since we had ever heard a bell except one that summoned us against the enemy. And that morning when they rang for mass it was at the same time that we had grown used to expect the call to arms. All the more solemnly then did we give thanks to God, and to His Blessed Mother, for the gracious favour that they had shown us.'

A solemn *Te Deum* was offered to the God of Victories, and then for the first time in all that long infernal summer the gates were opened. Knights, men-at-arms and townsfolk walked out of their fortresses over the rocks blistered by explosives and Greek fire, past bodies which there had been no time to bury, and into the lines and the trenches where abandoned guns pointed their empty mouths to the air. Soon the first rains would come and wash the island clean. But it was an island that, thin-soiled and part-barren as it had been before, now looked as if the God of War himself had singed and scorched every nook and cranny of it. Mustapha Pasha, when he learned the true figures of the relief force that had reached Malta from Sicily, attempted to recall his troops, many of whom were already embarking in Piali's fleet which lay at anchor in St. Paul's Bay on the east coast. Despite a last valiant attempt to stem the retreat, and to give battle to the new-comers, Mustapha Pasha had to resign himself to the inevitable. For the second time in his life, he and the Sultan's army had been defeated by those 'Sons of Satan', the Knights of the Order of St. John.

This time the defeat was of an order that had never before been experienced in the reign of the all-conquering Sultan. Less than a third of his army finally reached the safety of the Golden Horn. Mustapha and Piali trembled for their heads. They were spared, possibly because they had been intelligent enough to send on their despatches in a fast galley a long way ahead of the fleet. Suleiman's temper had had time to abate before his commanders arrived—on the Sultan's orders bringing the army and the fleet into Constantinople after dark, so that the people could not see what ruin had been inflicted upon them.

'I see now,' said Suleiman, 'that it is only in my own hand that my sword is invincible.' He gave orders for the preparation of a new expedition against Malta in the following year—'one which I will lead myself against this accursed island. And I swear by the bones of my fathers—may Allah brighten their tombs—that I will not spare one single inhabitant!'

22

Aftermath and city

'IT HAS PLEASED GOD THIS YEAR, 1565,' THE SPANISH ARQUEBUSIER
Balbi had written at the beginning of his journal, 'that under the good
government of the brave and devout Grand Master Jean de la Valette, the
Order should be attacked in great force by the Sultan Suleiman, who felt
himself affronted by the great harm done to him on land and sea by the
galleys of the Knights of the Order.' The Sultan might indeed have failed
in his objective, 'the extirpation of this nest of serpents', but he had
certainly inflicted more than 'great harm' upon the Order and its island
home. La Valette as he rode round the island with Don Garcia de Toledo
could only ruefully reflect that if the Turks returned to the attack next
year there was practically no chance of the island and the Order surviving.
His small kingdom lay in ruins about him and, however hard they worked
over the winter and spring months, it was very unlikely that the defences
could be made good before the return of spring brought once again the
return of campaigning weather. As a first measure he had all available men
put to filling in the Turkish trenches and destroying all the earthworks
that they had erected. At least, if they returned, they would not find anything left to assist them.

Innumerable problems confronted him, not least the lack of men to
garrison the defences adequately. Out of a force that had originally consisted of little more than 9,000 the Grand Master had only 600 left who
were capable of bearing arms. During the siege 250 Knights of the Order
had died and of those who survived nearly all were maimed, wounded or
crippled for life. Not even the last siege of Rhodes had taken such a toll.
Of the Maltese militia and the Spanish and foreign mercenary soldiers

some 7,000 had died. Had Mustapha Pasha prevailed over Piali and brought all the troops back, he might well have defeated the relief force. There can be no doubt that another week, or at the most two, would have seen the fall of Senglea and Birgu. Perhaps the greatest single piece of good fortune that befell the Knights during the course of the siege was the death of Dragut. It was Dragut who, by his siting of the batteries around St. Elmo and by his cutting off the nightly boat ferries that brought relief to the garrison, had finally contrived the fort's capture. There can be little doubt that, if his had been the guiding hand during the siege of the two main fortified positions, both Birgu and Senglea would have fallen long before the relief arrived.

There was another aspect of the affair, however, which, in his gloomy contemplation of his ruined island and decimated forces, may have escaped the Grand Master's notice at that moment. The Turkish losses had been immense, quite out of proportion to the value of their objective—even if they had attained it. Out of the various authorities who left their records of the siege of Malta the most conservative estimate gives the Turkish losses as 25,000 men, while most put them at 30,000. None of these figures take into account the losses suffered by the Algerians, the Egyptians or the corsairs of the Barbary coast, for whom no records are available. But even taking the most conservative estimate of the Turkish dead, it would seem likely that the total was probably in excess of 30,000 men. As W. H. Prescott commented in his *History of the Reign of Philip II*: 'The arms of Soleyman the First, during his long and glorious reign, met with no reverse so humiliating as his failure in the siege of Malta. To say nothing of the cost of the maritime preparations, the waste of life was prodigious . . .'

Although no one could have foreseen it at the time, this was the last real effort of the Ottomans to break into the western Mediterranean and complete the encirclement of Europe from the south. Had Malta fallen, the face of Europe might have been completely changed within the next decade. That perspicacious ruler, Queen Elizabeth of England, had observed during the course of the siege that 'if the Turks should prevail against the Isle of Malta, it is uncertain what further peril might follow to the rest of Christendom'. In Protestant England, where in 1534 King Henry VIII had expropriated all the lands and possessions of the English Langue, the victory of the Knights was seen as the salvation of Europe. The Queen ordered the Archbishop of Canterbury to appoint a special form of Thanksgiving to be read out in all the churches throughout the land, thrice weekly for three weeks, after the lifting of the siege.

The Knights, those who had survived, and the Grand Master—but above all the Order itself—suddenly found that their defence of their barren, rocky island had brought them a world-wide fame, a lustre so enduring that even after centuries it has not dimmed. Although there were still those who hankered after a return to Rhodes it was not too difficult for the pro-Malta party to have their way and, since the Grand Master himself was in favour of retaining the island as their home, the opposition was discredited. But the fact remained that the siege had clearly shown that the two peninsulas of Senglea and Birgu, however much their defences were improved, were unsuitable for a permanent base. They were overlooked from the high ground behind them, and in the case of Birgu also from Mount Salvatore to the east. Above all else they were dominated by the bony ridge of Mount Sciberras on the far side of Grand Harbour and, with the steady improvement in the range of guns, it was clear that in any future siege both peninsulas could be rendered completely un-tenable by massed batteries sited opposite them. The suggestion had been made earlier by two military engineers, Ferramolino and Strozzi, that, if the Knights wanted an ideal site for a fortified city—one that would not only rival but surpass that of Rhodes—then Mount Sciberras was the place to build it. Only a few years before the siege another distinguished engineer, Bartolomeo Genga, had confirmed the opinions of his pre-decessors and had gone so far as to make a model of a fortified city embracing the whole of Mount Sciberras and extending as far as the area now known as Floriana; a point from which the whole of the Marsa area could also be brought under gunfire. Even before the siege La Valette had been in favour of moving the home of the Order to Sciberras, but shortage of money and a knowledge that the attack would come too soon for the proposed city to be completed had caused the plans to be shelved.

The time was now ripe for raising the issue once again, and for securing the good will of the Pope—at a moment when the Order stood so high in his esteem—for a project which, though it would undoubtedly be costly, would ensure that the Order was securely housed and protected against any further incursions by the enemies of Christendom. La Valette, fore-stalling the dissentients in the Order, who were all in favour of leaving the island at once (a number of the Order's relics and other valuable possessions had already been packed for shipment), despatched ambassadors to the Pope to plead for his help. Pius IV, a practical man who was well aware how important the Order in Malta was for the defence of Sicily and Italy, decided to despatch one of the best military architects of the time to make a study of the problems involved and to advise on the construction of a more permanent home for the defenders of this outer bastion of Christendom. His choice fell on Francesco Laparelli, a pupil and assistant of Michelangelo, and an expert in military architecture who had already carried out a number of commissions for the Vatican.

Laparelli arrived in the island late in December and immediately began to make a survey of Grand Harbour and its defences. He proposed first of all that both Birgu and Senglea should be further strengthened—this with a view to the fact that the Turk might return before the new city was built. The city which Laparelli proposed was to be built exactly where his predecessors had envisaged it, running right along the top of Mount Sciberras and guarded at the seaward end by a new and greatly strengthened Fort St. Elmo. It would command the entrance to Grand Harbour and Marsamuscetto, thus relegating the roles of Birgu and Senglea to that of secondary defensive positions which would guard the southern flank of Grand Harbour. Laparelli grasped the whole problem with such speed that he had laid a draft of his proposals before La Valette and the Council within three days. He forcibly expressed the view—which was shared by La Valette—that the whole island of Malta was by its very nature a fortress and that, in view of its superb harbours and fine building stone, it would be criminal folly to think of retiring elsewhere. Opposition was thus overcome and on March 28th, 1566, the first stone was laid by the Grand Master. The city was to be named Valetta after him and, in the custom of the time, the descriptive adjective *Humilissima* was attached to it—*Civitas Humilissima Valettae*, 'The Most Humble City of Valetta'. In later days, when the grandeur of its buildings and the arrogance of its knightly defenders had somewhat changed the original image that La Valetta had had in mind, it was commonly referred to throughout Europe as *Superbissima*, 'The Most Proud'.

The cost of the whole project was daunting. Indeed it was this which had prevented any action being taken in previous years. But the great difference now was that the Order stood in such high renown throughout Europe that, from the Pope down to the most obscure Catholic nobleman, there was a unanimous feeling that these saviours of Europe and Christendom should at all costs be provided with money and help. They must be given the means whereby, if the enemy should come again, they could once more repeat, or even better, the feats of 1565. Apart from a large subsidy from the Pope, considerable sums were voted to the Order by the kings of France and Portugal as well as by Philip II of Spain. The latter had seen that his predecessor Charles V had chosen wisely when he had installed the Knights in Malta, and that this fortress-island was the best guarantor of the security of his other Mediterranean dominions. Individual members of the Order cheerfully gave immense sums to further the work on the new city and commanderies throughout Europe gave literally everything they had to ensure that the expenses could be met. The city of Valetta may be said to have arisen on a sudden surge of enthusiasm throughout Europe for the almost forgotten ideals of the Crusades. It owed its birth also to the purely natural instinct of self-preservation—of regarding the Knights in their small limestone island as a good investment against further Turkish inroads into the Continent.

In all of this the astounding popular fame which the Siege of Malta had acquired played no small a part. La Valette himself was offered a cardinal's hat, an honour which he wisely declined, maintaining that as Grand Master of the Knights Hospitallers (and he undoubtedly had the militant side of the Order in mind) he must often of necessity be involved in actions which were hardly suitable to a cardinal. Within the very year of the siege ballads and broadsheets were being sold throughout Europe, depicting the until then little-known island, the features of La Valette and of his opponents Mustapha and Piali, as well as incidents of the siege. At that moment in its more than usually troubled history, with nation divided against nation and with the Turk firmly established in eastern Europe and his shadow growing daily longer over the West, the Continent badly needed a victory. Great though their losses may have been, the Order of St. John profited enormously from the fact that the siege occurred at the moment that it did. Nothing could have been more opportune. East of Malta, in another island which lived under the shadow of Turkish power and which was one day destined to fall within the Ottoman Empire, some Cypriot ballad-maker coined a song that was destined to become famous throughout the sea, and to be sung wherever men needed to remind themselves that the Turk was not all-powerful:

'Malta of gold, Malta of silver, Malta of precious metal,
We shall never take you!
No, not even if you were as soft as a gourd,
Not even if you were only protected by an onion skin!'
And from her ramparts a voice replied:
'I am she who has decimated the galleys of the Turks—
And all the warriors of Constantinople and Galata!'

The Abbé de Vertot in his history of the Order, published in the eighteenth century, gives as the reason why there was no further attack on Malta in the following year the fact that the main arsenal in Constantinople was blown up by a spy or spies employed for that purpose by La Valette. Certainly nothing could have suited the Grand Master better, and it is just possible that the account is true, but unfortunately Vertot does not give any sources for his statement. It has been repeated by a number of historians, among them Whitworth Porter:

. . . La Valette, feeling that he was unable to oppose force by force, decided on having recourse to stratagem to avert the danger. He availed himself of the services of some of his spies at Constantinople to cause the grand arsenal of that city to be destroyed by fire. Large stores of gunpowder had been accumulated for the purpose of the approaching expedition, the explosion of which utterly wrecked the dockyard and the fleet which was being equipped within it. The blow put a complete stop to the undertaking, and the death of Soleyman, which occurred on September 5th, 1566, whilst invading Hungary, prevented any renewal of the attempt.

Certainly the great Sultan did die next year while campaigning in Hungary, and certainly there was no further attack on Malta in 1566, but the real truth of the matter will never be known. In any case, whether by La Valette's design or by sheer accident (common enough in powder magazines in those days when safety precautions were little understood), the destruction of the arsenal in Constantinople saved the Order from a further siege which it could never have withstood.

In July 1568, three years after the siege, La Valette suffered a stroke from which he never recovered. His last few years had not been particularly happy. Apart from the pleasure of seeing his new city rising in white limestone blocks under the brilliant southern sun, his time had been taken up with resolving innumerable disputes among the young Knights who, when not absent on their caravans, found time lie heavy on their hands in the soft and indolent atmosphere of Malta. This was a problem that had already beset a number of Grand Masters (including d'Aubusson). It was one that was to cause them more and more concern in the centuries to come, when the harsh demands of warfare were felt less and less, and when the inevitable decline in the standards of the Order was to lead to interminable 'town and gown' quarrels between Knights and Maltese, and to gaming, wenching, drinking and duelling—anything to enliven the soporific seasons of the south.

La Valette was buried in the city that bore his name. A Latin inscription on his tomb, composed by Sir Oliver Starkey, translates as follows: 'Here lies La Valette, worthy of eternal honour. The scourge of Africa and Asia, and the shield of Europe, whence he expelled the barbarians by his holy arms, he is the first to be buried in this beloved city which he founded.' Few other Grand Masters, even given the circumstances of the time, could have attained the pre-eminence of La Valette. If ever justification was needed for the ideals of old-fashioned chivalry the life of this most unusual man provides it.

In the very year that he died the new city had progressed so well that its chief architect, Laparelli, could afford to apply to the Pope for leave to return to Italy. While La Valette was succeeded as Grand Master by an Italian, Pietro del Monte (as enthusiastic about the whole project as the founder himself), Laparelli's place was taken by his talented Maltese assistant, Gerolamo Cassar. Cassar was the first of a long line of Maltese architects who were to embellish their island not only with the dignity of fortresses but with some of the most superb baroque architecture to be found anywhere in Europe. The restraint imposed by the limestone blocks, coupled with the skill of the native stone masons, gave Maltese baroque a dignified austerity not to be found in other lands. The city which was to dominate not only Grand Harbour and Marsamuscetto but the whole island and the imagination of many travellers in the years to come was based on the mathematical grid principal that had first been evolved in ancient Greece. This system could in some places lead to a rather heartless rigidity, but Valetta was redeemed from this by the fact that, although it had been the original intention to level off the top of Mount Sciberras, the tools, the labour and the money were not available. The result was that the rectangular street pattern was enlivened by a series of dips and rises, with always—as one looked east towards Fort St. Elmo at the end—a prospect of the Mediterranean framed between palaces, houses, or the Auberges of the Knights. On the landward side, the only side from which any real attack could come, the city was divided from the slope beyond by a massive ditch cut in the sheer limestone. It has been claimed as the largest man-made ditch in the world.

As Quentin Hughes describes Valetta in *The Building of Malta*:

The plan of the city provided for a rectangular pattern of streets, running along and across the peninsula, twelve in the length and nine in the breadth, excluding the perimeter track. The main street ran from the gate of St. George . . . direct to the gate of Fort St. Elmo: there the axis of the fort turned more to the north. The principal square of Valetta was placed about half-way between the main gate and the fort, and another square opened off the south side of the street in which the Conventual church was built . . . Valetta differed from the two previous capitals of the Order in three major respects. The new city was laid out on a rectangular grid pattern. The idea of having a citadel containing the Magistral palace, capable of making a final stand, was abandoned, and instead the palace was built in the city. The Collachio, an area set aside for the exclusive privileges of the Knights and in which all the public buildings of the Order were situated, was not used in the new city and the auberges of the Knights were dispersed throughout Valetta, each being built near the bastion defended by its respective Langue.

Over the centuries, as the prospect of being besieged receded ever further into the realms of improbability, what had begun as an austere fortress-city became embellished with innumerable private buildings of strength and dignity, largely styled in that Maltese baroque which is florid without ever being over-ornate. This was the city that for nearly two centuries was to be the home and headquarters of the Order of St. John. Here they would establish their Great Hospital, which would be the envy of Europe for its size, its design, for its medical proficiency and for the conditions available for the treatment of patients. Here in Valetta, as it became more and more a worldly capital, the austerity of that military-monastic life which the Knights had known in Birgu and Rhodes and under the hot skies of Syria and the Holy Land would gradually yield to an increasingly secular form of existence. The pomps and ceremonies of a miniature European court would gradually conceal from view the original ideals of their founder, Brother Gerard. Yet, even in their days of ease, the Knights could never look across Grand Harbour at the frowning grandeur of Fort St. Angelo without being reminded of the Great Siege, and of the fact that the continued existence of the Order stemmed directly from the terrible summer of 1565.

23

Lepanto and Malta

SIX YEARS AFTER THE SIEGE OF MALTA THE KNIGHTS COULD FOR THE first time feel assured that, although much remained to be done, they had in Valetta a city which could successfully resist any further siege. The opportunity now occured for a major stroke against the Turkish fleet in its home waters. In the famous battle of Lepanto that followed in 1571, the navy of the Order was only represented by three galleys. This was due to the fact that they had recently suffered a major disaster—rare in the Order's history—when the general of the galleys, Saint-Clement, in command of four transports had been overhauled by the Algerian corsair Ochiali. Saint-Clement had lost three of his vessels in an action in which it would appear that he had not only broken his vows but took to his heels in the face of the enemy.

On arrival in Malta Saint-Clement was brought to trial, found guilty of cowardice, and stripped of his habit. So great was the popular indignation against him that he was handed over to the civil authorities for punishment. (It was not within the jurisdiction of the Order to condemn one of its members to death.) Saint-Clement was strangled, his body put in a sack, and thrown into the sea off Malta. Ochiali, the victor of this engagement, was an Italian from Calabria, one of the many renegades who contributed to the success of the Moslems at sea during this period in history. He had learned his trade under the formidable Barbarossa and he himself was more than an adequate match for most Christians. Ochiali was undoubtedly one of the best commanders afloat.

The Order of St. John was completely right to try the unfortunate Saint-Clement and to expel him. In view of the smallness of the Knights' fleet the whole of their reputation rested upon the fact that it was more efficient than any other, and that the Knights and the men aboard it would always fight to the death rather than surrender. On an earlier occasion, summoned before the Sultan Suleiman prior to the siege of Malta, a Turkish sea captain had said of the Knights: 'Their vessels are not like others. They have always aboard them great numbers of arquebusiers and of knights who are dedicated to fight to the death. There has never been an occasion when they have attacked one of our ships that they have not either sunk it, or captured it.' If the Knights had lost this reputation—if they had not constantly justified it—then their time in Malta would have been short indeed.

The combination of European naval forces that brought the Turkish fleet to battle off Lepanto was led by Don John of Austria, the natural son of Charles V. His command consisted of the Spanish Mediterranean fleet, a squadron from the Papal States, the Order's three galleys, and two squadrons from Genoa and Venice. Altogether the allies mustered six galeasses, 212 galleys, and twenty-four large sailing transports. The largest contingent was pr.. vided by Venice—the six galeasses, 107 galleys, and two of the transports. Venice's interest in the Aegean and the Levant was, as always, the preservation of her trade route with the East. But on this occasion the Venetians had more at stake than usual, for the Turks were engaged in trying to annex that Venetian preserve, the great island of Cyprus. And without Cyprus Venice was well aware that most of her interests in the East would founder. The Knights would always fight the Moslems anywhere they could be found, and as for the other states— particularly Spain—it was to their mutual interest to keep the Turks out of the central and western Mediterranean. One crushing victory, it was felt, would clear the sea of the Turkish menace and, without the power of the Ottomans to back them, the corsairs of North Africa could soon be dealt with. Pope Pius V had been largely instrumental in welding the coalition together, but even so it was always something of an uneasy alliance. As Admiral Ubaldini has commented in his history of the Order's navy:

Although the types of ships involved were well balanced one with another, there was no such homogeneity among the allies. Jealousy, misunderstandings about matters of precedence, mutual reproaches, and facile resentments—all these made themselves only too plainly evident while the fleet was still assembling at Messina. It was only due to the warm understanding between Don John of Austria and Marcantonio Colonna that the Christians were able to reconcile their differences and acquire a uniformity of purpose sufficient to confront the power of the Turk with any kind of confidence.

On September 16th, 1571, the combined fleet moved across the Ionian Sea to the island of Corfu. It was not until October 7th that the great engagement between East and West took place in the narrows of the Gulf of Patras, just off the small port of Lepanto. The Turkish fleet consisted of 250 galleys, backed up by a number of smaller sailing craft and oared vessels. The great significance of Lepanto was that it was the last action in history in which the oared galley predominated. For thousands of years, since Greek had fought Persian, and Roman had fought Carthaginian, the naval history of this sea had been dominated by the galley. It was fitting somehow that it should end in a contest worthy of the innumerable other great sea-battles that had been fought and determined by the muscle-power of men.

The Turks were drawn up in an excellent defensive position that forced the allies to deploy round the northern headland at the mouth of the narrows. But, despite initial tactical success, they failed to take adequate advantage of it. Before long the impetuous advance of the allies had begun to shatter the Turkish centre. The Ottoman flagship, the great galley of Ali Pasha, was taken by storm. As Don John of Austria was to report in his account of the action:

The fighting on the galley went on for a whole hour. Twice our forces reached the mainmast of the Turkish ship, only to be forced back again by Moslem charges which drove our men back to the forepart of our own vessel . . . But after an hour and a half God granted us the victory, and the Pasha as well as five hundred other Turks were captured. His flags and his standards were taken and the Cross hoisted to the mainmast. Don John caused the cry of victory to be raised.

Among those serving aboard the Spanish vessel *Marquesa* in this action was Miguel de Cervantes, the future author of *Don Quixote*. Wounded twice in the chest by gunshot, he was also maimed in his left hand—'for the greater glory of his right' as he put it later.

The three galleys of the Order of St. John had been given the honour of holding the extremity of the right wing, a position which was soon attacked by a squadron under the command of El Louck Ali, Viceroy of Algiers. Although heavily outnumbered the Knights fought with their usual gallantry. One account of the action describes how:

> The Knights and their men defended themselves with a valour worthy of their heroic Order. A youth named Bernadino de Heredia, son of the Count of Fuentes, signally distinguished himself, and a Zaragozan knight, Geronimo Ramires, although riddled with arrows like another St. Sebastian, fought with such desperation that none of the Algerine boarders cared to approach him until they saw that he was dead. A knight of Burgundy leaped alone into one of the enemy's galleys, killed four Turks, and defended himself until overpowered by numbers.

One of the Order's galleys was captured and was being towed away as a prize when a counter-attack forced El Louck Ali to abandon it. On board it the rescuers found three survivors, two Knights senseless from their wounds, and the Prior who had five arrows in his body. Around these three lay the bodies of other Knights, men-at-arms, and seamen, together with 300 Turks who had been killed while trying to seize the galley.

By the close of day it was clear that the Battle of Lepanto was destined to go down in history as a great Christian victory. Only El Louck Ali, who had nearly driven in the right wing of Don John's fleet, managed to extricate himself with honour. When the centre of the Turkish fleet collapsed under the weight of the Christian attack, El Louck Ali, whose position had now become untenable, managed to withdraw his squadron successfully and escape 'to fight another day'. Elsewhere the Turkish losses were enormous—fifty ships burnt or captured and as many as 20,000 men killed or taken prisoner. The allies for their part lost 8,000 dead and almost twice as many wounded. A most important outcome of the battle was the release of tens of thousands of Christian slaves from the oar-benches of the Ottoman fleet.

Lepanto was rightly celebrated throughout Europe as an outstanding victory—the greatest that had ever been achieved over the Turks at sea. The victories of Lepanto and Malta were seen throughout Europe as a sign that the hitherto irresistible force of the Turks was contained. It is certainly true that, after these two famous actions, the Ottoman navy was never again used in force in any attempt to break into the western

Mediterranean or invade Europe itself. On the other hand, as Moritz Brosch has pointed out in *The Cambridge Modern History*:

The Battle of Lepanto proved the superiority of Christian arms, its results that of Turkish diplomacy . . . The maintenance of this position was facilitated by the divisions, nay hostility, which broke out not only between the cabinets of the three allies, but between the crews of the different nationalities, which had united to win the victory but went asunder over the division of the spoil.

It is undoubtedly a fact that even at this moment of victory the allies could not reconcile their differences. As Marcantonio Colonna, the commander of the papal squadron and the man who in company with Don John had managed to unify the fleet sufficiently to get it to Lepanto at all, was to write in a despatch: 'Only by a miracle and the great goodness of God was it possible for us to fight such a battle. But it is just as great a miracle that the prevailing greed and covetousness have not flung us one against the other in a second battle.'

The battle of Lepanto, the victory of Don John of Austria, has often enough been celebrated in European history. It was hailed at the time in such extravagant terms that the people of western Europe might well have believed that the power of the Turk—at any rate at sea—was extinguished for ever. Even as late as the nineteenth century a historian could write that, 'The results of the victory were so great that for many years the naval power of the Turks in the Mediterranean was almost annihilated.' Later research has shown that this was certainly not the case. Only three years after Lepanto the Ottoman navy sailed down unopposed and reoccupied Tunis, out of which Barbarossa had been driven by Charles V. The fleet was under the same El Louck Ali, who had already proved his ability at Lepanto, and it numbered no less than 150 vessels—all of them brand new. The Ottoman Empire was rich enough in money, men, and timber to make good its losses in a way that astounded the princes of Europe. The French ambassador in Constantinople wrote at the time in a despatch to France, 'I could never have believed that this monarchy was so great, had I not witnessed it with my own eyes'.

Lepanto was certainly a victory, and one in which the Knights of St. John could take a justifiable pride since their three galleys had sustained the attack of the ablest Moslem seaman afloat. They had managed to hold the crucial right wing of the fleet at the moment when Don John was breaking through the Turkish centre. Lepanto did not mean, however, that the central basin of the Mediterranean was cleared of the enemy. On the contrary, the new Turkish occupation of Tunis meant that the Knights' caravans out of Malta were to become even more necessary. If Southern Italy, Sardinia, Sicily, and indeed Malta itself, were to be secured against the corsairs from the Barbary coast, then it was the duty of the Order—the sole policemen of the area—to ensure that the corsairs were not only contained but put on the defensive. Great battles, great sieges, these are remembered by historians, but the steady year by year 'police work' carried out by the Order of St. John during the century and more after the battle of Lepanto is often only too easily forgotten.

One of the most important events in the Order's history during their Maltese years occurred in the late sixteenth century during the rule of Grand Master La Cassière. A proud, arrogant, and obstinate man, he had shown himself a brave and capable commander, but the nuances of island politics were beyond his comprehension or capability to deal with. He offended the Maltese in many ways, not least through his dislike (which he did not bother to conceal) of the local Maltese bishop. There had always been a potential source of friction between the islanders' elected bishop and the Grand Master who, as head of this great religious Order, considered himself the equal of a cardinal. All this came to a head under La Cassière, and it ended—after his appealing to the Pope against the bishop—in the establishment in Malta of a member of the Inquisition. The latter was an extremely important figure in the time of the Counter-Reformation. To the Grand Masters he was almost inevitably an odious one, since he was responsible only to the Pope. He constituted, therefore, a third form of authority in the island. The Maltese, who had learned over the centuries how to exist under one foreign overlord after another—Carthaginian, Roman, Byzantine, Arab, Norman, Siculo-Spanish, and now the Order of St. John—were quite devious enough by nature, without having the peculiar cat's cradle of their island's secular-cum-religious politics complicated any further. The Knights, with their aristocratic and arrogant attitude towards their largely peasant subjects, were hardly likely to be tolerant towards the intervention of the Pope (through his grand inquisitor) in the affairs of their island. The result was that in this trinity of interests —at the head of which stood the Grand Master—there was ample scope during the years to come for every possible kind of petty jealousy, political and religious in-fighting, and Machiavellian intrigue. The arrival of the Inquisition in Malta was an unhappy occasion for the island.

In one sense the most important event during this period was the building of the Conventual cathedral of St. John the Baptist in Valetta. It is one of the great buildings of southern Europe, and one of the greatest architectural monuments of the Order. Built during the grandmastership of La Cassière to the design and under the supervision of Gerolamo Cassar, the cathedral was completed in 1578. Outwardly it is austere—a fortress of the Faith—designed in the Mannerist style. Inside, it is one of the great Baroque buildings of the world, and successive Grand Masters and other members of the Order spent fortunes upon its side chapels, upon their monuments of marble, and upon the treasury of the church which was constantly being enriched by gifts from all over Europe. As the decades passed, so the whole floor of St. John's became a monument in coloured marbles to the noble houses of Europe whose sons had died in the Order's service. Each Langue had its own side chapel, and here as elsewhere there was inevitable competition between the Langues, each eager to make its own chapel the richest and the most decorative. At a later date the Spanish Cotoner brothers secured the services of the Calabrian Mattia Preti to paint frescoes for St. John's: frescoes which Sir Osbert Sitwell described as 'one of the finest decorative exploits of Baroque painting'. Towards the end of the seventeenth century, Grand Master Perellos enriched the church with twenty-eight magnificent Flemish tapestries, woven in Brussels and based on cartoons by Rubens. The austerity of the cathedral's exterior served like an iron-bound treasure chest to protect and conceal the sudden explosion of light, colour and richness that met the eye inside. St. John's shows, as it were, the two faces of the Order; the military dedication of purpose and the aristocratic love of the sumptuous.

But, as was almost inevitable, the glamorous reputation that had come to surround the Order ever since the siege of 1565, coupled with a decline in the crusading spirit (something which had happened in Europe centuries before), gradually resulted in a weakening of the Order's morale. In the original rule of Raymond de Puy members of the Order had been enjoined that 'whenever they are in a house, or a church, or wherever women may be present, they are mutually to protect one another's chastity. Neither may women wash the brethrens' hands or feet, or make their beds, and may the High God protect them and watch over them in this matter.'

These enjoinments to the chaste life were to have less and less meaning for the young Knights as the centuries passed. The very proximity of Malta to Europe meant that the tone and pattern of life as it was lived on the Continent were quickly absorbed into Malta. And life for the nobility in seventeenth- and eighteenth-century Europe was a far call from the asceticism which the rules of the Order ordained. Drinking, whoring, gambling and duelling were the leisure activities of young nobles, and it was hardly likely that members coming from the easy-going courts of Europe would suddenly put on the face of medieval knighthood. Certainly they would go out whenever required upon the caravans, and certainly they would do battle against the infidel whenever the opportunity offered, but they were not going to wear hair shirts and behave like monks when they were back at home in Malta. Rhodes had been cut off, isolated geographically and spiritually from the western world, and it had been possible there to maintain an anachronistic society. Malta was quite different. Before very long even the statutes of the Order, although frowning upon open immorality, more or less admitted that the sins of the flesh existed—and that it was only the open display of them that must at all costs be avoided.

The following, quoted in Porter's *History*, gives a fair indication of the attitude which of necessity had to be adopted towards the private lives of the Knights.

It has been very rightly ordained that no member of our brotherhood, of whatever position or rank he may be, shall be permitted to support, maintain, or consort with women of loose character either in their own houses or abroad. If any one, abandoning his honour and reputation, shall be so barefaced as to act in opposition to this regulation, and shall render himself *publicly* [my italics] infamous, after having been three times warned by his superior to desist from this vice, we decree, after the expiration of forty days from the date of his first warning, he shall, if a commander, be deprived of his commandery, and if a simple brother of the convent, he shall lose his seniority. If any member of our Order shall be so barefaced as to adopt as his own a child who may be born to him from an illegitimate connection (such as is not recognised by law), and attempt to bestow on him the name of his family, we decree that all associates of loose women who may be ranked as incestuous, sacrilegious, and adulterers shall be declared incapable of possessing any property or of holding any office or dignity in our Order. And we designate as an associate of loose women not only those who are notorious evil livers and have had judgement passed upon them as such, but also any who, without sense of shame or fear of God, and forgetting his profession, shall entertain and support a woman of doubtful character, notorious for her bad life and evil conversation, or shall reside with her constantly.

As is quite clear, this injunction was such that one could, in the Maltese expression, 'Drive a horse and carriage through it or around it'. The city of Valetta, that monument to the siege and to the greatest Grand Master in the Order's history, soon became a byword in Europe for the laxity of its morals and the availability of its women. Many a traveller making the Grand Tour during the next two centuries would find himself happily accommodated in Malta with a mistress and a house overlooking the splendour of Grand Harbour. To quote Porter again, whose prose has the true Victorian ring: 'The streets were thronged with the frail beauties of Spain, Italy, Sicily, and the Levant, nor were the dark-haired houris of Tripoli and Tunis wanting to complete an array of seduction and temptation too strong for aught but a saint to resist . . .' And there were few saints among the Knights.

The notorious promiscuity of the island provoked two reactions. The first was the arrival of the Jesuits bent on reforming the Knights (thus bringing a fourth element into the power politics of Malta), and the second was the widespread dissemination of the pox, or the 'French disease' as it was generally termed by all those who did not belong to the Langue of France. A chaste Knight, as another saying has it, was as rare as a black swan. A French visitor writing in the late seventeenth century warned his correspondent that the Maltese pox was the worst in the world, 'being a compendium of every possible kind'. Earlier in the same century, an English traveller, George Sandys, wrote in his memoirs that 'there are three nunneries in Valetta: the one for Virgins, another for penitent Whores (of impenitent here are a store) and the third for their Bastards'. The Maltese name *Spitiri*, a corruption of the Italian *Ospedale* (the Hospital or Foundling Hospital) is said to derive from the fact that illegitimate children were automatically designated 'Of the Hospital'.

Patrick Brydone in his *A Tour through Sicily and Malta* (1776) recorded witnessing the departure of a caravan of three galleys on its way for a raid on Tunis, and described how the Knights were all waving from the galleys at their mistresses who 'openly weeping for their departure' thronged the bastions of Valetta. Despite innumerable efforts over the next two centuries to curb the amount of prostitutes in Valetta the authorities were never successful for long. If the Maltese themselves could be shamed and disciplined into abandoning their trade, then it was only too easy to import 'hordes of priestesses of Venus from every nation'.

24

Seventeenth century

ALTHOUGH THE RELATIONSHIP BETWEEN THE KNIGHTS AND THE Maltese was nearly always a somewhat distant one, there can be no doubt that under the autocratic rule of this foreign body the Maltese islands flourished in a way they never had before. From being an 'obscure rock', a small archipelago of insignificant islands whose natives spoke a tenth-century dialect of Arabic, Malta became one of the most famous places in the Mediterranean. As the headquarters of the most powerful and richest fraternity in Europe, whose Grand Masters vied with one another for the splendour of the monuments that they left behind, Malta became a jewel-box of architecture. Fountains sparkled at its street corners; the magnificent Auberges of the various Langues competing in grandeur and magnificence gleamed white under the southern sun; an aqueduct brought down water from the rocky hills where the ancient city stood; and ramparts and forts sprang up at every corner of the island. Great underground granaries ensured that, if ever the Turk came again, the population would be more than adequately fed on the grain that came down regularly from Sicily. All of this prosperity was reflected in the villages of the Maltese themselves where great churches, large enough often to be called cathedrals in most countries, dominated the small cube-shaped, North African style houses of the countrymen. Village competed against village in the splendour of the *festas* in honour of their patron saints, a large part of the money for these extravaganzas, so dear to Mediterranean hearts, being provided by the public treasury. The island had indeed become 'Malta of gold, Malta of silver . . .'

The money for fortifying and embellishing the island did not only come from the Order's holdings and commanderies in Europe. It was also a by-product of the lucrative *corso*, those caravans or excursions against the Moslems in which the Knights could enjoy the sense of fighting for their Faith at the same time as acquiring valuable plunder—silks, spices and slaves, precious metals and gems, together with more mundane but equally acceptable cargoes such as wine, grain, and fruit. The agriculture of the island itself improved greatly during these centuries with the benefit of improved irrigation, the introduction of better types of vines, the extensive cultivation of citrus fruits (Maltese blood oranges became famous throughout Europe), and—at a later date—the introduction of cotton. The latter was for quite a long period to dominate the island's economy and Maltese sails became renowned throughout the Mediterranean both for the quality of the cloth and for the skill of the island's sailmakers.

The prosperity of Malta was in marked contrast to the condition of most other Mediterranean islands during the seventeenth and eighteenth centuries. All those in the East which had come under the sway of the Ottomans slumbered in dusty dejection, their spirits broken by the taxgatherers from Istanbul and by regular forfeiture of their young men and women: some to the Janissaries and others to the homes and harems of their masters. Corsica far to the north, although administered in theory by the Republic of Genoa, was in fact farmed out to an unscrupulous commercial corporation, the Banco di San Giorgio, which wrung from the island all that it could and put nothing back in return.

Sardinia, a subject state of Spain, was equally exploited and the misery of its inhabitants provoked innumerable revolts which were stamped out with callous brutality. Both of these islands were ill-protected and lay too far from Malta for the Knights to shield them—as they did Sicily—with the result that they were regularly visited by the Barbary corsairs who regarded them almost as their own provinces which they could enter freely and loot at their pleasure. Sicily itself was little better off, for the Spanish viceroys bled the island dry, while themselves living in their comfortable court at Palermo regardless of the sufferings of the peasantry.

In marked contrast to all these areas of the Mediterranean—areas which from their natural wealth and resources should have been comparatively prosperous—the little archipelago to the south presented a scene of orderliness, comfort, richness, and even splendour. Although Maltese historians

have often enough decried the Order of St. John, pointing to its aristocratic exclusiveness and the *droit de seigneur* attitude that the Knights were
inclined to display towards their womenfolk, the fact remains that no
other island in the Mediterranean was so well-governed or so prosperous.
In the accounts of numerous European travellers one comes across their
pleasure, and indeed astonishment, at finding after the squalor and poverty
of Italy and Sicily the well-ordered state of Malta. Thackeray, although
writing in the nineteenth century when the island had come under British
rule, only echoes the views of many predecessors:

> Nor does [Valetta] disappoint you on a closer inspection, as many a foreign
> town does. The streets are thronged with a lively comfortable-looking population;
> the poor seem to inhabit handsome stone palaces, with balconies and projecting
> windows of heavy carved stone. The lights and shadows, the cries and stenches,
> the fruit-shops and fish-stalls, the dresses and chatter of all nations . . . the shovel-
> hatted priests and bearded capuchins; the tobacco, grapes, onions, and sunshine;
> the signboards, the statues of saints and little chapels which jostle the stranger's
> eyes as he goes up the famous stairs from the Water-gate, make a scene of such
> pleasant confusion and liveliness as I have never witnessed before.

The best indication of the island's prosperous and healthy condition is to
be found in its population figures. In *The Story of Malta* Robin Blouet
comments:

> During the next two and a half centuries [after 1530] the knights of St. John
> spent lavishly on fortifications, ordnance establishments, new towns, palaces and
> villas. The Maltese prospered on this spending and on the spending necessary to
> maintain the high standard of living which the knights enjoyed. During the Order's
> rule the number of Maltese increased fivefold, new trades and industries were
> developed and the islands became the home of one of the most prosperous
> communities in Europe . . .

One source of the island's wealth lay in the slave trade. In their early
days the Knights had been content if they could but fill the oar-benches of
their galleys and have a work-force of slaves available for building and
maintaining the fortifications. Gradually, however, as they acquired a
surplus, they began to follow the practice of the Turks, the Tunisians, and
the Algerians. Slaves were regularly sold to traders from Genoa, Venice,
and other Italian cities. Even as late as the eighteenth century there were

still about two thousand slaves employed in Malta. They were either Turks captured from Ottoman trading or fighting vessels, Arabs or Berbers from the North African coast, or Negroes who had themselves been enslaved to the oar-benches of Arab galleys.

The chronicles of historians of the Order such as Bosio and Vertot reveal quite clearly that, even if the lives of the Knights had lost the salt tang of asceticism in Malta, they still remained the finest seamen afloat. In action after action the Cross of St. John triumphed over the Crescent, and the news that the Maltese galleys were cruising off the Barbary coast was enough to send all the Moslem sea captains scuttling back to their ports and harbours. In 1638, for example, six galleys of the Order came up with a Turkish convoy underway from Tripoli for Constantinople. The Turkish merchant ships were escorted by three large men-of-war, sufficient had they been well handled to drive off the much lighter and less heavily armed galleys. But the Knights pressed home their attack with such efficiency, and diverted the fire of their opponents so successfully, that they managed to capture not only the whole convoy but the men-of-war themselves. An action which, in theory at any rate, should certainly have been won by the Turks was turned into a triumph for the Knights, even though their cost in dead and wounded was a high one.

It was actions like these that enabled the Order's small fleet to exercise for decade after decade an influence throughout the Mediterranean quite disproportionate to its size. Two years later, on an offensive sweep off the Tunisian coast, the Order's galleys even managed to burst into La Goletta, the fortified harbour of Tunis, and cut out from under the guns of the fortifications six corsairs' ships. Such an action was successful not only in its immediate result but in its long-term effect of demoralising the enemy. Had a similar raid been made upon the harbour of Valetta by the Turks there can be no doubt what the result would have been. Watchtower after watchtower along the coast would have reported the enemy's advance, the galleys would have put to sea to meet them, and every gun commanding the entrance to Grand Harbour would have been manned within minutes of the first sighting reports. The whole of Malta was run like a large warship; a floating fortress anchored in the centre of the Mediterranean. Close to North Africa though it lies, south indeed of the latitude of Tunis, Malta was not permitted to relax into the languorous torpor of the Lotus Eaters.

In 1644 the Knights captured a large Turkish galleon in which, among other distinguished passengers, was none other than a sultana of the imperial seraglio. The Sublime Porte was sufficiently irritated and disturbed to dream of reviving the ambition of the great Suleiman, and attempt another invasion of Malta. But nearly a hundred years had passed, and the power of the Ottoman was not what it had been in the days when the whole of Europe seemed to lie helpless before the onrushing Janissaries and the innumerable galleys of the Ottoman fleet. The Grand Master at this time was a Frenchman, Jean de Lascaris, who on receipt of the news that a serious attack was threatened against Malta despatched messengers to all the commanderies in ⌐urope requesting the immediate presence of every available member. The invasion scare, like so many others throughout the years to come, proved false. No Turks advanced over the blue acres of the Ionian to attempt what Suleiman the Magnificent had failed to achieve. The last real invasion in fact, although only on a modest scale, had taken place in 1615 when sixty galleys had come to the assault of Malta and had landed several thousand men. They had been daunted, however, by the immensity of the fortifications and by the inaccessibility of any suitable harbours. (All the bays and inlets were now dominated by watchtowers or fortresses.) After a few inconclusive skirmishes the raiders had withdrawn.

Although Malta was often enough in the future to raise the alarm throughout Europe that the island was threatened, this served more to remind absent Knights and others of their responsibilities—financial and otherwise—than to arouse any great interest among the European powers. Most of them in any case had already established a *modus vivendi* with the Ottomans. As early as 1536 Francis I had concluded a Franco-Turkish alliance, this at a time when the Turks were without doubt Europe's greatest enemies. In later years, as Sir Godfrey Fisher writes in *Barbary Legend,* there arose

the discreditable state of affairs created by the duplicity and insatiable ambition of the princes, popes, and republics who showed no hesitation in paying tribute to the Sultan for his favour and projection, or invoking his aid against each other. The mutual recrimination and public washing of dirty linen must have been largely responsible for the contempt in which, according to Haedo and later writers, the Turks held the Christians.

It might indeed be said that the only Christians for whom the Turks continued to hold any respect throughout this period were the Knights of St. John, of Rhodes and of Malta. Firmly entrenched in their rocky little island they were as dangerous to provoke as a desert scorpion.

Quite apart from their constant incursions into the water off the North African coast, the galleys of the Order challenged the Turks as far afield as Greece, the Dardanelles, Oran, and Algiers. But more and more it was the corsairs to the south of them that became the main target of the galleys of Malta. As Roderick Cavaleiro records in *The Last of the Crusaders*:

As long as the unprincipled states of Barbary . . . continued to menace Christian shipping, the galleys of St. John maintained a regular *Corso*, thrice-yearly cruises in search of the squadrons and pirates of Algiers, Tunis and Tripoli; they seldom failed to make prizes. The record of the Order throughout the seventeenth century showed a vast credit list of captures, firings, sinkings and forcings aground. The number of Moslem slaves in Malta far outnumbered those in other lands.

It might well have been thought that a combination of Christian powers —as at Lepanto—could quite easily have cleared the seas and exterminated the Barbary pirates for ever. But the fact was that, in the divided state of Europe, it suited not only the pirates but the Europeans themselves to continue to allow the sea to remain in a state of anarchy. In the uneasy balance of power (and one that was always changing) between the European kingdoms, the Moslem seafarers provided a useful makeweight. They could tip the balance one way or another. It was with this knowledge in mind that most of the states—whether papal, republican, kingdoms, or princi- palities—continued to bribe and barter with the corsairs; now securing protection for their own ships, and now inciting the Moslems to cause the utmost damage to some European rival.

Because they were neither rich enough nor powerful enough to mount a large-scale sea-offensive against their enemies, the Knights throughout the seventeenth century—as they had done long ago at Rhodes—tended to ally themselves with other Christian naval powers in order to inflict the maximum damage upon the Moslems. Their assistance was constantly sought. Not only did they know the whole sea-basin like a book familiar since childhood, but their help could always be solicited on the ground that it was a war against the enemies of the Faith. The Knights' dedication to a religious war (in which of course they were entitled to their pickings) meant that they were not seeking territorial aggrandisement for themselves. It was for this reason that the Knights of St. John were constantly to be found throughout the seventeenth century working in concert with the Venetians in attempts to restrain the Ottoman power in the eastern basin of the sea. For the Venetians this was a simple financial matter— their trade with the East was the source of the wealth of their proud republic. For the Knights, comparatively few of whom had any Venetian connections, it was a question of increasing the striking power of their fleet against their eternal enemy. Such a compact suited both allies very well. 'The Venetians,' writes Kelf-Cohen in an essay on *The Knights of Malta*, 'were the one power who continued to resist the Turks at sea. They were still lords of the great island of Crete, which lay athwart the trade routes of the Levant, and only by its conquest would the Ottoman control of the Eastern Mediterranean be complete.'

It was not until 1645 that the Turks finally declared open war on Crete, the principal reason for their doing so being that the Venetians had allowed the galleys of the Knights to take shelter in their waters after they had been attacking Ottoman shipping. Landing an army of 50,000 men, the Turks were soon successful in reducing the town of Khania in the north-west of the island. It was Candia, the capital, however, which they needed to secure before all else. Candia (from which the English language derives the word 'candy' from the sugar cane that was one of Crete's main exports) was a strong and well-walled city, and it was to resist the Turkish attack off and on for over twenty years. This, although not an entirely continuous siege, nevertheless probably rates as the longest siege in history. Throughout these years the Knights of St. John were constantly active in company with their Venetian allies. Hardly a year passed in which there was not either some major, or a series of minor engagements at sea, with the banner of St. John invariably present. One of the more important of these, but typical in essence of so many others, occurred in 1656 at the mouth of the Dardanelles. A contemporary report, based on Venetian despatches and published in London the same year, records how:

After the Venetian fleet had made a month's stay at the mouth of the Dardanelles to wait for and fight the enemy, in the meanwhile arrived the squadron
of Malta, which consisted of seven galleys. On the 23rd. of June the Captain

Bassa [Pasha] appeared in sight of the castles; his fleet consisted of twenty-eight great ships, sixty galleys, nine galeasses, and other small vessels.

The navy of the republic was composed of twenty-eight great ships, twenty-four galleys, and seven galeasses, to which joyned (as was said before) the galleys of Malta, commanded by the lord prior of Roccella. The navy of the republic kept in the narrowest part of the channel, so that the Turks could not come forth without accepting the battel which was offered . . . About ten of the clock it pleased God to send a small north-west wind which occasioned the Venetian navy to move, and the honourable Eleazer Mocenigo found means to advance with the *Sultana of St. Marke,* wherein he was, and passing beyond the Turkish fleet, endeavoured to hinder its retreat, keeping the mouth of the channel, and fighting valiantly.

The battel being thus begun, the captain general, Laurence Marcello, accompanied with the general of Malta, came up, intermingling with the rest of the Venetian commanders and vessels, fell to it pel mel. After the Turks had used their utmost endeavour to avoid the fight, being hemmed in by the Venetian fleet, and having no place left to escape, they were forced to fight, with the more eagerness because they had lost all hope of making a retreat, and so commended their safety to the conflict, whereby they gave the means to the Venetians the more to exalt their triumph and glory over their enemies, all the enemy being totally routed by the sword, by fire, and by water, the captain Bassa only saving himself with fourteen galleys, which hath crowned the republick with one of the greatest victories that ever was heard of in former times.

The number of the enemies' dead cannot be known nor discovered among so many ships and galleys taken and consumed by fire and water. About the shore there were seen huge heaps of bodies, and in the bay of a certain little valley there appeared so great a quantity of carcases that it caused horror in the beholders. The number of Christian slaves freed on this occasion is near upon five thousand. That of the Venetians' men killed and wounded doth not amount to three hundred, which makes the victory memorable to all ages . . . The Venetians having reserved some of the enemies' ships of all sorts in memory of the success, besides eleven which those of Malta had taken, it was resolved upon by the Venetian commanders to burn the rest, to free themselves from the trouble of sailing with so numerous fleet . . . The valour, courage, and magnanimity wherewith all the Venetians and Maltese did behave themselves in this occasion may better be understood by the action than by the discourse.

A tablet in the Auberge of Italy in Valetta also commemorated this notable action, recording how the prior, Gregory Caraffa, was 'The first to attack the enemy', and how the Maltese squadron 'seized three large ships, and eight other smaller galleys together with a large amount of brass guns, and captured 300 Turks as well as liberating 2,600 Christians'.

It was not until 1669 that the city of Candia finally fell to the Turks, after a last continuous siege of twenty-seven months. As was to be expected the Knights of St. John were there until the end, embarking in their ships for Malta only at the very last moment when the fate of Candia was clearly sealed. Morosini, the Venetian commander of the city, in a despatch to the Republic referred to them as follows: 'I lose more by the departure of these few, but most brave, warriors than by that of all the other forces.' During the course of this long drawn-out war (which finally sealed the fate of Venice in the East), the Republic, to show its regard for all the assistance that the Order had given them, passed a decree which authorised any Knight of St. John to appear fully armed at any time within Venetian territories—a unique privilege since it was not even conceded to native Venetians. The Knights, with their hauteur and arrogance which so upset the *nobilità* of Malta, were nevertheless aware of the meaning of the words *Nobless oblige*. Even in the days of their decline they never forgot their obligations to fight for their Faith wherever the opportunity offered.

25

More medical than military

THROUGHOUT THESE CENTURIES WHEN THE ORDER OF ST. JOHN IS mainly heard of in history through its incessant warfare against the Moslem Mediterranean, the Knights nevertheless continued to practise their ancient and foremost function—that of Hospitallers. At the time of the siege of 1565 there existed three hospitals in Malta. One was a very small foundation up in the old city, which had inadequate bed space even for normal victims of illness. The second was a slightly larger hospital kept by the Knights of the Italian Langue as an adjunct to their Auberge in Birgu. The third was the sacred Infirmary itself, the descendant of that original hospital in Jerusalem where Brother Gerard had first formulated the rules of the Order.

The Infirmary was sited on the east side of Birgu peninsula, only a little way back from the long curtain-wall that connected St. Angelo at the far end with the Post of Castile at the landward end of Birgu. Unfortunately, quite apart from the immense weight of gunfire that was directed at Castile, the whole of this curtain-wall came under heavy fire from Mount Salvatore on the eastern side of the creek, where the Turks had massed some of their largest batteries. Soon after the capture of St. Elmo, when the main Turkish attack fell upon Birgu and Senglea, the Sacred Infirmary found itself in the front line. Indeed, at one moment, when the wall had actually been breached and when La Valette in person had led the counter-charge that saved the city, the hospital itself all but fell into the hands of the enemy, whose troops had forced their way into the town.

Shortly after this, when the ranks of the defenders were so depleted that great sections of the fortifications were practically unmanned, La Valette visited the hospital and enjoined all those who could even walk to leave their beds and lend a hand at the defences. He showed them the grenade wound in his own leg, pointing out that he too could do with a rest but that such a thing was unthinkable when the situation was so desperate. The effect of his action and his words was such that all except those who were totally incapable of walking left their beds and made their way to the defences. In any record of the great siege of Malta it must always be borne in mind how important a part the Infirmary played in restoring men to action who would, under most conditions of war at that time, have certainly died from their wounds. Despite the cramped conditions under which the defenders lived it is remarkable that no pestilence or plague broke out in the two beleaguered cities. The Turks, on the other hand, with their field hospitals erected in the Marsa seem to have suffered far more heavily from sickness and disease. A regular line of transports passed between Malta and Tripoli evacuating the sick and wounded who could not be dealt with on the spot.

When the Order moved, the old hospital continued to function for about ten years, by which time a great new hospital had been built in Valetta. This, as W. Bedford writes in his history of *Malta and the Knights Hospitaller,*

was unfortunately placed on the south-eastern seafront close to the Grand Harbour, the inducement to choose this site being that patients might be landed from ships at the mouth of the harbour, and brought in by a covered way below the sea wall into the lower ward of the hospital, without making a tedious and dangerous circuit of the streets. Unfortunately it is thus completely sheltered by the high ground behind it from the healthy north and north-east winds, while it is exposed to the enervating sirocco.

Little enough was known in those days about the effects of climate, wind and weather upon the human constitution. It was natural enough that the designer of the hospital should place it on the southern side of Mount Sciberras, with a view to sheltering it and its patients from the strong—and at times tempestuous—northerlies. But even if the site was ill-chosen, the hospital in all other respects was the envy of Europe. In its day it was without any doubt the greatest hospital in the world. The Order, despite its militant role, had never at any time forgotten its principal function in the world—the care of the sick. This was at a time when, throughout most of Europe, the sick were no more than sad casualties abandoned on the battlefield of life.

The main or 'great' ward of the Valetta hospital was (and still is) one of the longest rooms in Europe, 185 feet overall by nearly thirty-five feet wide, and thirty-one feet high. The height of the ward was all-important in Malta where summer heats of ninety degrees are quite common and, in the days before fans, the only method of keeping a room cool was to have as high a ceiling as possible. Curiously enough, although the hospital was in essence the raison d'être of the Order, the name of its architect is unknown. Erected when La Cassière was Grand Master it might be expected that Gerolamo Cassar would have been chosen to design it, but among the numerous other works with which he is credited there is no mention whatever of his having been concerned with the Valetta hospital. The hospital largely follows the design of that of Santo Spirito in Rome and it is almost certain that, whoever in fact was the architect, he had seen this fifteenth-century Roman hospital. One of the best descriptions we have of it during its seventeenth-century days comes from the diary of a British naval chaplain, Henry Teonge, who visited Malta aboard H.M.S. *Assistance* in 1674. 'The hospital is a vast structure, wherein the sick and wounded lye. This so broade that twelve men may with ease walke abreast up the midst of it; and the bedds are on each syde, standing on four yron pillars, with white curtens and vallands, and covering, extremely neate, and kept cleane and sweete . . .' Everyone who visited the hospital over the years commented on its cleanness—rare enough in Europe at that time—and upon the fact that the Knights themselves attended the patients, who were all served off silver plate. The use of silver was not so much a matter of ostentation as of hygiene. At a later date in the eighteenth century, when the finances of the Order were at a low ebb, pewter was substituted for silver.

Surgery was still primitive, as indeed in the rest of Europe, but the Order's physicians were at least better educated in matters of hygiene than most of their contemporaries. The Greek doctor-philosophers, Galen and Hippocrates, still provided the basis of medical knowledge, transmuted by the works of the Arab Avicenna, whose *Canon of Medicine*, one of the principal treatises of the time, was itself based on the doctrines of the two famous Greeks modified slightly by those of Aristotle. Anaesthesia prior to surgery was also rudimentary—alcohol and the narcotic sponge being the main methods of inducing loss of consciousness. The latter was soaked in opium-poppy solution and other drugs, the patient taking it in his mouth and sucking it until the combination of the fumes and ingested opiates made him unconscious. Dr. Paul Cassar in his *Medical History of Malta* also mentions a simple but efficacious method of 'putting a patient out'—probably the world's original anaesthetic. 'The hammer-stroke was also practised. The patient's head was encased in a sort of helmet on which the surgeon delivered a good blow with a wooden hammer in such way as to stun the patient into insensibility and thus enable him to go through the operation without suffering any pain.'

On other aspects of medical treatment Dr. Cassar adds that 'wounds were cleaned and washed with salted water as a first aid measure. [During the siege La Valette had butts full of salt water placed at various points along the fortifications.] Splinting and traction were employed in the treatment of fractures; broken skull bones were treated by the elevation of the depressed fragments and trephining was resorted to when necessary. Wounds involving soft tissues were sutured and severed blood vessels were ligatured as the tying up of bleeding arteries had begun to replace the cautery as a haemostatic. The wound was then dressed with tow or wool. In injuries of the mouth which rendered the intake of food difficult or impossible, the necessary nourishment was administered by means of nutrient enemas.'

One of the sovereign remedies used as a cure for wounds, haemorrhages and dysentery was a curious black fungus (*Fucus coccineus melitensis*) which grew on the top of a small island, 'Fungus Rock', just off the western coast of Gozo. So important was this considered that the fungus was a perquisite of the Grand Masters and a permanent guard was maintained in a tower opposite the rock to prevent anyone from stealing it. The only means of access was by a basket which was suspended on ropes stretched between the rock and the mainland of Gozo. Even after the Knights had left Malta, as late as 1815, this strange form of transport was still used to collect the fungus, and an Englishman, Claudius Shaw, described how he went out to the rock in 1815:

The passage to this rock is rather curious, if not dangerous; two ropes are made fast on each shore, on which a box with grooves on its edges passes over. A Maltese first works his way across, then the person desirous to go over draws the box back and seats himself in it, when he is hauled over by the guide; in this manner as many as please can go, one at a time. It is not a very pleasant sensation to be suspended some hundred feet above the water, and if there is any wind, the movement of the box is anything but agreeable, and all that can be obtained are a few pieces of fungus. I was well pleased to be back again, and made a determination never to risk my precious carcase in that conveyance again. It seems very strange to be swinging up in the air between two rocks, with sea-gulls and other aquatics flying about below you.

It would seem that the plant—perhaps because of its dark colour rather like congealed blood—was more of a homoeopathic remedy than a scientific one. An analysis carried out in 1968 by the British Naval Hospital at Bighi in Malta disclosed no curative properties in the plant at all.

Quite apart from the work in the hospital the medical service of the Knights was also carried out at sea. No galley or sailing vessel belonging to the Order ever left Malta without a doctor, a surgeon and an assistant surgeon on board. One of the reasons why the Order's ships suffered less from disease than those of most other maritime powers was the fact that strict attention was paid to cleanliness and hygiene. This in itself was difficult enough, for the average galley (which might be no more than 125 feet long between perpendiculars) had to provide accommodation for about 500 men. There were thirty to thirty-five knights, 300 oarsmen or more, and 200 soldiers, as well as a number of sailors, a professional pilot, and artificers such as carpenters and riggers. It was small wonder that the great plague first reached Europe via some Venetian galleys coming from Egypt and making their first port of call at Messina in Sicily. The records of the Order show that, even with their attention to medical care, fevers were common among the crew. Since medical definitions were in their infancy it is almost impossible to know what is meant by 'malignant fevers' although this may well have been malaria which has been prevalent in many parts of the Mediterranean right up to the twentieth century. The Maltese galleys suffered also from undulant fever carried in goats' milk, a disease which was so prevalent in the island that it was for a long time commonly known in Europe as 'Malta Fever'.

Sufferers from 'contagious diseases' as well as venereal diseases were not allowed to embark in the Order's vessels although, with the limited medical knowledge and inspection of the time, some sufferers must inevitably have come aboard and passed on their ailments to others. Despite the fact that the oarsmen had their heads shaved, lice and fleas inevitably abounded under the cramped conditions in a galley. So beautiful at a distance to the eye, the galley with her flags and banners, her bright colours, her gingerbread work and her lean greyhound lines was in fact a breeding ground of disease.

One observer commented: 'It is not necessary to look far to find an extreme contrast with the galley's appearance. At the very moment that the galley dazzles one's eyes with her sculptures, her draperies and her movement through the water, she horribly affronts one's nostrils, and exudes throughout her whole length the utmost misery . . .' It was not until canvas finally triumphed over the oar that it was possible within the increased breadth and depth of a sailing ship to introduce healthier and more humane conditions for both officers and crew. The young sprigs of European nobility who came out to Malta and did their first 'caravans' in the galleys very soon became acquainted with a harshness of life that was unknown even to a European peasant of the time.

The Order's obligations to their duty as Hospitallers was far from confined to their work in Malta alone. They provided in the Mediterranean the first equivalent to what would now be an international 'mercy' or relief force. In January 1693, for instance, when the town of Augusta in Sicily was destroyed by earthquake five galleys were immediately despatched to render all possible assistance to the local inhabitants. This particular earthquake had also caused a considerable amount of damage in Malta (an island which is relatively free from seismic disturbances), yet the Order nevertheless attended to its Christian duties, taking surgeons and medicines, food and clothing to the Sicilians. Similarly in 1783 when the seaport of Reggio in Southern Calabria together with Messina in Sicily had been devastated by an earthquake the Order's whole fleet was despatched to aid and succour the survivors.

The records show that the Sacred Infirmary in Valetta sent aboard the ships the best surgeons in the island, together with twenty medicine chests, a great number of tents to accommodate the homeless, and some 200 beds. It is evidence of the wealth and prosperity of Malta under the rule of the Knights that an island so small could afford to render assistance to its considerably larger neighbour. On this occasion the Bourbon government at Naples was so embarrassed at its own inefficiency, when contrasted with the active humanitarianism of the Knights, that a protest was delivered to Grand Master Emmanuel de Rohan, stating that the Kingdom of the Two Sicilies had never asked for help and requesting the Order to withdraw its ships. De Rohan replied that his Order was doing no more than it had done for centuries, 'helping all Christians in distress'. This reply seems to have mollified King Ferdinand, for no further obstructions were placed in the Knights' way and they were allowed to set up a temporary hospital in Messina for the relief of the sick and injured.

As in the Sacred Infirmary itself, where great attention was paid to a wholesome diet, the Order's fleet was given far better rations than was customary in other navies during the seventeenth and eighteenth centuries. Bread, vegetables, biscuit, oil and wine were all issued to the crew—wine especially when the oarsmen were showing signs of flagging in the long hot calms of Mediterranean summer, or if they were called upon for a special burst of speed in order to come up with an enemy. Fresh meat, 'beef on the hoof', was always embarked before leaving Malta and whenever possible, as the cattle were slaughtered, replacements were obtained at other ports of call. Poultry was also carried on board and chicken broth, as well as eggs, enlivened the diet. A basic iron ration of biscuit, salted meat and fish, together with wine and oil, meant that any galley could if necessary stay at sea for two months without provisioning.

The crews of Mediterranean galleys, whether Maltese, Genoese or Venetian, were lucky in one respect compared with the French, Dutch, English and Spanish operating on the long ocean voyages to the New World and the Far East. Their voyages never took them far away from land for any great length of time, with the result that they were nearly always able to revictual within a fortnight or so with fresh fruit and vegetables. Scurvy, that plague of the East Indiamen and the Atlantic trader, scarcely ever bothered these Mediterranean sailors. Their simple healthy diet, coupled with an indulgent climate, meant that despite the cramped conditions aboard they were in many respects better off than the sailors of the North. It must always be borne in mind that, because the galley was basically so fragile a craft, the sailing season was never very long. During the hard gales of winter and the rainy seasons of autumn and spring, the galleys were laid up and their crews were all ashore.

26

Decline . . .

DURING THE EIGHTEENTH CENTURY THE ORDER OF ST. JOHN, ALTHOUGH it never actually slumbered, went into a slow but steady decline. The fact of the matter was that the Order which had been formed to assist and protect Christian pilgrims to the Holy Land inevitably lost its raison d'être as The Age of Reason supplanted the Ages of Faith. Protestantism had long ago cost the Order one of its most powerful members in the dissolution of the Langue of England, and Lutheranism generally had made massive inroads throughout Europe on what had once been the monolithic stability of the Catholic Church. In the eighteenth century the onslaught of the philosophers and savants in France—the principal source of the Order's members and finances—was bound in the long run to bring a weakening of resolve and a gradual loss of faith. But, over and above all this, it was the decay of Ottoman power and of militant Mohammedanism that induced a similar situation in the Order of St. John. If Malta was, as the traveller Patrick Brydone described it, 'the epitome of all Europe', it must inevitably therefore have come to epitomise a Europe where the crusaders were hardly a memory, and where the concept of militant Christianity and an eternal war against the enemies of the Faith were almost incomprehensible.

The fact that the Order, even at its most lax and worldly, never quite forgot either its vocation or its historical role may perhaps be traced to the influence of the small island which was its home. The term 'insular' has become almost synonymous with conservative, and in Malta the Knights had one of the most conservative societies in the world. The people themselves were devout Catholics, 'More Catholic than the Pope' as they have subsequently been known to boast, and as a community largely composed of peasant-farmers, fishermen and boat-builders, they inherited the innate conservatism of these age-old patterns of life. It was among the Knights rather than among the Maltese that the new ideas stirring in Europe began to circulate: fashionable cults such as Mesmerism, the scepticism of the French philosophers and, at a later date, even the downright atheism or agnostic deism of Voltaire. It is more than doubtful that Voltaire's *Philosophical Dictionary* of 1764 ever got into the island (and it would certainly have been impounded and burned had it done so), but ideas are less easy to check. The questioning of the credibility of many of the Bible stories, both in the Old and New Testaments, coupled with a hatred of religious intolerance whereby people kill one another in the name of different theological systems—these were part of Voltaire's legacy to the new Europe that was in due course to spring from the French Revolution. Even Malta of the Knights could not be completely cut off from the intellectual ferment that was brewing in Europe in the second half of the eighteenth century.

Newcomers were now active upon the Mediterranean sea, the British and the Dutch among them, and it was clear that even though the Order had almost entirely gone over to sail by the early eighteenth century the maritime balance of power was shifting. By 1705, when the Spaniard Ramon Perellos was Grand Master, the navy of the Order consisted of five ships-of-the-line and only five galleys. But the trouble about the new and far heavier sailing vessels was that, though they needed less crew to man them, they were enormously expensive to build and to maintain. Perellos was an extremely rich man and like so many other rich Grand Masters during this period spent lavishly from his own resources in the Order's interests. It was calculated when he died that he had spent nearly a quarter of a million *scudi* out of his own pocket, mainly upon the navy. Even so, the Order was immediately compelled to raise an immense loan with the Bank of Genoa, which could only be met by a general tax on all its lands. The Order was living above its income, and its income was dwindling.

The great new maritime powers who were beginning to interest themselves in the trade and affairs of the Mediterranean did not have that respect for the Order of St. John which its Catholic neighbours had accorded it over the centuries. They were rather inclined in their bluff, northern—and, one must remember, Protestant—manner to treat these noble defenders of the Faith in a somewhat cavalier fashion. Here, for instance, is the Rev. Henry Teonge again, writing about his visit to Malta aboard H.M.S. *Assistance* in 1675:

This morning wee com near Malta; before wee com to the cytty a boate with the Malteese flagg in it coms for us to know whence wee cam. We told them from England [and] they asked if wee had a bill of health for prattick viz entertaynment, our captain told them he had no bill but what was in his guns mouths. Wee cam on and anchored in the harbour betweene the old toune [Birgu] and the new [Valetta] about nine of the clock, but must wait the governours leasure to have leave to com on shoare which was detarded because our captain would not salute the cytty except they would retaliate. At last cam the consull with his attendants to our ship, (but would not com on board till our captain had been on shoare,) to tell us that we had leave to com on shore six or eight or ten at a time, and might have anything that was there to be had, with a promise to accept our salute kindly. Whereupon our captain tooke a glass of sack and drank a health to King Charles, and fyred seven gunns, the cytty gave us five again, which was more than they had don to all our men-of-war that cam thither before.

It is interesting to note from a further page in the chaplain's diary that, when a number of Knights of the Order visited the English ship, the chaplain was used as an interpreter, the *Lingua franca* being Latin.

Throughout this period, from the late seventeenth century to the close of the eighteenth, the Order kept on building assiduously. Malta is in fact a giant stone-quarry ('The whole world might come here to sharpen its knives,' D. H. Lawrence was later to remark), and from neolithic times onwards it seems as if this mass of easily-quarryable stone has induced a paroxysm of building in the island's inhabitants. It was not only chapels and churches, palaces and summer resorts, dykes and ditches, towers and forts, but works of immense complexity like the extension of the Valetta fortifications into the area and suburb of Floriana. Most impressive of all, and not in fact entirely completed until the nineteenth century by the British (who had by then become the guardians of Malta), were the Cotonera lines. These were named after the Spanish Grand Master Nicolas Cotoner, who almost exhausted the treasury in his determination to raise a huge linear defensive system to protect the Three Cities of Birgu, Cospicua, and Senglea from the south—guarding those slopes from which the Turks had made their main attacks during the siege of 1565. Designed by the distinguished military engineer, Maurizio Valperga, these were a huge semicircular ring, designed to shelter up to 40,000 people (almost the entire country population of Malta), and having a circumference of 5,000 yards. As Quentin Hughes writes: 'The foundation stone was laid by the Grand Master on 28 August 1670, and a flowing inscription recording the gift of the works by Cotoner was placed over the arch of the Zabbar gate, which leads the main road into the Cities. The Grand Master announced his undertaking to the princes of Europe and received, in exchange, their disapproval of his extravagance and criticism of the size of the new fortifications.' The Cotoner lines remain to this day one of the most impressive works of fortification in European history.

There can be no doubt that these works provided continuous and useful employment in the island, but it would be difficult to justify their existence. By the eighteenth century any real Ottoman threat to Malta had almost entirely faded. It is quite true, as we know from the records, that even into the late eighteenth century the traveller by sea to Malta was never entirely free from the danger of being taken prisoner and enslaved by one of the Barbary corsairs who, despite the Order's vigilance, still roamed the Middle Sea. But these were individual ships or at the most small squadrons. They were certainly never capable of transporting and landing the kind of army that would have been necessary to threaten Mdina even, or Birgu or Senglea, let alone the giant walls and defences of Valetta.

One of the most unusual Grand Masters of this period was the Portuguese Manoel Pinto, who reigned from 1741–73—the longest reign of any Grand Master in the Order's history—dying at the age of ninety-two. Remarkable though he was, and in a sense quite unlike any other Grand Master—being more of a sovereign monarch than in any way *primus inter pares*—Pinto somehow represents the Order in the eighteenth century better than most of his predecessors or successors. Patrick Brydone, who met Pinto a year or so before his death, describes him as follows:

He has now been at the head of this singular little state for upwards of thirty years. He received us with great politeness, and was highly pleased to find that some of us had been to Portugal . . . He is a clear-headed, sensible little old man; which, at so advanced a period of life, is very uncommon. Although he is considerably upwards of ninety, he retains all the faculties of his mind in perfection. He has no minister, but manages everything himself; and has immediate information of the most minute occurences. He walks up and down stairs, and even to church, without assistance; and has the appearance as if he would live for many years. His household attendance and court are all very princely; and as grand master of Malta, he is more absolute, and possesses more power than most sovereign princes.

This observation was accurate enough, and a portrait of Manoel Pinto by the French artist Favray shows him clad in scarlet, pointing with a royal gesture to a crown. It is symbolic of the change that had come over the Order, and indicative of his own aspirations to all the dignity not of a prince of the church, but of a king.

Pinto's long reign, quite apart from the general circumstances of the time, undoubtedly did much to accelerate the Order's decline. His authoritative manner, his regal pretensions, his determination to rule without the assistance of ministers or council, all contributed to a feeling of hopelessness, since all the offices appeared to be vested in him. The other senior Knights and Grand Crosses abandoned their own ambitions for advancement in the face of this seemingly indestructible old man. More often than not in the Order's long history Grand Masters had been elected who were already of an advanced age, with the result that the office was quite often turned over every few years. But Pinto who, on reading his obituary notice in a Paris journal when he was seventy-seven, only laughed and remarked, 'Ah, then it is not Pinto but his shade who rules Malta,' completely changed the normal pattern. Like a giant old tree, beneath whose shade nothing can grow, he effectively stifled all ambition in those around him.

Perhaps the most important event in Pinto's reign was an attempted insurrection by all the slaves in the island. Both those who were employed ashore as house servants, as well as those in the galleys, were in the conspiracy. The plot was betrayed by a Jew, himself a member of the conspiracy but who had fallen out with some of his fellows, who unveiled the whole plot to the Grand Master. Sixty of the ringleaders were hanged, and the security regulations were rigidly tightened up, even the house slaves being compelled to retire at night to the bagnio or slave quarters. Pinto was accused by later chroniclers, anxious to find some excuse for the disaster that finally overtook the Order, of every kind of malpractice, from misuse of the Order's funds and other public moneys, to gluttony and even sexual excess. Ovide Doublet, who became French secretary to the next Grand Master but one, Emmanuel de Rohan, maintained that the old man had died *in flagrante delictu* with his mistress, and attributed the entire breakdown of the morale of the Knights to the vicious influence of Pinto. This of course was absurd, but it was natural enough for a Frenchman, seeking to excuse what was indeed a predominantly French organisation, to place the blame on one of the 'odd men out', a Portuguese. Manoel Pinto, in fact, seems to have been a severe old disciplinarian, an ascetic who conformed punctiliously to his religious duties, and who would tolerate no backsliding or religious unorthodoxy among the young Knights. It was probably as much for this as for his unprecedented longevity that he was hated while alive, and maligned when dead.

During the brief reign of Pinto's successor, François Ximenes of the Langue of Aragon, an event occurred which showed only too clearly the increasing discontent felt by the Maltese people for these feudal overlords. In the past, however much they may have disliked being second class citizens in their own island, they had nevertheless enjoyed the prosperity, and indeed fame, which their small island enjoyed because of the presence of the Order. Maltese sailors and merchants visiting other Mediterranean countries could not fail to observe the want and misery to be found in nearly all of them. But in recent years, as the *corso* practically ceased to exist, and as heavier taxes were laid upon the Maltese to shore-up the declining fortunes of the island, they began more and more to see their masters as outmoded tyrants. A tax on bread—always the staple diet of the Maltese working man—was unwisely levied by Ximenes, while a further insult (rather than injury) was an edict forbidding the clergy to take part in any secular activities, in particular field sports. Now the rocky Maltese islands provided little enough opportunity for sport or outdoor activity, and one of the great pleasures of the parish priest had long been the shooting of quail and other birds during the migratory periods of spring and autumn. A plot was hatched to overthrow the Knights, in which the priesthood took the lead, and an insurrection took place in September 1775. The Order's fleet was away blockading Algiers, and, taking advantage of the occasion, the rebels managed to seize one of the main defensive positions inside Valetta as well as the all-important fort of St. Elmo. Yet, despite these initial successes, the insurgents were not joined by a sufficiently large number of the population to ensure success. The rebellion finally petered out with the capture of several hundred men, a few of whom were executed and a number of others given life imprisonment. The attempt had failed, but the insurrection of 1775 showed clearly enough which way the wind was blowing. Not even the death of the unpopular Ximenes in the same year could disguise the fact that Malta of the Knights was nearing its end. Even the efforts of his energetic and statesmanlike successor, François de Rohan, could not stem the tide of events. Despite considerable measures of reform, wise changes in the law, and the establishment of public schools, de Rohan was destined to fail in his efforts to put the Order of St. John back on a financial and administrative footing capable of riding out the storm that was to follow. The prime cause of this was the French Revolution.

It was inevitable that an aristocratic Order of Knights would be anathema to the French revolutionaries, and equally inevitable that it should side with Louis XVI in his attempt to retain his throne. When the king's finance minister, Jacques Necker, appealed in 1789 to all landowners for a voluntary contribution, the Order of St. John was the first to come forward, giving him one third of the revenue from all its French commanderies. This in the long run would have been quite enough to ensure the destruction of the Order once the revolutionaries had come to power. But their error was compounded when they pledged their credit to the tune of 500,000 *francs* in order to assist the king in his attempted flight. The flight of Louis, which ended so disastrously at Varennes, heralded not only his death, but that of the Order of St. John in Malta. The French Constituent Assembly now declared that the Order was a foreign power holding property in France, and that it was therefore liable to the same taxes as French citizens. Very shortly after this a further decree was passed, declaring that any Frenchman belonging to an order of knighthood which required proofs of nobility from its members could no longer be considered a French citizen. The final blow fell on September 19th, 1792. It was formally decreed that all the property of the Order of St. John in Malta within the limits of France was automatically annexed to the French national domains. The axe had struck at the roots of this ancient oak.

27

. . . And fall

ON THE DEATH OF DE ROHAN IN 1797 THE CHOICE FOR THE NEXT Grand Master fell upon Ferdinand von Hompesch—the first German to be elected as Grand Master in the history of the Order. He was also to enjoy the melancholy distinction of being the last Grand Master of Malta. It is said that he was unwilling to be a candidate for the post. This seems to be belied by the fact that he had spent a considerable amount of money in promoting his own cause, and that after the election he was permanently hampered by the debts he had incurred.

The situation for the Order in Malta looked desperate after the confiscation of all their French possessions, but a gleam of light came from a somewhat unexpected quarter. The Tsar Paul I, who had recently succeeded Catherine II, was now in possession of the Priory of Poland, and it happened that the Tsar, among his numerous other eccentricities (which were to end in outright insanity), was a passionate enthusiast for the concepts of Knighthood and Chivalry. He had long been an admirer of the Order, and he now proceeded to change the Polish Priory into a Russian one. He gave it a revenue of 300,000 florins and incorporated it into that curious hybrid which had sprung up in 1782, the Anglo-Bavarian Langue, George III of England having given his consent to this part-revival of the defunct Langue of England. The Tsar, as it were, now took Malta under his protection. This was made clear by the fact that he was granted by the Order the title of 'Protector of the Order of Malta'.

Russian interest in this small island was not new in itself. As far back as the seventeenth century Peter the Great had announced: 'I am not looking for land, I am looking for water.' One of his close friends, the Boyar

Czeremetev, who had been an active campaigner against the Turks, was permitted by Peter to make a visit to Rome in fulfilment of a vow—but only on condition that afterwards he went to Malta and inspected its fortifications and cast an eye over its fleet. He had been received by Grand Master Perellos, had attended High Mass in St. John's, and had been invested with the Gold Cross of Devotion by the Grand Master. Nothing further came from this initial Russian probe into the island and its affairs, for events in Russia immediately engaged the attention of both Peter and Czeremetev. The word 'Malta', however, had found its way into the Russian archives, and an interest in the island as a possible outlet for Russian involvement in the Mediterranean had been excited.

This was to be revived during the reign of Catherine the Great, who despatched an Italian nobleman, Cavalcabo, to Malta to ingratiate himself with the aging Pinto and to act as her *chargé d'affaires* in Malta. Cavalcabo became involved in a plot against the administration and was very nearly dismissed the island in disgrace. He managed, however, to survive through the brief reign of Grand Master Ximenes and was then involved in yet a further plot in the early months of the reign of de Rohan. The latter acted quickly, a cache of arms was found in a cellar below Cavalcabo's house, and he was recalled in disgrace by his sovereign. These incidents, though petty in themselves, showed that Russia had definite designs upon this Mediterranean island with the object of furthering her ambitions not only against the Turks but against the European powers. The Tsar Paul's interest in the Order, although it probably stemmed from his own delusions of grandeur and passion for orders of chivalry, was no doubt prompted by ministers who had a more practical eye to affairs.

But despite the fact that the Tsar had clearly indicated that he regarded the Order (which in effect meant Malta) as within the Russian sphere of influence, the French were determined to act—and act quickly. Two hundred of the Knights, out of a total of about 300, were members of the three French Langues. They were therefore readily susceptible to influence from the new France, and keenly aware of the attractions of the French empire that Napoleon was so busily constructing. Against the glamour of the rising star of French imperialism even the aristocratic prejudices of a number of these Knights were bound to yield. Meanwhile, Napoleon had sent a cousin of the French consul at Malta, Possielgue by name, to keep him posted as to the state of affairs in the island. Possielgue found the native Maltese disaffected, the treasury almost bare, and in von Hompesch a man who deserved no more than the title of 'Grand Master of Indecision'. Clearly the moment was ripe for French intervention. It happened to coincide perfectly with Napoleon's plans for his expedition to Egypt. Malta lay right in the path of his fleet's invasion course, and it would be unthinkable to leave it in its present state when it might so easily be occupied by the English, who would use it as a base from which to cut the French line of communications.

A decree published by the French directory on April 12th, 1798, signed the death-warrant of the Order of St. John in Malta. This time it was not the Turks, not the eternal Moslem enemy, but the French—once the foremost of all crusaders—who achieved more or less by the stroke of a pen what all the cannons, fleets, sappers and miners, Janissaries, Generals, and Admirals of the Sublime Porte, together with the innumerable private raiders of the Barbary coast, had failed to do. After declaring that the Order in Malta had clearly proclaimed itself an enemy of the French Republic, the edict went on to issue its specific instructions to 'The General in Command of the army of the East'. He was to 'take possession of the island of Malta . . . for which purpose he will immediately proceed against it with all the naval and military forces under his command.' It went on to say that these orders were secret, 'not to be printed', and added the rider that General Bonaparte as commander-in-chief of the army destined for Egypt was 'to obtain possession of the island of Malta' unless for any reason he found this objective might interfere with the main purpose of the expedition.

A sad characteristic of the Knights in their latter days was that something of the fatalism of the East, the ennui of the Lotus Eaters, had overtaken them. The Maltese themselves are prone to say 'X'Tista Taghmel?' (What can you do?), and there is another local saying, 'Even St. Paul was shipwrecked on Malta'. This conviction of the inevitability of things, and of the inability of man to do anything against them, seems to have written itself into the hearts of the Knights during their last days in Malta. As Whitworth Porter wrote in 1883, in his History of the Knights of Malta, 'One power alone continued careless and inactive in the midst of the general alarm. Whilst the note of preparation arose in every other country in Europe the island of Malta remained in a state of supine and indolent security.'

Von Hompesch had been warned that the expedition against Egypt was also directed to capture Malta en route. He failed to take any action at all. It was as if he, like the whole island, was hypnotised by the magnitude of its prowess in the past, by the certainty that 'Malta of Gold, Malta of Silver' would forever remain inviolate. He looked around him at the massive fortifications of Valetta, at the scarps and counterscarps of Floriana, at the restored star-shaped fortress of St. Elmo. He put his trust in these just as much as the Order had done for centuries in the hand of St. John the Baptist in its jewelled reliquary in the cathedral. Under the inactive sky and the bright sun of early June, when the whole island shrugged its shoulders and prepared for the long mid-summer sleep, its German Grand Master sat indolent as a peasant in the shade.

On June 6th, 1798, the advance guard of the French fleet, consisting of over eighty vessels, sailed up to the island and a launch was sent ashore asking for permission for some of the vessels to enter Grand Harbour and water. The Order's position throughout this period of history was a difficult one. They had endeavoured—as they did now—to maintain a position of strict neutrality between the warring powers, according watering facilities equally to ships of whatever nation might ask for them. Permission was therefore granted for two transports to come in and water, as well as for a frigate which was in need of repairs. Three days later there hove up on the horizon a fleet such as not even Suleiman the Great at the height of the Ottoman Empire's powers could have envisaged. As Doublet wrote, 'Malta had never seen such an enormous fleet in its waters. For miles around the sea was covered with ships of every size. Their masts looked like a huge forest.' Under the command of Napoleon, the whole French fleet and army destined for Egypt was now assembled off the eastern coast of Malta. It consisted of fourteen ships-of-the-line, thirty frigates and 300 transports. One of the largest warships in the world, the battleship L'Orient, held the commander-in-chief, a man who, however active ashore, disliked the sea intensely. Napoleon regarded this whole part of the expedition as no more than an unattractive prelude to the glories awaiting him in the shadow of the pyramids. While he perused an account of the voyages of Captain Cook, Napoleon had also brought with him, among innumerable other volumes on the East, a copy of the Koran. It was a strange quirk of fate that it should be a Frenchman who now read the words of Mohammed as he prepared to capture the island that had resisted the onslaughts of the followers of the Prophet for so many centuries.

A message was promptly sent by Napoleon via the French consul asking the Grand Master to admit the whole fleet into the harbour for water. Von Hompesch called the Council who, with only one dissentient (a Spaniard who pointed out that his country was an ally of France), unanimously declared that in accordance with a treaty made some years beforehand between the Order and the governments of France, Naples, and Spain, only four warships at a time might enter harbour. Napoleon no doubt had been expecting just such a refusal, for the entrance of the whole fleet and army would in itself have been an admission of the island's capitulation. 'They have denied us water,' he said, 'then we shall take it.' His reply to von Hompesch's courteous answer was couched in the words of the all-conquering warlord: 'The commander-in-chief is extremely indignant to learn that permission to water is restricted to only four vessels at a time . . . How long at this rate would it take for 500 sailing vessels to water and victual? General Bonaparte is determined to take by force what ought to have been given him freely under the rules of hospitality which govern your Order.'

This was an open declaration of war, and Napoleon had made all necessary plans well in advance of sending his original request to von Hompesch. General Reynier was assigned to the capture of Gozo, General Baraguey-Hilliers was to land at Mellieha Bay in the north-east of Malta, General Vaubois at St. Julian's Bay a little to the north of Marsamuscetto, and General Desaix at Marsasirocco in the south of the island. Even if the Knights, even if the soldiers, even if the Maltese militia, had been of the frame of mind and calibre of their forbears in 1565 there can be little doubt as to what would have been the outcome against the massive numbers of men and artillery at Napoleon's disposal. True, Valetta itself, with its fantastic defensive system, should have been able to hold out for weeks if not months, but the strongest battlements are useless unless those who man them have an equal strength of purpose. But Malta had long had its fifth column. Even while von Hompesch irresolutely paced the floors of the Grand Master's palace, the agents of the French Republic were everywhere urging the inhabitants to join the victorious Tricolour, to adopt the new principles of liberty and freedom which all Europe was embracing, and to discard the Order of St. John, that unwanted relic of feudalism.

Historians of the Order have sometimes been too inclined to attribute its successes in warfare—whether in Rhodes or in Malta—to the unswerving dedication of the Knights, and to their unconquerable courage. Much is to be said for this outlook—for if an army lacks good officers it is useless. But an army is nevertheless composed of a number of non-commissioned officers and a vast bulk of men. These need training, need a sense of purpose, and need above all to believe that the men who are leading them are worthy of their trust. At Malta in 1798 all these ingredients were lacking. As Roderick Cavaleiro puts it:

Of the 200 French, 90 Italian, 25 Spanish, 8 Portuguese, 5 Bavarian and 4 German Knights, 50 were either too ill or too old to fight. The ancient guns, repeatedly painted up to look like new, but unused for nearly 100 years except for ceremonial purposes, were wheeled out. The powder was found to be rotten, the shot defective. The urban militia, drilled on Sunday afternoons by officers too lazy to learn the language [Maltese], ill-disciplined, given over to obstinate stupidity and malingering, shuffled into place terrified at the prospect of fighting the French.

Even if he had not had very adequate information about the state of things in Malta long before his expedition had set out, Napoleon might have deduced from the reports of random travellers that the Order and the island were as soft as rotten fruit.

They fell into his hands with disgraceful ease, von Hompesch displaying an irresolution that seems scarcely credible. He sat alone in the palace, except for one aide-de-camp, making no attempt to coordinate the resistance or even to give orders as to what resistance, if any, was to be offered. Everything was left to the individual commanders of the various fortresses and strong points, who for their part having received no orders, were indecisive as to what to do—which meant that most of them did nothing. Before nightfall Desaix moving up with his forces from the south had invested those formidable Cotonera lines upon which Grand Master Cotoner had lavished his fortune, and was in possession of Fort Ricasoli which guarded the southern point of Grand Harbour. Elsewhere the story was much the same. Reynier had landed at Ramla Bay on the east coast of Gozo and, although he came under fire from the heights surrounding this sandy beach, he too by nightfall had captured the citadel of Gozo's capital, Rabat, as well as taking Fort Chambrai which guarded the entrance to Gozo's one small harbour. The only real resistance that seems to have been offered in any part of the island was by members of the Maltese Militia. But, ill-disciplined and ill-officered as they were, they could hardly be expected to be a match for the finest troops in Europe. At one point, outside the massive fortifications of Floriana, the French were for a time held at check. A Knight of the Langue of Auvergne led a sally which brought his militia men under a murderous cross-fire, driving them back to Floriana. At this point the Standard of the Order of St. John fell into the hands of General Vaubois.

Throughout the night there was firing all over the island and a scene of indescribable confusion in Valetta where, as Doublet wrote, 'From every balcony one could hear the women lamenting in their houses, and cursing the French and the Grand Master all in one breath.' Inevitably the many saints revered in the island were being implored on all sides to protect the faithful, while the statue of the Apostle Paul (who is said to have converted the Maltese to Christianity in A.D. 60) was paraded throughout the streets of Valetta. Finally a deputation of leading Maltese citizens went to the palace and insisted on seeing von Hompesch, demanding that he should sue for peace. Everywhere there were scenes of mutiny and un-disciplined panic, while many members of the Maltese mob took it upon themselves to have their revenge upon individual members of the Order. These aristocrats, who were now apparently surrendering with cowardice, inspired only contempt. Throughout the thirty-six hours which was all that it took for the French to capture the once proud island-fortress, Napoleon remained impassively aboard *L'Orient*. He was quite confident that his men outside the walls, and his supporters within, would give him this rich prize, so important to the success of his main venture.

On June 11th, 1798, the armistice was signed. The main terms agreed upon were as follows: Malta and its sovereignty were surrendered to the French army by the Knights. The French Republic for its part would endeavour to procure for the Grand Master a principality equivalent to the one he was surrendering and would pay him an annual pension of 300,000 French *livres*. At the congress of the various powers assembled at Rastadt the French would use their influence to ensure that the Knights of each nation should be allowed to exercise their rights over such property of the Order as existed within their respective countries. French Knights would be allowed to return to France, but those who preferred to stay in Malta would receive an annual pension of 700 *livres,* those over sixty years old, 1,000 *livres.*

It was the end of the Order in Malta. Bonaparte in person entered Valetta on the twelfth and was astonished at the size of the fortifications which had fallen to him so easily. But he commented later in his memoirs that, 'Malta was not able to withstand a 24 hour bombardment. Certainly it possessed vast physical powers of resistance, but no moral strength whatsoever.'

Throughout all these scenes of chaos and confusion there moved the shadowy and irresolute figure of the Grand Master, that unhappy descendant of men like L'Isle Adam and La Valette. The Standard of the Order which had waved so proudly over unnumerable battle fields in the Holy Land and the East, and which had been the terror of the Moslem in a thousand sea-battles, was ignominiously lowered and in its place was raised the French Tricolour.

Six days later, on June 18th, von Hompesch and all the Knights who had not volunteered to serve with the French were dismissed the island. The plate, the jewels, and all the rich trappings of the Order became the property of the victors. (One sad irony was that nearly all the loot from Malta was sent aboard *L'Orient,* and went to the bottom with her at Aboukir Bay.) The Grand Master was only allowed to take with him the three most venerable relics of the Order—the splinter of the True Cross, the hand of John the Baptist despoiled of its bejewelled reliquary, and the icon from Rhodes of Our Lady of Philermos. Even this had been removed from its silver frame. The Order of St. John was once more homeless. But this time it was not with honour and with pride that the small band of Knights who accompanied the Grand Master into exile could look back upon their former island and their city.

28

A phoenix from the ashes

AFTER THE EXPULSION OF THE ORDER FROM MALTA IT MIGHT HAVE BEEN expected that an organisation so incongruous in the Europe of Napoleon was doomed to extinction. That it managed to survive at all was something of a miracle—and certainly not attributable to its broken-spirited Grand Master. Von Hompesch took refuge at Trieste, where he and those with him were taken under the protection of Austria. The Polish Knights in the Grand Priory of Russia, together with a number of French emigrés, looked to the 'Protector of the Order' for their salvation. The Tsar welcomed them with open arms. He now wished to have something more than his formal title, to become in fact the Order's Grand Master. Without waiting for any note of resignation from von Hompesch the Knights who were at St. Petersburg, acting with the Grand Priory of Russia, proclaimed von Hompesch deposed. In the September of the very year in which Malta was lost, Tsar Paul I became its head The fact that he was not a Catholic, not professed, nor recognised by the Church, does not seem to have troubled him.

There can be no doubt that the Tsar's nomination was quite illegal, for the post was neither vacant nor were the necessary members present for a genuine election. Implied, of course, in the Tsar's new office was the sovereignty of Malta—something about which the French, and later the British, were to have plenty to say. Autocratic Russia was inevitably the enemy of revolutionary France, and although allied with Britain by a mutual desire to see that the French did not become sole masters of

Europe, the two countries had little else in common. The British, indeed, were as determined as their French enemies not to have the vast land power of Russia turning into a maritime one in the Mediterranean.

Paul was formally invested with the insignia of his office in December 1798, announcing shortly afterwards that he was establishing a second non-Catholic Priory of Russia, so that his nobles of the Orthodox Faith could also become Knights of St. John. Von Hompesch was finally prevailed upon to resign. He ended his life poor and disgraced, dying at Montpellier in France in 1805—a man no weaker perhaps than some of his predecessors, but one who had been placed in a completely intolerable position. The authors of a recent commentary, *A Modern Crusade*, remark:

De Facto, thus, though not *de jure,* Paul I of Russia was the 72nd Head of the Order, and St. Petersburg, its momentary headquarters. Very likely the Emperor of Russia helped the Order to survive both the hostility of the revolutionaries and the rapacity of the monarchs.

But Russia did not get Malta. By September 1800, the British had set up their control over the island and showed no inclination to turn it over to the Emperor Paul who now claimed it. Russo-British relations then speedily deteriorated. On the eve of a war with England, however, on the night of the 11th March 1801, Paul was murdered.

Despite the fact that Paul's successor, Alexander, nominated one of his generals as head of the Order, Russian interest in both it and the island of Malta rapidly declined. The Maltese people who had risen in courageous revolt against their French masters (finding that the revolutionary and atheistic attitudes of the French were anathema to their conservative feelings) called in the British to help redress the balance. The result was that, with the renewal of the war between France and Britain in 1803, the latter became to all intents and purposes the successors to the Order of St. John as rulers of Malta. This was formally confirmed in 1814 by the Treaty of Paris when the island became part and parcel of the British Empire. In the Palace Square in Valetta the following inscription proclaims that the new ownership of the island was given (as it had not been to the Knights in 1530) with the full consent of its people: 'To Great and Unconquered Britain the Love of the Maltese and the Voice of Europe Confirms these islands A.D. 1814'.

In 1803 Pope Pius VII chose John Tommasi, the chief candidate of the Russian Priories, as Grand Master. After Tommasi's death two years later at Catania, there followed an interval during which the Order was ruled by Lieutenants who were elected by its Knights but ratified by the Holy See. The Convent remained in Catania for twenty-two years until in 1826 it moved to Ferrara, and a few years later to Rome, where it has remained ever since. During this period, when the surviving Knights were scattered throughout Europe, attempts were constantly made to obtain from the European powers some new base from which the Order might operate in something of its old capacity as a shield of Christendom and protector of the poor and sick. Islands were considered in the Baltic and in the Aegean, to which it might return and once again set up a sovereign state. But no one was particularly eager to cede even some relatively unimportant island or promontary to the once famous but now threadbare Order of St. John. The Order in fact had largely become what it had so often been accused of being—an exclusive club of old Catholic noblemen living in a dead past.

Whilst various splinter branches had established themselves in the countries from which the eight Langues had formerly been drawn, the real revival of the Order began in Rome. Here one of its members had bequeathed it a palace, the Palazzo di Malta, which is still its home. Crusading warfare was clearly a thing of the past, and its members turned to their original vocation which Brother Gerard had established, that of Hospitallers. The Grand Mastership was restored by Pope Leo XIII in 1879 and the seventy-fourth Grand Master since Raymond du Puy was installed, an Italian, John Baptist Ceschi a Santa Croce.

The Order's revenues, however, were slight and they had only this one small piece of territory over which flew the flag of the Order of St. John, 'the white cross of Peace on the blood-red field of War'. The question of the sovereignty of the Order was also a matter of interminable discussion and it has troubled many historians ever since. In 1862 the Italian Minister of Justice and Ecclesiastical Affairs declared that, 'It is to a certain extent a World Order . . . Deprived of the sovereignty which it exercised first in the island of Rhodes, and then in that of Malta, it continued to preserve, and still does, a character which no European power has ever ceased to recognise and respect.'

Some historians, among them Kelf-Cohen, have argued that the Order lost its sovereignty after leaving Rhodes. 'There can be no doubt whatever that, after 1530, the Order was no longer independent and sovereign, and that L'Isle Adam, despite all his efforts, had become a feudatory, though the service demanded was very slight. [The annual payment of one Maltese falcon.] The Act of Donation of Malta put them definitely into the position of feudal vassals of Charles V, as King of the two Sicilies.' If one examines the Charter itself it is clear that the Order through its payment of a pepper-corn rent had in fact become tenants of Malta. Rhodes they had won for themselves by force of arms, and had been accepted by the Pope as its sovereigns. However, the feudal tie was so very weak that after 1565 the Grand Masters were to all intents and purposes internationally recognised as the sovereigns of the Maltese islands. Vassalage in no way militated against sovereignty. The Kings of Naples and Sicily, for instance, were vassals of the Pope. The issue was finally resolved a few years ago, when on January 28th, 1961, a judgment was given by the Civil Courts of Rome that the Order was *un ente sovrano internazionale . . .*' ('an international sovereign society').

One of the most interesting features of the Order's revival during the nineteenth century was the reconstitution of the Langue of England. A number of French Knights of the Tongues of Auvergne, France, and Provence, proceeded on their own authority, without the consent of the Grand Magistry of the Order, to resuscitate the English branch in 1831. The Order, while always cooperating and remaining on friendly terms with the English branch, never agreed to recognise this organisation as a branch of the original Catholic Order founded by Blessed Gerard. This English Priory was converted by a Royal Charter of Queen Victoria into a British Order of Chivalry in 1888. The Queen became its Sovereign Head and appointed her son, later Edward VII, as its Grand Prior. The latter, with his love of wine, women, gambling and song, may seem a somewhat incongruous Grand Prior, but not all that much so, perhaps, when compared to some of his eighteenth-century predecessors. Ever since then, the reigning monarch has been Sovereign Head of the Order in England, while the Grand Prior has always been a member of the Royal House. Priories and commanderies have been established throughout the British Commonwealth overseas, and membership of the English branch of the Order now totals over 16,000. As its historian Sir Hannibal Scicluna writes: 'It is the only Order of St. John which admits Christians of all denominations.' Its objects and purposes are: 'The encouragement and promotion of all works of humanity and charity for the relief of persons in sickness, distress, suffering, and danger, without distinction of race, class or creed . . .'

These ideals, which accurately reflect the original intentions of Brother Gerard, are identical with those of the Catholic Order in Rome and the other branches of the Order in Ireland, Germany, Sweden, and the Netherlands. The Order is also strongly represented in the United States of America both by its Catholic members and by representatives of the English Order which was established there in 1960. In Jerusalem itself the English Order maintains an ophthalmic hospital which carries out research on trachoma, the eye disease which has been the scourge of the Middle East for centuries. The teaching body of the English Order is the St. John Ambulance Association, which has over 4,000 doctors on its staff. An extension of this is the St. John Ambulance Brigade which operates not only in the United Kingdom but throughout the British Commonwealth. Including men, women, and cadets, the grand total involved in its voluntary work amounts to nearly a quarter of a million people.

One of the most active branches of the Order of St. John is the Johanniterorden in Germany, which was re-established in 1852 by King Frederic William IV. The Johanniterorden separated from the Order founded by Brother Gerard through adherence to Protestantism in the fifteenth century. Like their British associates they are prominent in running first aid stations and ambulance brigades, and in training people in first aid work. The *Malteser Hilfsdienst* is an organisation of the German Knights belonging to the Order of St. John founded by Brother Gerard.

A press release from the Palazzo di Malta, dated December 1969, shows how these modern Knights of St. John of the German branch are still in the forefront of the battlefields of the world.

Three young voluntary members of the Order of Malta hospitaller team, the German *Hilfsdienst*, serving in the hospital at An Hoa, have died in a North Vietnamese prison camp. Two others still remain prisoners . . . A report of the imprisonment and subsequent deaths was officially reported to the U.S. Government by returning soldiers who had been imprisoned in the same military camp in North Vietnam. They confirmed that the deaths had been due to malnutrition and starvation and the plight of the remaining two young members of the medical team was desperate. The names of the young people who have died are: Georg Bartsch, age 25—nursing assistant; Hindrika Kortman, age 29—nursing assistant; Marie-Louise Kerber, age 20—dental assistant.

For nearly four years, from September 1966 until March 1970, the German branch of the Order maintained a team of about forty-five doctors, nurses and relief workers in Vietnam. Their average age was twenty-five. They had a network of thirty-four bases under their supervision, and gave hospital care to both sides without any discrimination. In three years they had given medical aid and rehabilitation treatment to over 200,000 Vietnamese.

The Order of St. John was always international, but it is now international in a way that neither its founder, nor any of the successive Grand Masters throughout the centuries, could ever have envisaged. Its work is no longer concerned only with the battlefields of Europe—and it is certainly no longer concerned with warfare. Much of its work, indeed, is carried out in the Near and Middle East, and is designed to assist the poor and the sick of those very countries against which the Knights once waged incessant warfare. But the Order now looks to spheres that were once totally unknown to the inhabitants of Europe. In November 1970, for instance, when Pakistan was devastated by a great cyclone the Order sent immediate financial aid to the Pakistan Government. Just as they had done in the great earthquake that devastated Messina and Reggio in 1783, so in 1970 they despatched innumerable crates of medicines and antibiotics (more efficacious than the once-famed Maltese fungus) to Bengal. Similarly, in the Peruvian earthquake disaster of 1970, a team of seventeen members of the Order worked in the worst-hit area for six weeks. When they left they had trained up a Peruvian staff to take over from them, to whom they donated their field hospital and all their equipment and medical stores. The Order is also increasingly active in Africa, especially in the battle against leprosy.

In common with most religious orders of the Church, that of St. John has had a second Order—its Hospitaller Sisters. These almost certainly originated at about the same time as the Hospital of St. John in Jerusalem, and worked there in the Hospital of St. Mary Magdelene. A group of nuns of the Order of St. John was established in England as early as 1180, and there were a number of other convents of Hospitaller Sisters in France,

Italy, Spain, Portugal, Bohemia, Denmark, the Netherlands and Malta. Although they are not Hospitaller Sisters, the nuns who work in the Hospital of St. John and Elizabeth in London still wear upon their habit the eight-pointed Cross of Malta, of Rhodes and of St. John.

From its headquarters in Rome today the Grand Master, His Most Eminent Highness Frà Angelo de Mojana, the seventy-seventh Grand Master in over 900 years, presides at the head of a world-wide service for the relief and prevention of disease. He himself is a fully professed Knight, of whom there are some fifty others. He and they have taken the full vows of poverty, chastity and obedience. He is not a layman but a 'religious'. He also ranks for ceremonial occasions at the Vatican as a Cardinal. There are 8,000 Knights in the Order, most of the members being married, while a number of their wives are Dames of the Order. There are in fact more Knights in the Order of St. John now than there were in the days of its material prosperity and grandeur in the eighteenth century; when Grand Master Pinto could so imperiously point towards a closed crown, indicating that he was as much a monarch as any other on earth.

The battlefield is now the world. The Order's activities range from centres for the treatment and rehabilitation of lepers in Africa, South America and Polynesia, to ambulance units in Ireland and Germany, hospitals and research clinics (including one in the Palazzo di Malta itself) and field units which are flown to any disaster area. All the more remarkable in the second half of the twentieth century is the fact that all this is *personal*, and privately financed. In Biafra the French branch of the Knights has organised a special settlement for children, after having air-lifted in thousands of tons of foodstuffs in 1968. In the Lebanon, an anti-diabetic clinic is maintained, in Malta a blood bank, and in the Philippines, Colombia, Abyssinia and Equador, volunteers work on the prevention and treatment of leprosy. Even at the height of its earlier fame it is impossible that the Order could have been so widely recognised. It maintains diplomatic relations with over thirty-eight states, ranging from Europe to South America, to Asia and to Africa, as well as a number of official delegations in other countries.

Today's work in hospitals and clinics, in disaster areas, and on Far Eastern battlefields, may seem a far call from Grand Master Roger des Moulins falling under a shower of arrows at Sephoria in 1187, from L'Isle

Adam embarking from Rhodes in 1522, or La Valette in the breach at Malta in 1565. Yet it is in essence nearer to the aims of its founder Brother Gerard than at any time in the intervening centuries. The Order has been wrongly called anachronistic. It is in fact traditional—so traditional that it is back where it started in 1099. The wheel has come full circle. After its apparent dissolution at the hands of Napoleon in 1788, the Sovereign Military Order of St. John of Jerusalem, of Rhodes and of Malta, is more vigorous than ever before. The Phoenix has risen from the ashes.

The Order since the loss of Malta

The complex politics following upon the expulsion of the Order of St. John from Malta in 1798 merit a little more detailed analysis than has been given to them in the main body of the text. So too, but for quite different reasons, does the remarkable efflorescence of the Order in recent years. The latter is one of the more singular phenomenon in the whole history of this remarkable organisation. For close on 900 years the Order has been both a shield and a sword to Christendom. It is easy enough to find high drama in the desert campaigns, the sieges, and the innumerable naval battles in the Order's history, but it is important to remember that the kernel of the Order has always been its Hospitaller work.

The whole arena of politics involving the Order, from the loss of Malta up to the mid-twentieth century, has been most adequately dealt with in the *Histoire politique de l'Ordre souverain de Saint-Jean de Jérusalem (Ordre de Malta) de 1789 à 1955*, by Le comte Michel de Pierredon (Paris, 1963).

Certainly the most interesting episode during this period is that in which the Emperor Paul I of Russia attempted to secure Malta in order to further Russian ambitions in the Mediterranean—principally directed against the Ottoman Turks. The occupation of Malta by the French and the dispossession of the Order seemed to have forestalled any further Russian ambitions in this direction. The previous *rapprochement* or treaty of amity between Grand Master Emmanuel de Rohan and Paul I, in which a new grand priory—the Grand Priory of Russia—had been established nevertheless still gave the Emperor a legitimate interest in the Order. This had been reinforced in 1782 when the Anglo-Bavaro-Polish Langue had been formed, George III of England ratifying the re-establishment of the English Langue in 1785.

After the partition of Poland, during the reign of the Emperor's mother Catherine II, the Polish Langue came under Russian control. In 1797 this whole curious portmanteau was renamed the Anglo-Bavaro-Russian Langue. The proclamation by Grand Master Ferdinand von Hampesch in the same year, making the Emperor Paul a Protector of the Order, meant that, even after the Napoleonic conquest of the island of Malta, the Emperor could still lay claim to Malta—if only he could get himself made the Grand Master. This was effected in 1798 when the Grand Priory of Russia, possibly with the connivance of a number of French emigré Knights, declared the Grand Master von Hampesch deposed.

In the November of the same year Paul I was proclaimed Grand Master of The Sovereign Military Hospitaller Order of St. John of Jerusalem, of Rhodes and of Malta. The whole episode is summed up in a portrait of Paul I by Borovikovsky (a copy of which hangs in the Palazzo Malta in Rome) showing Paul dressed as Emperor of Russia and Grand Master of Malta. There could never be any doubt that the whole transaction was completely illegal—for one thing Paul was not even a Catholic. However, as has been seen, the Maltese uprising against the French, coupled with the English intervention in the affairs of the island, caused the miscarriage of all Paul's Mediterranean policy. The whole of this curious and fascinating episode in the Order's history is succinctly dealt with in *The Order of Malta and the Russian Empire* (Rome, 1969), by Frà Olgerd de Sherbowitz-Wetzor and Frà Cyril Toumanoff.

Although much ink has been spilled over the question of the Order's sovereignty following the loss of Malta, the general consensus of opinion would seem to be that the fact the Order continued diplomatic relations with other States (including Napoleon's Empire), and that these relations were never interrupted in the case of the Court of Vienna, proves a continued sovereignty from the period of its residence in Rhodes right up to the present day. Certainly it does, from the Palazzo Malta in Rome, maintain at this moment diplomatic relations with thirty-eight sovereign States—a considerable advance even upon the days of its greatest material grandeur in the eighteenth century.

After the rule of Lieutenants from 1805 to 1879 (referred to in the text) the restoration of the Grand Mastership by Pope Leo XIII in 1879 was the beginning of the renewed life of the Order in Europe. The seventy-fourth Grand Master was Frà John Ceschi à Santa Croce. He died in 1905 and was succeeded first by Grand Master Thun-Hohenstein (1905–31) and then by Grand Master Chigi della Rovere Albani in 1931. It was during the reign of this distinguished Italian nobleman that the Order ran into considerable difficulties regarding its position with the Holy See—a powerful cardinal of the Sacred College being ambitious to secure control of the Order. The whole affair was, in effect, although on a smaller and more discreet level, somewhat reminiscent of the attack launched against the Templars by Pope Clement V in the fourteenth century. But the Knights of St. John were to prove, as they had done on great occasions in the past, that they were well capable of withstanding a siege—whether politico-ecclesiastical or military. The whole story has been admirably and wittily told by Roger Peyrefitte in *Chevaliers de Malte* (English trans. *Knights of Malta*, London, 1960). It ended with the position of the Order being clarified and confirmed, and in 1961 Pope John XXIII approved the new Constitutional Charter of the Order. On May 8th, 1962, after an interregnum during which the Order had been governed by Lieutenants, the seventy-seventh and present Prince and Grand Master, Frà Angelo de Mojana di Cologna, was elected.

The subsequent activities of the Order of St. John, which have been briefly outlined in the last chapter of this book, represent an astonishing renaissance. They are indeed more than what is implied by the word, for they are not so much a re-birth as the birth of a completely new international concept of hospitaller and charitable activities. The *Annuaire* of 1972, issued by the Palazzo Malta, gives detailed information on the present governmental structure and organisation of the Order as well as particulars about the various Grand Priories and the National Associations and Diplomatic Representatives throughout the world. An excellent outline of the Order's history and of its present government, together with a list of its hospitaller and charitable activities, is contained in *A Modern Crusade* (Palazzo Malta, Via Condotti, Rome).

List of the Grand Masters of the Order

1. Bx. Fra' Gérard, founder	† 3 sept. 1120
2. Bx. Fra' Raymond de Puy	1120–1158/60
3. Frà Auger de Balben	1158/60–1162/3
4. Frà Arnaud de Comps	1162/3
5. Frà Gilbert d'Assailly	1163–1169/70
6. Frà Gaston de Murols	c. 1170–c. 1172
7. Frà Joubert	c. 1172–1177
8. Frà Roger des Moulins	1177–1187
9. Frà Ermengard d'Asp	1188–c. 1190
10. Frà Garnier de Naplous	1189/90–1192
11. Frà Geoffroy de Donjon	1189/90–1192
12. Frà Alphonse de Portugal	1202–1206
13. Frà Geoffroy Le Rat	1206–1207
14. Frà Garin de Montaigu	1207–1227/8
15. Frà Bertrand de Thessy	1228–c. 1231
16. Frà Guérin	c. 1231–1236
17. Frà Bertrand de Comps	1236–1239/40
18. Frà Pierre de Vieille-Bride	1239/40–1242
19. Frà Guillaume de Châteauneuf	1242–1258
20. Frà Hugues de Revel	1258–1277
21. Frà Nicolas Lorgne	1277/8–1284
22. Frà Jean de Villiers	1284/5–1293/4
23. Frà Odon de Pins	1294–1296
24. Frà Guillaume de Villaret	1296–1305

25.	Frà Foulques de Villaret	1305–1319
26.	Frà Hélion de Villeneuve	1319–1346
27.	Frà Dieudonné de Gozon	1346–1353
28.	Frà Pierre de Corneillan	1353–1355
29.	Frà Roger de Pins	1355–1365
30.	Frà Raymond Bérenger	1365–1374
31.	Frà Robert de Juilliac	1374–1376
32.	Frà Jean Fernandez de Heredia	1376–1396
33.	Frà Richard Caracciolo	1383–1395
34.	Frà Philibert de Naillac	1396–1421
35.	Frà Antoine Fluvian de la Rivière	1421–1437
36.	Frà Jean de Lastic	1437–1454
37.	Frà Jacques de Milly	1454–1461
38.	Frà Pierre Raymond Zacosta	1464–1467
39.	Frà Jean-Baptiste Orsini	1467–1476
40.	Frà Pierre d'Aubusson, Cardinal	1476–1503
41.	Frà Emery d'Amboise	1503–1512
42.	Frà Guy de Blanchefort	1512–1513
43.	Frà Fabrice del Carretto	1513–1521
44.	Frà Philippe Villiers de L'Isle-Adam	1521–1534
45.	Frà Pierre del Ponte	1534–1535
46.	Frà Didier de Saint-Jaille	1535–1536
47.	Frà Jean de Homedes	1536–1553
48.	Frà Claude de la Sengle	1553–1557
49.	Frà Jean de La Vallette-Parisot	1557–1568
50.	Frà Pierre del Monte	1568–1572
51.	Frà Jean L'Evêque de la Cassière	1572–1581
52.	Frà Hugues Loubenx de Verdala, Cardinal	1581–1595
53.	Frà Martin Garzez	1595–1601
54.	Frà Alof de Wignacourt	1601–1622
55.	Frà Louis Mendez de Vasconcellos	1622–1623
56.	Frà Antoine de Paule	1623–1636
57.	Frà Jean de Lascaris-Castellar	1636–1657
58.	Frà Martin de Redin	1657–1660
59.	Frà Annet de Clermont-Gessant	1660
60.	Frà Raphael Cotoner	1660–1663
61.	Frà Nicolas Cotoner	1663–1680

62. Frà Grégoire Carafa   1680–1690
63. Frà Adrien de Wignacourt   1690–1697
64. Frà Raymond Perellos y Roccaful   1697–1720
65. Frà Marc Antoine Zondadari   1720–1722
66. Frà Antoine Manoel de Vilhena   1722–1736
67. Frà Raymond Despuig   1736–1741
68. Frà Manuel Pinto de Fonseca   1741–1773
69. Frà Francis Ximenes de Texada   1773–1775
70. Frà Emmanuel de Rohan-Polduc   1775–1797
71. Frà Ferdinand von Hompesch   1797–1799
72. (*de facto*) Paul I, Empereur de Russie   1798–1801
73. Frà Jean Baptiste Tommasi   1803–1805
74. Frà Jean-Baptiste Ceschi a Santa Croce   1879–1905
75. Frà Galeazzo von Thun und Hohenstein   1905–1931
76. Frà Ludovic Chigi della Rovere Albani   1931–1951
77. Frà Angelo de Mojana di Cologna   1962

LIEUTENANTS OF THE GRANDMASTERSHIP

Frà Innico-Maria Guevara-Suardo   1805–1814
Frà André Di Giovanni   1814–1821
Frà Antoine Busca   1821–1834
Frà Charles Candida   1834–1845
Frà Philippe di Colloredo-Mels   1845–1864
Frà Alexandre Borgia   1865–1871
Frà Jean Baptiste Ceschi a Santa Croce   1871–1879
Frà Antoine Hercolani Fava Simonetti, *ad interim*   1951–1955

LIEUTENANTS OF THE GRAND MASTER

Frà Pius Franchi de' Cavalieri (during the illness of the
     75th Grand Master)   1929–1931
Frà Ernesto Paternò Castello di Carcaci   1955–1962

A Military Glossary

Basilisk. A large cannon which fired an iron, stone or marble ball weighing from 50 to 200 pounds. (After the legendary monster whose breath and glance were fatal.)

Bastion. A defence work which consisted of two faces and two flanks, all the angles of which were salient.

Breastwork. A defence or parapet a few feet high, designed for the protection of arquebusiers.

Caravan. A term used by the Order of St. John to denote a year's seagoing duty on active service in the galleys of the Order.

Cavalier. A defensive work, sometimes shaped like a V, usually within the main fortifications. Any defensive work that stood higher than the main ramparts.

Chain-shot. Two cannon balls or half-cannon balls, joined by a length of chain. On leaving the gun, chain-shot whirled round in a parabola. Used against massed troops, and in sea warfare against masts and rigging.

Counterscarp. The slope of a ditch opposite the parapet.

Counterwall. Any wall erected against the enemy. In siege terms, usually a wall erected inside the main defences as a secondary defensive system.

Culverin. A long cannon, firing a comparatively small ball but with a great range. Generally, any large cannon.

Curtain-wall. The part of a rampart, bordered by a parapet, that connects two bastions or main defensive towers.

Demi-bastion. A half bastion, with a single face and flank.

Embrasure. A gun-port, or any opening in a parapet widening from within and designed for gun or arquebus fire.

Enceinte. The main enclosure or principal area of a fortification.

Fascines. Bundles of sticks, rods or brushwood, bound together and used in the construction of earthworks.

Gabion. A cylinder of wickerwork filled with earth, used for fortifications. Also a large barrel used in a similar way.

Galleas. A large galley with three masts, and fifteen or more oars each side.

Galleot. A galley propelled both by oars and sails, but smaller than a galleas.

Galley. A vessel principally propelled by oars. Almost invariably a warship.

Outwork. A defensive work constructed outside the main enceinte, either in or beyond the ditch of a fort.

Pasha. An Ottoman title signifying an Admiral, General, or Governor of a province. It was divided into three grades of one, two or three horsetails—the latter being senior.

Portcullis. A frame or grating made of wooden or iron bars. Sharp-pointed at the lower end, it slid vertically in grooves at the portal of a main exit of a fortified place.

Ramp. The gradual slope from the interior of a fortification to the level immediately inside the parapet.

Ravelin. A defensive work detached from the main structure, with two faces meeting in a salient at the front, and open at the rear. It was usually placed in front of a curtain-wall to protect it, as well as the shoulders of near-by bastions.

Sally-Port. Any small opening, usually masked or concealed, in a fortification, from which the defenders could sally out and catch the attackers by surprise.

Spur. A wall crossing part of a rampart and connecting it to the interior work. The projecting apex of any salient.

Traverse. An earthwork or parapet protecting a covered way. A double right-angle in a trench to prevent enfilading. A gun-port designed in connection with another one to give protective cross-fire.

Trump. A type of flame-thrower handled by one man, and discharging a form of liquid fire. Sometimes combined with a musket so that small shot was also discharged. Similar but smaller was the 'fire-pike', which could be used as a pike when its combustibles had run out.

Appendix   IV

Select Bibliography

Abela, F. G. *Della Descrittione di Malta* (Malta, 1647).

D'Aleccio, M. P. *I veri Ritrati della guerra & Dell'Assedio dali alla Isola di Malta dell'Armata Turchesa l'anno 1565* (Rome, 1582).

Balbi, F. di Correggio. *La Veradera relaçion de todo lo qui el año de MDLXV ha succedido en la Isla de Malta* (Barcelona, 1568).

Barber, R. *The Knight & Chivalry* (London, 1970).

Baudouin, J. *Histoire des Chevaliers de l'Ordre de S. Jean de Hierusalem* (Paris, 1624).

Boisgelin, L. de. *Ancient and Modern Malta & the History of the Knights of Jerusalem* (London, 1805).

Bosio, G. *Dell'Istoria della Sacra Religione et Illma. Militia di San Giovanni Gierosolimitano* (Rome, 1594).

Brantôme, L'Abbé de. *Oeuvres du Seigneur de Brantôme* (Paris, 1740).

Brockman, E. *The Two Sieges of Rhodes* (London, 1969).

Brydone, P. *A Tour through Sicily and Malta* (London, 1773).

Cassar, P. *Medical History of Malta* (London, 1964).

Catalogue of the Records of the Order of St. John of Jerusalem (Malta, 1964).

Caoursin, W. *Le fondement du S. Hospital de l'Order de la chevalerie de S. Jehan Baptiste de Jerusalem. Recueil des hitoriens des croisades* (Paris, 1822).

Cavaleiro, A. *The Last of the Crusaders* (London, 1960).

Cambridge Modern History. Vol. III. The Wars of Religion (1907).

Crema, Cavaliere F. T. da. *La Fortificazione, Guardia, Difesa e espugnatione delle Fortezze* (Venice, 1630).

Curione, C. S. *Nuova Storia della Guerra di Malta*, trans. E. F. Mizzi (Rome, 1927).

Currey, E. H. *Seawolves of the Mediterranean* (London, 1910).

Denon, N. *Voyage en Sicilie et à Malta* (Paris, 1788).

Downey, F. *The Grande Turke* (London, 1928).

Gravière, J. de la. *Les Chevaliers de Malte et la Marine de Phillippe II* (Paris, 1887).

Hammer, J. Von. *Histoire de l'Empire Ottoman depuis son origine jusqu'à nos jours,* trans. J. J. Hellert (Paris, 1841).

Hughes, J. Quentin. *The Building of Malta 1530–1795* (London, 1956).

Hughes, J. Quentin. *Fortress* (London, 1969).

King, E. J. *The Knights Hospitallers in the Holy Land* (London, 1931).

King, E. J. *The Rule, Statutes and Customs of the Hospitallers* (London, 1934).

Laking, Sir G. F. *Catalogue of the Armour and Arms in the Armoury, Valetta* (London, 1905).

Lane Poole, S. *Saladin and the Fall of the Kingdom of Jerusalem* (London, 1898).

Lucini, A. F. *Disegni della Guerra, Assedio et Assalti dati dall'Armada Turchesa all'Isola di Malta l'anno MDLXV* (Bologna, 1631).

Macarata, P. F. *Defesa et Offesa della Piazze* (Venice, 1630).

Mifsud, A. *Knights Hospitallers of the Venerable Tongue of England in Malta,* (Malta, 1914).

Molle, S. *L'Ordine de Malta la Cavalleria* (Rome, 1928).

Porter, W. *The History of the Knights of Malta* (London, 1883).

Pozzo, B. *Historia della Sacra Religione Militares di. S. Giovanni Gerosolimitano* (Verona, 1703).

Prescott, W. H. *History of the reign of Philip II* (London, 1855).

Recueil des historiens des Croisades (Paris, 1841–1906).

Riley-Smith, J. *The Knights of St. John in Jerusalem and Cyprus* (London, 1967).

Runcimen, Sir S. *A History of the Crusades,* 3 vols. (Cambridge, 1951–5).

Scicluna, Sir H. P. *The Order of St. John of Jerusalem* (Malta, 1969).

Seward, Desmond, *The Monks of War* (London, 1972).

Smail, R. C. 'Crusaders' Castles in the Twelfth Century' (*Cambridge Historical Journal* X, 1951).

Smail, R. C. *Crusading Warfare (1097–1193)* (Cambridge Medieval Studies, 1956).

Spreti, C. *A Treatise of Knightly Behaviour and Description of the Island of Malta* (Valetta, 1949).

Schermerhorn, E. W. *Malta of the Knights* (London, 1929).

Taafe, J. *History of the Order of St. John of Jerusalem* (London, 1852).

Ubaldini, U. M. *La Marina del Sovrano Militare Ordine di San Giovanni di Gerusalemme di Rodi e di Malta* (Rome, 1970).

Vertot, L'Abbé de. *Histoire des Chevaliers Hospitaliers de S. Jean de Jerusalem* (Paris, 1725).

Index